Christian Liberal Arts

Christian Liberal Arts

An Education That Goes Beyond

V. James Mannoia Jr.

ROWMAN & LITTLEFIELD PUBLISHERS, INC.
Lanham • *Boulder* • *New York* • *Oxford*

ROWMAN & LITTLEFIELD PUBLISHERS, INC.

Published in the United States of America
by Rowman & Littlefield Publishers, Inc.
4720 Boston Way, Lanham, Maryland 20706

12 Hid's Copse Road
Cumnor Hill, Oxford OX2 9JJ, England

British Library Cataloguing in Publication Information Available

Library of Congress Cataloging-in-Publication Data
Mannoia, V. James.
    Christian liberal arts : an education that goes beyond / V. James Mannoia Jr.
        p. cm.
    Includes bibliographical references and index.
    ISBN 0-8476-9958-7 (alk paper) — ISBN 0-8476-9959-5 (pbk. : alk. paper)
    1. Church colleges—United States. 2. Education, Humanistic—United States. I. Title.
    LC427 .M26   2000
    371.07—dc21   99-053840

Printed in the United States of America

∞™ The paper used in this publication meets the minimum requirements of
American National Standard for Information Sciences—Permanence of Paper
for Printed Library Materials, ANSI/NISO Z39.48–1992.

To Jimmy and Eva Marie,
whose character is my great passion and
whose love is my great strength.

Contents

Foreword

Throughout history the Christian church has been involved in shaping education. When Clement of Rome wrote to the Corinthian church shortly before 100 A.D. about "*paideia* in Christ," he was simply echoing the apostle Paul's words about "the *paideia* of the Lord." And when Origen added theology and Christian ethics to his teaching of the liberal arts in Alexandria and later in Caesarea, he was pursuing the same ideal. So too Augustine the teacher of rhetoric, after his conversion, and the monastery schools to which his work eventually gave rise; in fact, his little book *On Christian Doctrine* shaped higher education for over a thousand years. The Reformers for their part reformed not only the church but higher education as well, helping move it from a seemingly pointless scholasticism to the more widely practical Christian humanism that Puritan colleges in England and in this country inherited. The story of American higher education until the nineteenth century is therefore about Christian colleges and, in large measure, about the relationship of Christianity to colleges and universities in general.

Over the last decade or so a variety of books have appeared on this general subject. Some are about major universities, like George Marsden's account of their secularization in *The Soul of the American University*, or Williman and Naylor's discussion of student values and conduct in *The Abandoned Generation*. Others are about explicitly Christian colleges, like *Models for Christian Higher Education*, edited by Richard Hughes and William Adrian. Books like these reveal the serious engagement of Christians with the problems confronting higher education today, and Jim Mannoia's work is no exception. He writes for parents and others advising college-bound students, and for Christian college teachers trying to clarify the distinctive mission of Christian liberal arts education. And he writes out of years of experience in college teaching and administration, in this country and abroad. Here then is the mature, systematically developed thinking of a man deeply dedicated to the mission he now describes.

One of the problems in higher education today is erosion of the liberal arts. In a quick-food culture with a utilitarian approach to learning, a technological society obsessed with its latest tools, how relevant are history and philosophy, rhetoric and the arts? Whatever can you *do* with liberal arts? Why should parents support such a seemingly impractical route? Mannoia traces the origin of liberal studies, examines their several emphases, and shows what they contribute both "to me" and "for me." Being, it needs to be said, should take priority over doing, and "who I am" over "what I do" for a living. But why *Christian* liberal arts? Because what we need is not just the critical thinking that liberal arts teach but "critical commitment"; and Christian commitment combines being and doing in a Christlike character committed to a self-giving life, tackling real-life problems. This is liberal arts education for a life of service, through the integration of faith with learning and learning with living. It goes a second mile, as the Master asked, in what the author calls "an education that goes beyond."

Much of the literature on Christian higher education reflects a reformed tradition with its emphasis on developing a Christian worldview, but Mannoia's emphasis on developing character and helping the needy of this world reflects his Wesleyan heritage. As such I think this book stands alone and makes a significant contribution. Different emphases often complement each other, and the present volume is to be welcomed for developing dimensions that enlarge and sharpen the picture, and make more explicit the challenging opportunities facing Christian colleges and those who teach or study there.

Arthur F. Holmes

Acknowledgments

This work has been far too long in gestation. But that is no fault of the many people who have constantly encouraged me along the way. David Winter got it started with his own fresh thinking about liberal arts in a number of chapel addresses at Westmont College and then nourished it at a bachelor's breakfast one Saturday morning many years ago. His support and friendship over more than twenty years, first as my employer and now as my colleague and mentor, has been unqualified and constant.

Many people have taken the time to read the manuscript in its entirety and have provided much needed criticism. Thanks to my colleagues at Westmont College—Stan Obitts, Shirley Mullen, Ed Potts, and especially Jeff Schloss—who not only read it but shaped the very ideas by long conversations, even in Yosemite National Park. I thank my colleagues at Houghton College—Carlton Fisher, Rich Perkins, and especially John Van Wicklin—for encouraging a busy dean to keep at his writing and even referred to the ideas in his manuscript often enough to make him think they were useful.

Arthur Holmes read the manuscript and even reread it, I think. The deep impact of his classic *The Idea of a Christian College* has made him the "dean" of Christian liberal arts, and so his personal support has been both moral and tangible. If this work is even a small footnote to his, I will be pleased.

My debt to Jean Piaget, Lawrence Kohlberg, William Perry, Carol Gilligan, and James Fowler is obvious. But to Dallas Willard, Nick Wolterstoff, and Sharon Parks I owe a personal thanks for the way their ideas have shaped mine both in their writing and by the way they have brought their thinking to life for me in personal conversation and friendship. I offer very little that goes beyond them.

Thanks to my son, Jim, for letting me steal vacation time from him on yet another visit to Yosemite, and to my wife, Ellen, for tolerating the same kind of theft in the Colorado Rockies. To my daughter, Eva Marie, I can only say that I hope for both our sakes that this is not the last word on character.

1

Introduction

The mailbox was full again. My son was a junior in high school and the trickle of college brochures had turned into a flood. Watching them come in, I found myself reflecting not only on the tremendous effort involved in the production and mailing of such materials but on the entire university education process from admissions to commencement. Despite over twenty years of university teaching, I sometimes felt bewildered by the rush of information. Parents and college-bound students are faced with what Alvin Toffler in his classic book *Future Shock* might have called a kind of educational "overchoice."

The decision about which college to attend is very important. It may be the first major decision for which young men and women assume primary responsibility. Their choice may shape and mold not only their career but perhaps their choice of a life partner and even their overall well-being for much of their lives. But this decision is also important for parents. Are the costs justified? The choice between elite private and large public universities or colleges often boils down to prestige: the doors that reputation can open. But choosing among lesser-known liberal arts colleges, and especially Christian liberal arts colleges, is not so simple. Offering neither price nor prestige advantage, these colleges can appear very much alike.

Despite the importance of the decision, many students and parents lack critical information concerning the crucial differences among institutions of higher education. Even families that research the subject beyond the college's own materials often lack adequate means to classify the choices. Unfortunately for many Americans, college has become a rite of passage that obscures the deeper questions about the purposes and distinctives of educational institutions.

But what is worse, even the faculty at many colleges and universities often are not clear about the distinctives of their own institutions. Faculty are products of graduate programs shaped by the priorities of national and international professional associations and journals. Graduate schools rarely provide opportunity for future college and university professors to reflect on the different kinds of institutions in which they might eventually serve. And fewer jobs mean that these differences become even more blurred, since scholars seeking faculty positions are glad to find any work at all.

Almost every college or university claims "excellence" for itself. It's hard to imagine one that would not. A cursory look at the flood of brochures, viewbooks, and catalogs shows that every college sees itself as an "excellent" institution. But one question is often overlooked: Excellent at what? Excellence is only a measure of something else. Yet frequently "excellence" itself, without any distinctive direction or purpose, becomes the end in itself. We hear empty phrases such as "a college of excellence" or "a quality academic program." But what *is* the standard of excellence? What *is* the particular educational quality sought?

In short, there is a crisis of identity in many educational institutions in the United States today. Ernest Boyer, in a special Carnegie Foundation report, described it as a "crisis of purpose." He said that for many institutions, "their mission becomes blurred, standards of research are compromised, and the quality of teaching and learning is disturbingly diminished."[1] As others have put it, "By believing themselves to be what they are not . . . institutions fall short of being what they could be."[2] *Newsweek* has reported that higher education has become a "commodity item" in the United States today. And this has meant a reduction in quality of almost every kind.

But good institutions know their distinctives. This is just as true of educational institutions as it is of business corporations. There are practical, pedagogical, and, for Christian institutions, even theological reasons why they should.

PRACTICAL REASONS

When the mission and distinctives of any corporation or project are clearly defined and universally understood, the chance of survival and of success in those areas is strengthened. If McDonald's ever lost sight of "cleanliness and low prices," the company's appeal would be diminished. If Holiday Inn ever gave guests too many "surprises," its future success might very well be compromised. A company must know what it does best and concentrate on that. This is true of educational institutions too. The educational "marketplace" has become highly developed and highly competitive. The large budgets and sophisticated techniques of admissions departments, as well as the closely watched rankings of colleges in national magazines, illustrate this well.[3] In this environment, the college or university that does not recognize its distinctives will be at a considerable disadvantage. I am talking here about recognizing a kind of "market niche." Without this, students, parents, and faculty will all be dissatisfied.

Students and parents will question their high tuition costs. They will wonder why anything but price should count in selecting one institution instead of another. Incredibly, the costs of higher education skyrocketed faster during the past two decades than even those of the notorious health care industry.[4] And not surprisingly, higher education has suffered the same dramatic loss of public confidence that has plagued health care.[5] As tuition costs escalate, expectations for educational institutions will only increase. "When there are pressures for tuition increases, students are going to come down with a vengeance about what they're getting."[6] "Parents are thinking long and hard about that four-year investment of time and money. . . . Many colleges will be out of business if they can't show students they have a special niche."[7]

But the practical reasons for clarifying distinctives extend to faculty as well. Faculty grow frustrated and even embittered by the often inconsistent pushing and pulling among colleagues and with administration over decisions of curriculum, staffing, and budget. In large research universities like Stanford University, frustration can come from renewed calls for attention to teaching.[8] On small liberal arts campuses the fear is that continuing pressure to do research will threaten the priority of teaching there.[9] Given the dissatisfaction among students, parents, and faculty alike stemming from the lack of clarity about what makes them distinctive, the very survival of institutions is at stake.

PEDAGOGICAL REASONS

But the need for clarity about distinctive strengths goes beyond practical survival. Clarity fosters pedagogical improvement. American higher education is under attack today as never before. The numbers of books and articles written decrying the decline of education in America is astounding.[10] The National Commission on Excellence in Education concluded that

> the educational foundation of our society has been eroded by a rising tide of mediocrity that threatens our very future as a nation. . . . If an unfriendly foreign power had attempted to impose on America the mediocre educational performance that exists today, we might well have viewed it as an act of war.[11]

Educators have responsibilities to students and to the mission of their institutions. If an institution has "no clearly conceived and articulated sense of itself, its efforts to design a curriculum will result in little more than an educational garage sale, possibly satisfying most campus factions, but serving no real purpose and adding up to nothing of significance."[12]

Clarity of distinctives brings a focus of purpose that gives substance to the search for improvement in education. The recognition of distinctive strengths will result in focused improvements in this distinctive area or in that distinctive area, not just empty publicity. Clear purpose will better allocate resources of time, curriculum, and personnel. When resources are targeted more precisely, the concentration of effort can create the critical mass sometimes needed for creative discovery and for real advance. In this way clarity advances knowledge in itself, the work of faculty, and the personal development of students. Some of the character virtues I believe should be among the outcomes of higher education are rarely born outside clearly intentional nurturing environments. One movement in corporate management theory, TQM (Total Quality Management), focuses on improving quality in a number of ways, including attention to the "customer" and the centrality of "vision statements." The movement seems to be taking hold in academia too, despite critics who say that "students are not customers" or "it's okay for corporations but not colleges."[13]

But educators are also responsible for consistency with the mission statements of their institutions. Accreditation agencies judge excellence by the institution's own mission statement, not primarily by outside criteria. So the responsibility to such statements is a matter of integrity. That job is made easier by clarifying the distinctives of the mission. Too many institutions shirk this responsibility by either failing to clarify these distinctives or, worse, by paying only lip service to them while chasing instead more popular or more profitable enterprises that border on academic prostitution.

THEOLOGICAL REASONS

Finally, the Christian educational institution wants clarity about its distinctives for more than practical and pedagogical reasons. For faculty, staff, and administrators in these places, their work is more than business and more than an educational responsibility. It is also a calling—a ministry in the Body of Christ. To keep that purpose clearly in view requires attention to the distinctives of the institution.

Christian institutions of higher education, and especially Christian liberal arts colleges, must assess their distinctive mission in the light of the call to follow Christ. Questions concerning two features of that call stand out and shape much of what I have to say. First, does the Christian liberal arts college actually teach its graduates to become more like Christ?[14] Second, insofar as Christ's mission was to humble Himself and become a servant, does the

Christian liberal arts college actually teach its graduates to humble themselves and serve others?[15]

My purpose in what follows is both descriptive and prescriptive. For those readers directly involved in the work of Christian liberal arts education, those who seek to do it—faculty, staff, administrators, and trustees—it is prescriptive. I hope to sharpen the vision of the distinctives of Christian liberal arts education. I want to provide glimpses of what that vision might be and why it should be and might be realized. In short, I want to address a confusion of identity.

For readers not directly involved in Christian liberal arts education but who seek to understand it and choose it—students, parents, pastors, and career counselors—my purpose is descriptive. I want to show what some Christian liberal arts colleges might aspire to become and how clear focus can distinguish them from competing institutions. For these readers I want to address a confusion of understanding.

This is not to suggest that there can be only one good kind of college or university, much less that there can be only one good kind of Christian college. There are places for many different kinds of institutions. Educational pluralism has been an asset and should not be lost. Few if any other countries have such a wealth of educational variety. But many decry the slippage in American education. Whether or not that has occurred, there has been an unfortunate "leveling" phenomenon because, in my opinion, too many institutions have failed to recognize their own distinctive strengths. Instead, they have tried to become something they are not.

We need research universities, for instance. The resources of equipment, facilities, talent, and time permit the faculty at such institutions to push back the frontiers of knowledge. And as "apprentice houses" for others—especially graduate students—looking to follow that path, they are unsurpassed. Likewise, we need institutions equipped to prepare professionals for specific vocations: law, business, medicine. Community colleges advance the working older adult, the commuter, those wanting technical skills, and those unsure of how far to pursue higher education. Similarly, among Christian educational institutions there must be seminaries and Bible colleges for providing distinctively religious professional and vocational training. Liberal arts colleges, however, provide something quite different. Of course, institutions can mix purposes to some degree. For example, comprehensive colleges aim to combine a liberal arts core with strong professional programs. But in such mixing lies the danger that concerns me most: the danger of diffusing the focus and falling into the crisis of identity I have described.

Among these varied institutions, I want to focus on the Christian liberal arts college. That is not because it is superior to the others but because, like each of them, it too must be clear about its distinctive role. And it is the kind of college I know.

For reasons that are elaborated below, the liberal arts college—whether Christian or not—is in jeopardy. As long ago as 1959, E. J. McGrath bemoaned the fragmentation of liberal education, concluding that "the liberal arts college must . . . regain and affirm a clear, feasible, and independent mission."[16] David Breneman asked, "Are we losing our liberal arts colleges?"[17] In a study of these institutions, he concluded that of the six hundred colleges in the United States classified this way, perhaps only two hundred continue to live up to that name. Kenneth Ruscio, referring to liberal arts institutions, said that the "undergraduate years are the forgotten years in American higher education."[18] It would be a tragedy to lose the liberal arts college.[19] And of course, of those 150–200 liberal arts colleges, only a small fraction could be called Christian. I am concerned that distinctively Christian liberal arts colleges may be on the verge of extinction!

Many books have been written about higher education, even liberal arts education. John Henry Newman's *The Idea of a University*, Elton Trueblood's *The Idea of a College,* and Arthur Holmes's *The Idea of a Christian College* foreshadow and even overshadow many of the topics of concern to me. Each of them models the finest in Christian liberal arts scholarship.

So what is left to be said? What differences do I have in mind in writing this book?

First, I expect my discussion will *not* be so general or philosophical as the others I have mentioned. While it is certainly crucial to ground the distinctive characteristics of Christian liberal arts in the essentials of Christian faith (chapter 2), I emphasize middle-level principles that can serve as guides for the practical choices that must be made by those choosing a college as well as those shaping it (chapters 3–8). Then I offer concrete suggestions to implement those middle-level principles in the formal and informal curriculum of the Christian liberal arts college (chapters 9–11).

I suppose my desire to bridge the gap between discussions that are too general or too specific comes from the fact that I am a philosopher who has found himself doing academic administration. I hope this gives me an advantageous perspective with which people on both sides can identify. But of course the attempt to overcome such differences can instead produce criticism from both sides.

Second, I hope what follows will be accessible. Discussions of Christian higher education can be filled with statistical studies, packed with theology, tightly reasoned, and abstract. Or they can be concrete journalistic reports chiefly for informational purposes. I want to address concrete and abstract matters in a readable way. Of course here too I may fail. Some may find it still too dense, general, and even abstract. Others may find it superficial and simplistic.

Finally, my discussion will not be exhaustive, as I could not expect to describe all of the features of a Christian liberal arts college. There are features of such institutions, some of them of considerable interest to students, parents, faculty, and trustees, about which I will say little or nothing. Instead I want to concentrate on two essential characteristics that I believe, if recognized and understood, can dramatically clarify the distinctive mission of the Christian liberal arts college for those who seek to understand it and renew the vision of those who seek to accomplish it.

These two characteristics arise from the Christian's call to become like Christ and to serve others, respectively. The first is my belief that Christian liberal arts colleges should produce graduates who are critically committed. That is to say, they are persons with a rare combination of passion and humility toward what they believe. They are strongly committed to these beliefs in spite of careful and ongoing critical reflection on them. To become a person of such character and virtue is an essential *intrinsic* value of Christian liberal arts education.

The second is my belief that Christian liberal arts colleges should produce graduates who are integrative, that is, persons able to address themselves to real human problems. To do this competently, willingly, and self-sacrificially wherever they may live and work is an essential *instrumental* value of Christian liberal arts education.

Each of these distinctives reflects my central conviction: that Christian liberal arts colleges can go a step beyond both secular universities and other kinds of religious institutions of higher education.

2

What Does "Christian Liberal Arts" Mean?

*Combining Intrinsic and Instrumental
Values in Christian Higher Education*

Recently I stumbled onto two faculty colleagues in the midst of a heated debate over lunch. The topic was Christian higher education but in perhaps its most practical incarnation. As I joined in, these professors at a Christian liberal arts college, one a chemist and the other a psychologist, were debating why the psychologist's own son had chosen to attend the state university instead of the Christian college where they both taught. The chemist wanted his friend's son to return because the young man was interested in chemistry and because he had known his friend's son for years. But the father reported that his son was not only doing well in his studies but was growing spiritually as well. "Would the son grow more at the Christian college?" the chemist asked. The psychologist was not sure, but he did not want to fix what was not broken. There were good reasons why a son might not want to study where his father taught. But the real question his friend in chemistry pressed was whether the psychologist saw enough distinctives in Christian colleges to urge his son to attend one. Were they real or were they only catalog propaganda? If real, were there trade-offs in academic rigor, in exposure to the real world, or in reputation? The psychologist wasn't sure. For my part, I found myself caught in the middle. I had never attended a Christian educational institution in my twenty years of education, yet I had given over twenty years of my professional career to Christian higher education. The debate resolved nothing. But the ambivalence startled me, coming as it did from veteran faculty at a Christian college.

Those involved in Christian higher education want to do Kingdom business. We do not want to merely prepare students to go out into the world to become standard evangelical Christian American yuppies. Kingdom values are much different from the world's. Unless this difference in values makes a difference in the graduates of Christian colleges, perhaps "Christian" is not applicable. Then the struggle and sacrifice required to keep them open would be unjustified, and we would all be better advised to become "salt and light" in secular—and perhaps academically superior—institutions. Faculty and administrators want to be associated with Christian colleges only if they recognize their distinctive mission, see their niche in higher education, know what they can do better than any other institutions . . . *and* are prepared to accomplish that mission, fill that niche, be that institution.

So what does the term "Christian liberal arts" mean?

LIBERAL ARTS: TWO TRADITIONS

The diversity of American institutions of higher education is astounding, for example, the University of California–Berkeley, Yale University, Massachusetts Institute of Technology (MIT), the University of Southern California, Santa Barbara City College, Claremont-McKenna College, Haverford College, California State University at Fullerton, Fuller Seminary, Asbury Seminary, Moody Bible Institute, LeTourneau University, Rosemead School of Psychology, Wheaton College (Ill.), Greenville College (Ill.). This short list includes institutions that are private and public;[1] undergraduate and graduate; research oriented and teaching oriented; prestigious and relatively unknown; Christian and secular; denominational, interdenominational, and nondenominational; academic and professional/technical; small and large; narrow and comprehensive. And of course these pairs of categories can be combined to produce hair-splitting distinctions. With so many possible ways of drawing lines, it is not hard to understand why there might be confusion about institutional distinctives among insiders and outsiders both.

Definitions

Attempts to define the liberal arts frequently become mired down in a swamp of confusion. Books are full of definitions of the liberal arts of many sorts. What makes matters worse, as Samuel Capen said as long ago as 1921, is that "nobody pays attention to literature of this sort in defining liberal arts."[2]

Four Approaches

Operational

One approach is operational, such as the following classification system used by the Carnegie Foundation:[3]

Carnegie Foundation Classifications
Research universities
  I. At least fifty doctorates per year and $33.5 million in federal support
  II. At least fifty doctorates per year and $12.5 million in federal support
Doctoral universities
  I. At least forty doctorates annually in five or more disciplines
  II. At least twenty doctorates annually in at least one discipline or ten annu-
     ally in three or more
Master's (formerly comprehensive) universities and colleges
  I. Fifty percent or more of baccalaureates in two or more occupational dis-
     ciplines, M.A., more than 2,500 students
  II. Fifty percent or more of baccalaureates in two or more occupational dis-
     ciplines, M.A., 1,500–2,500 students
Bachelor's (formerly liberal arts) colleges
  I. Forty percent or more of baccalaureates in arts and sciences, highly selec-
     tive, primarily undergraduate
  II. Forty percent or more of baccalaureates in liberal arts, less selective, pri-
     marily undergraduate (includes some with less than 50 percent in liberal
     arts, but less than 1,500 students and thus not comprehensive
Two-year community, junior, and technical colleges
  No baccalaureate degree, associate of arts degree or certificate only

David Breneman has argued that the foundation's liberal arts category became a kind of catchall category for other kinds of institutions whose size
does not permit them to be placed appropriately in the "comprehensive" category.[4] Interestingly, within three years of that assessment, the foundation
changed its categories to avoid use of the liberal arts label altogether.[5] Breneman goes on to say that if one is careful to hold to the definitions laid down,
the number of liberal arts colleges remaining in our country is less than two
hundred, or only about one-third of the number previously assumed. In
short the commission is saying that a liberal arts education is that provided
by a liberal arts degree. But if our concern is that institutions themselves are
not clear on their own distinctives, it will not do to define liberal arts circu-
larly in terms of the number of liberal arts degrees an institution grants.

Basket Approach

The basket approach defines the liberal arts by collecting lists of skills or competencies that seem important to the writer or the committee producing the definition. One project said liberal arts focused on enhancing critical thinking, aesthetic and cultural development, communication, breadth of perspective,
autonomy, social relations, and life goals.[6] Another collection included the following:[7] "the appreciation for the exact formulation of general ideas, for their
relations when formulated, for their service in the comprehension of life"
(Whitehead 1953); "the cultivation of the intellectual virtues, including intuitive

knowledge, scientific knowledge, philosophical wisdom, art, and prudence" (Hutchins 1936); "the capacity for wise decisions in those matters with which everyone must be concerned, to think for [oneself] . . . to establish an adequate relation of mind to the things which it undertakes to grasp, . . . to formulate clearly the difference between conflicting lines of argument and to locate the critical point at which determination of relative merit and soundness of different approaches may be profitably undertaken" (University of Chicago faculty 1950); "thinking effectively, communicating thought, making relevant judgments, and discriminating among values" (Harvard faculty 1945). Derek Bok, president of Harvard, said a general liberal arts education must be "built around the mastery of intellectual skills . . . [students must] learn how to learn." At MIT—an institution not generally thought to be much concerned about liberal arts—a faculty committee charged with development of curriculum described its approach to liberal knowledge as "contextual."[8] In a remarkable effort to provide *empirical* evidence of the value of liberal arts education, a group of behavioral scientists produced a "basket of baskets" from sources ranging from ancient philosophers to contemporary faculty committees, which was then used in a long-term study. They said the liberal arts consisted in enhancing analytic skills; learning to learn; thinking independently; empathizing and recognizing one's own assumptions; exercising self-control; showing self-assurance in leadership; demonstrating mature social and emotional judgment; holding egalitarian, liberal, proscience, antiauthoritative values; and participating in cultural experiences.[9]

A priori Approach

A priori definitions start with someone's idea of the overarching principle of liberal arts. For example, as Jacques Barzun says, in the 1920s and 1930s, "ten thousand commencement speakers annually explained that the liberal arts were liberating arts."[10] Those who follow the tradition of Cicero argue that the genius of the liberal arts is the education of the citizen, while followers of the platonic tradition insist that the liberal arts value learning for its own sake.

Historical Approach

Finally, there are almost innumerable histories of the liberal arts, some written from the point of view of each of the previous three starting points.[11] In these histories attempts are made to link the meaning of the liberal arts today to their roots in the past.

Two Traditions: Plato and Cicero

The confusion in defining the liberal arts is not new. Debates about the liberal arts go back a long time. Bruce Kimball finds the debate in the conflicts of two traditions; one philosophical and one oratorical, with exponents of each side stretching from ancient Athens to the present day. The tradition of the philosophers affirms the pursuit of knowledge for its own sake, freedom of thought, and emphasizes the use of speculative reason and dialectic. This has come to dominate current thinking about the liberal arts. The line stretches from Socrates, Plato, and Aristotle to Boethius, the "schoolmen" of medieval Paris, the philosophes of the Enlightenment, T. H. Huxley, modern science, and the great research universities of today. The tradition of the orators affirms "public expression of what is known," the centrality of text and tradition, and the importance of building a "community of learning and knowledge."[12] The line of this tradition stretches from Isocrates, Cicero, and Isidore to the "artes liberales" of the Middle Ages, Renaissance humanists, the vision of Matthew Arnold in his debates with Huxley, and the vision of many in the humanities today. This historic distinction is crucial so let us develop it further.

The natural place to begin in understanding the "liberal arts" is with the words themselves. This is true even though in the end their meaning may have changed dramatically. The term "artes liberales" can be found in the Renaissance, the late Middle Ages, Isidore in the seventh century, Cassiodorus in the sixth century, and Quintillian in the first century; apparently it first appeared in the writings of the famous statesman and orator Cicero in the first century B.C.[13] Seven specific subjects were taught in medieval institutions, including the Trivium of grammar, rhetoric, and logic as well as the Quadrivium of geometry, arithmetic, music, and astronomy. Later theology became a part of higher education and eventually science was added as it emerged in the seventeenth century. Knowledge of a classical language became essential to study the classic authors in each of these areas. So today the liberal arts usually comprise studies in the natural and social sciences as well as the humanities and languages, although usually modern and not classical languages. Clearly, the curriculum of the liberal arts has evolved. But how did these "artes liberales" come to be? What are the essential characteristics that cause these subjects to be included and not others, such as medicine, engineering, or business?

Since the earliest recorded use of "artes liberales" is apparently found in Cicero, one view is that the confusion about the liberal arts can be resolved simply by referring to his educational views. For Cicero, the term "liberal" (from *liberalis* "free") undoubtedly referred to the education of free men who were in that day citizens and not slaves and thus had the necessary leisure time. On this point there is considerable agreement. But what kind of education did he have in mind? What kind of education was suited to free men with free time?[14] We will return to Cicero below, but first a digression.

Cicero himself suggested that the term "artes liberales" was already in common usage. Thus some maintain that the liberal arts arose from the "pedagogical century" in Greece (450–350 B.C.), when Athens flourished. Liberal arts in this view simply referred to the education of that time, usually assumed to be the tradition of Socrates and his followers. But there was no single dominant approach to education in Athens during the pedagogical century. As Aristotle said, "The existing practice is perplexing; no one knows on what principle we should proceed—should the useful in life, or should virtue, or should the higher knowledge, be the aim of our training; all three opinions have been entertained."[15]

Socrates, Plato, Aristotle, and their followers favored contemplative dialectical (back-and-forth) reasoning and disagreed mightily with the sophists, such as Gorgias and Protagoras, who emphasized mainly the skills of oral communication so crucial to the politics of the Athenian city-state.[16] But Isocrates represented a third approach to education and disagreed with both. Like Plato, he criticized the sophists for their rhetorical display and their disregard for character virtue.[17] Both Plato and Isocrates condemned the moral disintegration promoted by the sophists, and yet many young people flocked to the sophists because of the power their "education" provided them in politics. Unlike Plato, however, Isocrates had no time for endless speculation and disagreed that a distinction could be made between the sophist's "sophia" and Plato's "philosophia." Instead, Isocrates affirmed, with little analysis, the traditional values of the community and promoted the ideal of the citizen who lived out the noble virtues and used oratorical eloquence to persuade others to do so as well. Thus the view that the essential characteristics of liberal arts can be found by tracing the use of the words "artes liberales" beyond Cicero to their Greek equivalents in the education of Athens must fail because there was no agreement even at that time about how education should be conducted. Both the philosophical and the oratorical tradition were already strong and strongly in disagreement. Attempts to link the Latin "artes liberales" to Greek root words is also unhelpful because these roots were associated with both of the Athenian traditions.[18] The confusion about what is meant by liberal arts remains.

A dominant mode of education did not emerge in Greece until the time of Alexander the Great, when the orators, such as Demosthenes and Aeschines, and not the philosopher-kings, dominated public affairs. It was the oratorical tradition of Isocrates, not the philosophical one of Plato, that was handed down to Cicero and the Romans. "Plato had been defeated. . . . The victor, generally speaking, was Isocrates, and Isocrates became the educator first of Greece and then of the whole ancient world."[19] So if the meaning of liberal arts is to be tied to the earliest dominant mode of education in Greece, or to the dominant mode of education at the time the words "artes liberales" were first recorded by Cicero, then the term "liberal arts" must refer to characteristics of the Isocratean oratorical ideal and not the philosophical model of Socrates, Plato, and Aristotle, as is often assumed.[20]

Which view of the liberal arts dominates today? Those who follow the oratorical tradition point to the excessive emphasis among contemporary faculty on esoteric research for its own sake (described in the next chapter) and conclude that the philosophical tradition has taken over the liberal arts. Those in the philosophical tradition point to excessive vocationalism among students and conclude the oratorical tradition has prevailed once again.

Two Questions: What Can Liberal Arts Do "for" Me and "to" Me?

Given this kind of confusion among those who actually study the matter, it is unsurprising that the most common understanding of liberal arts defines them negatively—in terms of what they are not. For many, the liberal arts are simply "leftovers." Liberal arts on many large university campuses are studied by those who can't yet figure out what else to do. "What is your major? Oh, just liberal arts?" For others, the liberal arts are the opposite of what is practical. And in a day when students (and their parents) are eager to be educated in a way that will prepare them for a vocation, the liberal arts have become unpopular. Between 1970 and 1985 majors in philosophy dropped 41 percent, in English 57 percent, and in history 62 percent. The vocational "trend" continued into the early 1990s, as over 25 percent of all incoming freshmen in the United States planned to major in business.[21]

The demand for vocational relevance or at least usefulness of some kind, as well as the dismissal of liberal arts as impractical, brings us to a crucial distinction that will provide the framework for the rest of this chapter and the following ones. This distinction represents the long-standing debate between the philosophical and the oratorical traditions described above and, if pressed, creates a dichotomy in approaches to education. It is my concern to show that the dichotomy is false and that even the earliest advocates of each tradition accommodate the other one.

Perhaps the most frequent question I am asked by students or their parents when they discover I am a philosopher is, "What is it good for?" It often also arises about what is commonly taken as the liberal arts in general. "Is this kind of education really worth having, especially when it is often much more expensive than the more vocationally oriented education offered elsewhere?" Leo Marx of MIT puts their question this way.

> How can we possibly justify, in this global arena of deadly serious economic and military power struggles, a policy that would expend more of our scarce educational resources on soft, imprecise, impractical kinds of liberal knowledge? . . . We might concede than an expanded program in liberal studies would be a good thing in some other, less imperfect world, but on planet Earth . . . how can we pretend that liberal knowledge is the kind the nation needs most? . . . Today, more than ever, advanced societies are committed to the Baconian assumption that knowledge . . . is the basis of national wealth and power. . . . Hence liberal

knowledge, however desirable, is a luxury our educational system can afford only after it fulfills its primary obligation to reproduce the expert knowledge required to maintain such vital nationwide systems as military security, industrial production, transportation, communication, etc. . . . On planet Earth . . . how can we pretend that liberal knowledge is the kind the nation needs most?[22]

The question goes back to the debate in England between those at Oxford University who held on to the idea of a liberal education and those in the empirical and scientific tradition who called for more practical education. Philosopher John Locke said, referring to the standard classical practice of learning Latin, "Can there be any thing more ridiculous, than that a father should waste his own money, and his son's time, in setting him to learn the Roman language, when at the same time he designs him for a trade."[23]

I usually answer the question by suggesting that the student is asking the wrong question. Or I may reply by saying that the question is only one of two the student ought to ask. The question is not only, What can a liberal arts education (or a philosophy major) do *for* me? but What can it do *to* me?[24]

Two Values: Instrumental and Intrinsic

In talking with my student, I go on to explain that this is just another way of making a distinction between two kinds of value that anything, including an education, might be said to possess. Some things are valuable because they lead to other things that are of value, that is, they are valuable as instruments or means to some other end. Roughly speaking, they are good because of what they can do *for* you. Tools of all kinds are valuable in this way. But things may also have intrinsic value, not because they lead to anything else but because they are inherently valuable. They are ends in themselves. Health and honesty or courage and perhaps friendship are examples.

Of course a particular thing may be valuable in both ways. Some tools may be valued for their own sake as some people collect automobiles or empty bottles. And some things of intrinsic value can be used as tools to other ends, as some people use friendship to achieve selfish gain. But the distinction still holds.

So the question comes down to whether an education is valuable as a means, as an end, or as both.

Can Liberal Arts Combine Both Values? A Working Definition

I believe it is simplistic to put the question as a choice between education that is instrumentally valuable or intrinsically valuable. My longer response to students is that by asking "what is this liberal arts education good for?" they have only inquired about half its value. I do agree with Newman that liberal arts have intrinsic value and that value must not be lost. But without

slipping too easily into facile compromise, I want to say that the instrumental and intrinsic values of liberal arts education can coexist without ceasing
to be liberal. With Bertrand Russell I want to say that a liberal education has
two purposes: to form the mind and to train the citizen. The Athenians, he
said, concentrated on the former while the Spartans emphasized the latter.[25]
Russell's history of Athens may be skewed but the belief that two traditions
can be brought together stands. The emphasis you make depends on what
you see more of around you. For every example of how vocationalism has
swamped the priorities of today's parents and students there are examples of
narrowness in esoteric research and teaching that neglect important instrumental values of education as well. The *philosophical tradition* sees vocationally oriented education, like that of the sophists, enslaved to the ends of
politics and life. It needs freedom. The *oratorical tradition* sees narrow
speculative research for its own sake—not unlike that of the philosophers—
impotent, wandering, and selfishly turned on itself. It needs application,
value, and community. Liberal arts seek to accomplish both sets of goals.
And Christian liberal arts in particular are distinctively equipped to do this.

If we adopt this as our working definition, the question becomes, In what
sense can the liberal arts be "useful" and yet remain "liberal"? Or, put in a
way that avoids Newman's insistence that the term "liberal" be reserved for
the philosophical tradition, In what sense can the liberal arts be true to both
Socrates and Isocrates, to both Plato and Cicero? In what sense can a liberal
arts education be valuable both instrumentally and intrinsically? I believe the
answer to this question depends on learning to walk the fine line between
marketing and prostitution.

Put this way, the issue predates Locke and his arguments against Latin. It
is found in the dramatically different conceptions of a university that developed in Germany and England. In Germany the preoccupation was with
scholarship, whereas in England it was with the development of the scholar-
statesman. But with Bruce Kimball, Arthur McGill agrees that "the conflict actually extends back through the entire history of the West." There was the
conflict between the champions of logic and the champions of classics and
history in the sixteenth and seventeenth centuries. There was the conflict of
classical humanism and new scholasticism in the twelfth century. And there
was "the conflict in Athens in the fourth century B.C. between Plato, who
wanted to perfect the rational mind, and the Sophists, who placed education
in the service of the social and political aspects of life."

> We are dealing with a conflict between two fundamental and incompatible ideals
> that have been in tension for twenty-four centuries. The question is this; should
> young people be given, before anything else, an initiation into the life of intellec-
> tual clarity, with all the disciplines and techniques that are involved? Or, before
> everything else, should they be taught how to participate in the community life?[26]

So let us ask in turn, What does a liberal arts education do *to* me? and then, What does it do *for* me?

Intrinsic Value: What Does a Liberal Arts Education Do to Me?

Cardinal Newman

Cardinal John H. Newman, writing in the nineteenth century, was one of the most articulate and outspoken advocates of the liberal arts. He spoke from the philosophical, not the oratorical, tradition. In his classic *Idea of a University,* he accepted the distinction drawn between the liberal arts and the vocations. "We contrast a liberal education with a commercial education or a professional."[27] As an initial suggestion he points out that "liberal" means the opposite of "servile," meaning physical or bodily employment. So liberal arts are, by contrast, intellectual or mental ones. But that definition falls short because he says there are physical activities that can be liberal (Olympic sports and even war) and mental ones that are not liberal (the practice of medicine).

Instead, Newman concludes that the distinctive knowledge arising from the liberal arts has intrinsic value. It "stands on its own pretensions, is independent of sequel, expects no complement, refuses to be informed by any end, or absorbed into any art."[28] "Knowledge is capable of being its own end."[29] Newman hereby aligns himself with the philosophical tradition. He does not, however, deny or decry the existence of "useful knowledge" stemming from what he calls "mechanical" arts.[30]

> Life could not go on without them; we owe our daily welfare to them; their exercise is the duty of the many, and we owe to the many a debt of gratitude for fulfilling that duty. I only say that Knowledge, in proportion as it tends more and more to be particular, ceases to be Knowledge.[31]

> That further advantages accrue to us and redound to others by . . . possession [of liberal knowledge], over and above what it is in itself, I am very far indeed from denying; but, independent of these, we are satisfying a direct need of our nature in its very acquisition.[32]

Newman's view is quite strong. He believes the value of the liberal education has little to do with whatever practical advantages it may or may not afford. Instead it has to do with the intrinsic value of enabling the mind to do what it is uniquely suited to do. Unlike the bodily eye that is *naturally* empowered to perform its unique task of "seeing," the mind requires educating. In summary,

> this process of training, by which the intellect, instead of being formed or sacrificed to some accidental purpose, some specific trade or profession, or study or science, is disciplined for its own sake, for the perception of its own proper object, is called Liberal Education.[33]

A strong Aristotelianism is evident here.[34] Aristotle understood the world to be purposeful; everything had a natural (i.e., proper) end. Good was defined by the achievement of the end to which a thing was intended. For rocks, it was good to be at the center of the earth; hence gravity needs no further explanation. For acorns, it was good for them to become oak trees; hence growth. For eyes, it was good for them to see well. For the human body in general, it was good to be healthy. For these objects it is unnecessary to ask, What is the use, the value, of their achievement? For these they were intended. If "intention" sounds too theistic for the Aristotelian, then for these they are suited. Their achievement is valuable in and of itself. And this is true whether or not gravity, growth, and health may also be useful as means to still other ends. Likewise, then, for the human intellect, it is good that it should be enabled (educated) to become what it is *uniquely* suited to become. That is enough reason for education, whether or not it may also be useful as means to still other ends. Newman himself summarizes his view quoting Aristotle:

> All that I have been now saying is summed up in a few characteristic words of the great Philosopher. "Of possessions," he says, "those rather are useful, which bear fruit; those *liberal which tend to enjoyment.* By fruitful, I mean, which yield revenue; by enjoyable, where nothing *accrues of consequence beyond the using.*[35]

Newman is quite adamant about this. If the most ordinary pursuits are done for their own sake, they become "liberal" (although not necessarily liberal *knowledge*). Likewise when even the learned professions become, for example, popularly beneficial, politically important, or intimately divine, they cease to be liberal. Theology *for the pulpit* or science *for the service of man* cease to be liberal arts; not for this reason less valuable, only not intrinsically valuable. The mention of science is particularly interesting because today we often confuse science and technology. The Baconian approach to science, and in fact to knowledge generally, was to value it for its usefulness, its power. And there is no doubt that science has led to a technology that has produced a wealth of material benefits. But science in this sense would not belong to the liberal arts.

So far little has been said about what this intrinsic good really looks like. This is the subject of chapter 3, but a brief description is in order here. If a liberal education is valuable in itself because of what it does to the one educated, then what are some of the things it does? In Aristotelian terms, what are the distinctive ends of the human mind that are achievable by the discipline of a liberal education in contrast with a vocational one?

One very important quality is *freedom.* Aristotle thought education was for free men for the wise use of their leisure time, not for slaves. Freedom was essential to humanity. Without knowing of Aristotle, Cicero also believed that liberal arts are those appropriate to humanity.[36] He agreed that freedom was at the heart of what is distinctively human. Education was, then, for free men in the exercise of their freedom as citizens. John Milton in *Of Education* described the course of studies and the nature of academic society that he believed essential for an advancing civilization. He was concerned with the "liberating studies."[37] Newman also includes freedom in his list of the qualities of the liberally educated human mind: "A habit of mind is formed which lasts through life, of which the attributes are, freedom, equitableness, calmness, moderation, and wisdom."[38]

Although the idea of education of free men for freedom does not exhaust the intrinsic value of liberal education, it can serve to open the discussion. If liberal education means liberation (i.e., freedom), then from what does it liberate and to what does it liberate? Let us consider what we might call both the negative liberation (freedom *from*) and the positive liberation (freedom *to*) of liberal education.

Liberation "From"

Liberal arts can liberate the mind in a number of ways. There are prisons of intolerance, of closed-mindedness and narrow-mindedness, and of parochial perspectives. Banishment to some of these may result from crimes of commission but to others from ignorance or omission.

Intolerance most often is deliberate and is directed against persons different from ourselves. The worst forms of discrimination (racism, tribalism, sexism, etc.) begin as intolerance. From such discrimination come some of humankind's worst crimes. But intolerance can also take the form of an intellectual inflexibility that stunts the mind's ability to conceive of things in new and creative ways. In whatever form, intolerance is ethically objectionable from the point of view of almost any value system, in part because of its effect on human relationships but also because it falls short of that of which the human spirit is capable.

Parochialism is perhaps a more benign prison. It represents merely a limitation of perspective. Often for lack of opportunity, people see things only one way. Their tradition has shaped the categories with which they see and classify their experiences all around. They are unable to "stand in other shoes." Maynard Mack of Yale University describes the parochialism of academics who have become narrowly overspecialized:

> We are narrowing not enlarging our horizons. And we communicate with fewer and fewer because it is easier to jabber in a jargon than to explain a complicated matter in the real language of men. How long can a democratic nation afford to support a narcissistic minority so transfixed by its own image.[39]

The liberal arts provide an escape. Wider exposure, disciplined thought, and models of maturity are among the keys.

Liberation "To"

Virtually all advocates of liberal education would affirm the need for liberation from prisons of the kind described. Yet liberation from such prisons is not enough unless it is liberation to something else. On this aspect of liberal arts as liberation there is much less agreement.

If the value of a liberal arts education is defined strictly in terms of what it is *not*, we have made no progress over the naive response of the confused student who saw it merely as "leftovers": what you study when you can't make up your mind what you want to do. Liberty becomes license, not just in behavior but in thought life as well. Liberation from a single authoritative reading of a text leads of necessity to the deconstructionist view that all readings are permitted. "Anything goes," so everything stays. In the name of avoiding discrimination, minds "liberated" only in this negative sense become indiscriminate. The titles of some existentialist works—*Flies, No Exit, Nausea*—suggest that even perfect freedom when it is only negative, only liberation from, is anguish. It's like Buridan's notorious donkey caught between two equally delicious bales of hay: it died for lack of a reason to prefer one over the other. It is like a nightmare in reverse. Instead of reasons to act but no power (our usual terror), one has instead all the power in the world but no reason, no truth. Without something to which one is liberated, the "liberation" becomes only a new kind of prison.

Sadly, some today are convinced that this is what has happened to American education. In his controversial book *Illiberal Education,* Dinesh D'-Souza wrote that most students enter college with excitement, anticipation, and idealism, eager to prepare themselves for lives as "shared rulers in a democratic society. In short, what they seek is liberal education."[40] But by the time these students graduate, universities by and large have failed to provide a liberal education. Instead they have taught students that all rules are unjust, that all preferences are as good as any others, that justice is simply the will of the stronger party, that standards and values are arbitrary, that the ideal of an educated person is a figment of ideology, that individual rights are only a cover for social privilege, and that knowledge should be pursued not for its own sake but for the political ends of power and so on. He concluded, "In short, instead of liberal education, what American students are getting is its diametrical opposite, an education in closed-mindedness and intolerance, which is to say, illiberal education."[41]

To what, then, does a liberal education liberate? First, and foremost, it is liberation to pursue truth instead of mere opinion. The fundamental purpose of education is the pursuit of truth, according to John Silber, president of Boston

University.[42] I am talking here about belief in objective values—standards of all sorts that exist independently of whether any persons actually hold them. In this sense the advocate of liberal education shares Plato's quest.

Some suggest we do not need truth and objective values, only tolerance. This is the gospel of political correctness. But this alternative collapses on itself. As an *attitude*, tolerance is beyond reproach, commendable, even crucial, as we will see. But as a value, as a prescription for life, as a goal for education, it is empty nonsense.[43] If as a value tolerance *excludes* anything (e.g., usually intolerance), then it is self-contradictory because it is intolerant tolerance. But if it *permits* everything, then it is self-defeating because it could never claim to be preferable to intolerance or that it ought to be the goal of education. Escape from the prison of intolerance to tolerance is only an unstable "halfway house" to more complete liberation. Advocates of this alternative kind of education reduce truth to opinion, ideology, or the "will to power." As Plato might have said, they perpetually chase shadows, like men chained in a cave.

A liberal education must teach us to recognize the good, the bad, and the ugly. "Yet what is the goal of liberal education if not the pursuit of truth? If education cannot teach us to separate truth from falsehood, beauty from vulgarity, and right from wrong, then what can it teach us worth knowing?"[44]

Put slightly differently, liberal education is intended to help the student discover truth and not only to create it. This claim is easily opened to misunderstanding. It certainly does not preclude creativity. And more will be said about how the liberally educated person handles truth. But the point is that apart from the affirmation of and pursuit of truth, there can be no liberal education.

Second, as a corollary, liberal education is liberation to virtue. What does a liberal arts education do to me? With Plato, the philosophical tradition in education says it inculcates a dialectical approach that is the crown of learning and enables us to discover virtue.

Robert Sandin wrote that the heart of the concept of virtue is excellence, but excellence is empty without a context; there can be excellence for a whole range of human activities.[45] In other words, "excellence" sounds like a noun but is actually an adjective or adverb in search of something to modify. What *is* the content of academic virtue, of academic excellence?

There is certainly more to academic virtue than just the possession of truth. In fact virtue is not any particular set of beliefs or behaviors at all. That would be casuistry of belief and action. As Georg von Wright wrote, "The path of virtue is never laid out in advance. It is for the man of virtue to determine where it goes in the particular case."[46] In Sandin's words, "Virtue concerns not the quality of particular actions in the specific circumstances of moral decision, but the traits of character that facilitate responsible and reflective decision making in complex moral situations."[47]

Those traits are states of being, not faculties or competencies. They are the foundation for belief and action. Collectively they comprise academic virtue, which "is the state of being that frees the human mind for thinking about the dilemmas of moral decision making."[48] This means that academic virtue is in large part an orientation toward truth and decision making as much as it is a particular set of beliefs, skills, or actions. This means that academic virtue is in large part attitude. A liberal education is liberation to a set of habitual attitudes.[49]

Perhaps the most important attitude liberal education produces—one which is essential to the way truth is handled—is that of intellectual humility. It is the kind of tolerance I described earlier as an attitude and not a value. As we shall see in the next chapter, without this attitude, liberation to affirm and pursue truth degenerates too easily into dogmatism.

Humility cannot easily arise in someone who adopts the view that truth is created and not discovered. Instead, this subjectivist view tends to produce pride and the politicization of all matters so that they come to depend on will and on power. Humility, on the other hand, is possible only with the affirmation of objective standards of truth and beauty higher than oneself. Humility arises in the recognition that believing that there is truth does not in any way guarantee the possession of it.

But affirming objective truth always raises the issue that there may appear to be several "truths" and, most seriously, the question of whether one can ever know the Truth at all. Clearly, negative liberation (liberation "from") and positive liberation (liberation "to") are inseparable. Liberation from the prisons of intolerance and parochialism requires objective standards of truth in order to avoid sheer arbitrariness. Negative liberation requires positive liberation. But because positive liberation—liberation to pursue truth—can never be certain it has found truth, it must fly from intolerance and parochialism. Positive liberation requires negative liberation.

Instrumental Value: What Does a Liberal Arts Education Do for Me?

Cicero

Cicero, writing in the first century before Christ (106–43), spoke from what we have called the oratorical, not the philosophical, tradition. He is sometimes seen as the champion of more practical education. He believed that the chief fault of the philosophical approach to education was that it remained forever an intellectual activity, rarely making a difference in the world or even in the character of the persons so educated. His educational program, in many ways like that of the sophists before him, was opposed to the overly abstract, "bookish" education of the philosophers. It was intended instead to promote public service largely through the exercise of speech. "Let those be ashamed," he said, "who have so buried themselves in books that they can offer nothing for the common good."[50]

Cicero believed that the crown of learning was rhetoric, not dialectic, and that by rhetoric, persons would be persuaded to act virtuously in society. Education had value not in itself but because it equipped one to be a good citizen. It was intended for the "free man" (i.e., the citizen) for the wise use of his leisure, the work of citizenship, the nonremunerative work that was, as Josef Pieper has described it, "the basis of culture."[51] For the Greeks as well as the Romans, leisure was the center point about which everything revolves.[52] In fact the Greek word for leisure *(skole)* is one of those from which "liberal arts" is said to be derived because it is the same one from which the word "school" is derived. Ironically then, "school" was not a place for work but for leisure—something most students today would find puzzling, to say the least! This so contradicts post-Reformation thinking about work as to seem almost nonsensical. We cannot digress here from confusions about liberal arts to those about work and leisure. But it is important to see that both Greeks and Romans believed the "leisure" of the citizen was the work for which the oratorical tradition took liberal education to be preparation. So what then is the liberal education preparation for? What is its instrumental value, its use?

Four Kinds of Usefulness

Useful for Graduate School

The usefulness of the liberal arts can be seen at a number of levels beginning at the most basic. Students in most places calling themselves liberal arts institutions are asked to take a wide range of courses outside their discipline. They ask how these courses will help them in their chosen profession. They assume that if they are headed for graduate school in a particular profession they should not "waste" their time in courses not obviously related to that field. At best, these general education courses are viewed as inconvenient "way stations" en route to a professional degree.[53] So it is both interesting and ironic that there is empirical evidence that students concentrating on liberal arts studies not directly related to their chosen profession often are better prepared for graduate work in that field than those who have specialized early. Reports on the scores of students taking the MCAT examination for admission to medical school, for example, show that students majoring in such disciplines as philosophy or mathematics tend to outperform those studying sciences more directly related to medicine. Jaroslav Pelikan, Sterling Professor of Philosophy and former dean of the Yale Graduate School, in *Scholarship and Its Survival,* says the best preparation for graduate work is, in fact, a broad-based field of study.[54]

Useful for Jobs

As well as being better preparation for graduate studies, broad studies in liberal arts are also better preparation for long-term advancement in most jobs. It is interesting that "most students do not use the content of their major directly in their careers."[55] Workers are likely to change jobs five times before they are forty.[56] And the typical college graduate will change professions (not just jobs) over three (and some say six) times in his or her career. Furthermore, with the pace of change in most professions, the specific training received during undergraduate years often becomes obsolete in a very short time, requiring on-the-job continuing education in any case. A study by AT&T some years ago confirmed that the education most suited to long-term advancement in most professions is not the narrowly specialized one but the one that provides the transferable skills crucial to a variety of jobs.[57]

Chief among such skills are those in thinking and communication. First, forming abstract concepts and second, tying them to concrete particulars is the basis for the kind of vision required of leadership in almost any situation from home to corporate life or politics. Third, differentiating, and fourth, classifying among a broad range of particular phenomena are organizational skills required in a wide range of managerial tasks. Fifth, grouping tasks and issues according to a framework is essential for supervising with vision. Sixth is the ability to identify assumptions—whether one's own or those of others—in the context of everyday oral and written discussion on the job or in the news, for example. This skill enables the one who possesses it to identify the various possible positions on important issues related to personal, family, community, or worldwide matters. Seventh, evaluation of evidence and eighth, revision of the abstract concepts hypothesized to encompass particulars are thinking skills critical in almost any walk of life. Ninth, articulation of one's thinking, especially of the abstract concepts that tie that thinking together, is useful in persuading others or even in working together with others on a day-to-day basis. This includes the ability to speak and write in such a way that the relevant audience will understand. And of course because what one knows or believes is always open to revision, it is essential, tenth, that one learn how to learn.

One study of the connection between work and education concluded that "our most consistent—though unexpected—finding is that the amount of knowledge one acquires of a content area is generally unrelated to superior performance in an occupation. . . . In fact, it is neither the acquisition of knowledge nor the use of knowledge that distinguishes the outstanding performer, but rather the cognitive skills. . . . The cognitive skills constitute the first factor of occupational success."[58]

The liberal arts claim all of these transferable skills as outcomes. They represent the instrumental value of a liberal arts education. They are among the most important things a liberal arts education does for you. But, you might ask, do not other forms of education—vocational, technical, or even more narrowly professional forms—also produce these outcomes at least as well? There is evidence that a liberal arts education improves these skills and improves them with greater effectiveness than other kinds of education.

One important empirical study was conducted in the mid-1970s with students from a range of institutions.[59] Freshmen and seniors were compared with regard to proficiency in a wide range of the transferable skills, including those mentioned above. Furthermore, after a period of years, longitudinal studies were also done to compare the same students as freshmen and as seniors with regard to the same skills. Careful attention was given to factors that might have interacted with the effect of the distinctively liberal arts curriculum and environment.[60] And perhaps most importantly, the study recognized that measuring the outcomes of a liberal arts education—including the kind of transferable skills we have been discussing—cannot be accomplished only with traditional objective tests that ask for choices and involve mere knowledge of facts. Since the critical issue is whether liberal arts are useful, it was important to measure the students' abilities to do things, for example, think in certain ways or communicate in certain ways. To this end, operant measures were introduced in addition to the usual objective tests and self-reports.[61]

The results of this study showed that seniors at the liberal arts institution had significantly improved their thinking skills. The freshman–senior differences at the non-liberal arts colleges were significantly smaller.[62] These skills included, specifically, the ten mentioned above as well as a range of motivational and emotional outcomes. The study went on to try to identify the specific aspects of the liberal arts curriculum and environment most closely correlated with these improvements. Those results are eye-opening.[63] But the point here is that a liberal arts education is at least as effective and probably more effective than other kinds of education for producing transferable skills useful in many walks of life.

Useful for Research

Specialized skills are also crucial in the performance of many occupations. Since its introduction into American education at Johns Hopkins in 1878, the disciplinary "major" has increasingly become the centerpiece of college curricula. Progress in some areas of research and development depend on this concentration and focus of effort. However deplorable the excesses and dubious results of some forms of expert knowledge, such specialization seems to be "an inescapable concomitant of the growth of knowledge."[64] But it is interesting that some of the best arguments for more general education of the kind found in liberal arts institutions are coming from those involved in some of the most technical fields.

One example comes from reports on recent attempts to create artificial intelligence (AI). According to Hubert and Stuart Dreyfus, the AI movement got under way in the early 1950s in research groups committed to two competing schools of thought.[65] One school (foundationalists/reductionists) derived its basic working assumptions from Western philosophy and believed that the brain and the computer were alike in operating according to fixed formal rules. The other school (connectionists/contextualists) assumed the best way to create intelligence was to build on the idea of pattern recognition. Both were initially confident but by 1970, the foundationalists seemed to have prevailed. More recently, however, the foundationalists have come to recognize that their failure to even come close to creating machines capable of original thought can be traced to the "contrast between expert (or reductionist) and liberal (or contextual) concepts of knowledge." The problem, according to Herbert and Stuart Dreyfus, is the limitation of the reductionist, analytic approach derived from the abstract atomistic method of Western rationalism. This approach assumes that the problem can be reduced to a set of "context-free elements" that stand in formal relationships. Although this approach has been eminently successful in solving problem after problem in science and technology, it is hardly a panacea for knowing of all kinds. Such an approach fails to recognize the centrality of analogy (pattern recognition) and of commonsense background understanding in "everyday real-world thinking."[66]

Karl Popper made essentially the same point in responding to philosopher of science Carl Hempel. Hempel had tried to reduce the process of how theories are confirmed by facts to a strictly logical one. In order to avoid a set of paradoxes about the amusing possibility of "indoor ornithology" that arose when scientific theories were expressed in formal logic, Hempel insisted that scientists should never attend to more information than the particular isolated data at hand. In other words, he said scientists should employ the "methodological fiction" of ignoring all the background understanding from years of experience. Popper correctly pointed out that this is simply not the way good scientists work. Choices among theories are often matters of judgment, and some of the most creative aspects of discovery are born out of analogy, pattern recognition, and synthesis of enormous amounts of contextual information.

The irony is that at least in the field of AI, the contextualist's case for liberal knowledge arises from neuroscientists specialized in brain research, whereas the foundationalist's failure is ascribed to the specialized, reductionist, expert approach of modern philosophy, a discipline that has always been associated with the liberal arts. If nothing else, this should raise questions about the wisdom of defining liberal arts merely by lists of disciplines traditionally associated with the liberal arts.

Useful for Citizenship

Perhaps the oldest argument for the usefulness of a liberal arts education is Cicero's: preparation for citizenship. The same transferable skills so important for doing a job well are central to responsible participation in community. Unless the citizen today is able to think and communicate clearly about issues pertaining to the community, democracy cannot work as it should. For Cicero and his predecessors in Greece, it was enough that the aristocracy be liberally educated; education was for the "free man," the citizen, not the common man or the slave. But the value of liberal education is even more important today. Unlike forms of government that restrict decision making to a few, modern liberal democracy requires everyone to envision frameworks for justice, discern assumptions, relate principles to particular concrete situations, make connections with precedent, revise hypotheses, form judgments independently, articulate opinions to others, and so on.

Graduate school, jobs, research, and citizenship then are some of the things a liberal arts education is good for. Many liberal arts institutions have come to recognize these instrumental values of the education they offer. It makes perfectly good sense for such institutions to affirm these values in a marketplace saturated with concern for usefulness. It seems reasonable to "market" a liberal arts education for its genuine instrumental value if that is what parents and students are looking for. A liberal arts degree in physics is excellent preparation for engineering or management in scientific corporations. A liberal arts degree in philosophy is one of the finest possible preparations for law school, for an M.B.A. program, for seminary. A liberal arts degree in anthropology or sociology is wonderfully useful in full-time cross-cultural Christian ministry.

But there is a fine line between "marketing" and "prostitution." When the instrumental values begin to distort and compromise the intrinsic values of a liberal education, that line has been crossed. When the process is no longer one of matching the instrumental values inherent in liberal education with the market demands for usefulness but becomes one of creating curriculum in response to the market, the line has been crossed. Economic pressures on educational institutions of every kind—large and small, public and private—undoubtedly furnish the greatest single motive to go whoring.

Combining Two Traditions

We have examined briefly the roots and characteristics of two traditions in education. Are the liberal arts to be associated exclusively with the view that asks what an education does *to* you or with the view that asks what it does *for* you? Is a liberal arts education distinguishable because of its intrinsic value or because of its instrumental value?

Both Kimball and McGill suggest the differences between these two traditions are irreconcilable. To McGill they have held "incompatible ideals" for
2,400 years. Although Kimball believes a liberal arts education ought to contain elements from both traditions, he insists they must be held in "open,"
"real" tension, not "flabby compromise." They cannot be reconciled without
confusion,[67] and accommodations that bridge the two must be inconsistent
and contradictory.[68] He concludes that the "useful" versus "liberal" arts distinction is simply not helpful because it leaves too small a step to the idea of
the liberal arts as useless.[69]

But I do not agree that these two traditions are really irreconcilable. I have
already said it is simplistic to put the question as a choice between education
that is instrumentally valuable or intrinsically valuable. Perhaps the liberal
arts can be true both to Socrates and Isocrates, Plato and Cicero. Perhaps a
liberal arts education can be both instrumentally and intrinsically valuable.
Derek Bok calls for the same thing: "The true mission of universities would
be to nurture a healthy balance between applied intellectual pursuits and the
search for truth and meaning for their own sake."[70]

But can these two traditions really be combined? First, I want to examine
evidence in the traditions themselves that they are more compatible than has
been acknowledged. Second, I want to look at how Christian liberal arts can
be especially, if not uniquely, positioned to bring these two together.

Evidence of Compatibility from Plato and Aristotle

Ancient Greek philosophers acknowledged the importance of the orator's
rhetoric even if it was of secondary importance when compared with dialectic (logic). Plato gave scarcely any value to rhetoric in earlier work but
later admitted it might be an art worth studying.[71] Rhetoric is a less precise
but more useful shadow of the dialectic. Of course the orators saw the matter in reverse. Rhetoric was basic, the art on which real life was based. Dialectic was merely the abstraction from this reality; the logical framework at
best. Plato's student Aristotle went beyond his master's almost grudging admission of value to say that rhetoric was the counterpart in everyday discourse to dialectic in philosophical exchange. One might say that Aristotle's
Rhetoric represents a kind of synthesis of the two traditions.[72] But even if this
goes too far, it can hardly be said that the Greeks saw the two as incompatible irreconcilable approaches to education.

Evidence of Compatibility from Cicero

Cicero also gives some reason to believe the two traditions have commerce.
He suggested that Plato had incorrectly divorced the tongue and the brain,
reducing rhetoric to mere eloquence—confusing the orators with the
sophists. This suggests that at least for Cicero, the proper view is one that

combines the elements of dialectic and rhetoric. Cicero himself states that knowledge without eloquence is preferable to eloquence without knowledge, although the ideal is the marriage of the two.[73] In fact, according to Newman, it is Cicero, who, in describing the hierarchy of knowledge, takes the pursuit of knowledge for its own sake as foremost.[74] Although the practical pursuits of life come first in order of necessity, "as soon as we escape from the pressure of necessary cares, forthwith we desire to see, to hear, and to learn; and consider the knowledge of what is hidden or is wonderful a condition of happiness."[75] Plainly, then, since it comes after the satisfaction of these needs, knowledge is not intended to be used for these practical ends. So even for Cicero, pursuit of this knowledge is not intended for the benefit of society.[76] His valuing knowledge for its own sake stood in contrast to the very strictly instrumentalist views of the elder Cato, who strictly forbade introducing Greek philosophy into the education of Roman youth. Cato judged everything by what it produced; this was certainly not the view of Cicero. In short, Cicero valued knowledge for its own sake as well as knowledge for practical pursuits. While his point of view raises questions about which kind ought to come first and whether certain classes can ever attain to knowledge for its own sake, it is apparent that for Cicero, the two kinds of learning are not incompatible.

Evidence of Compatibility from Newman

There is even evidence of the compatibility of the two traditions in the views of Cardinal John Newman, a staunch advocate of the philosophical interpretation of the liberal arts. Newman himself recognized the question of usefulness when he said, "And now the question is asked me, What is the use of it?"[77]

> What is the real worth in the market of the article called "a Liberal Education," on the supposition that it does not teach us definitely how to advance our manufactures, or to improve our lands, or to better our civil economy; or again, if it does not at once make this man a lawyer, that an engineer, and that a surgeon; or at least if it does not lead to discoveries in chemistry, astronomy, geology, magnetism, and science of every kind.[78]

Newman's chief response was that liberal education was valuable in itself: "There is a Knowledge, which is desirable, though nothing come of it, as being of itself a treasure, and a sufficient remuneration of years of labor."[79]

But he went much further. In an important section of his book *The Idea of a University,* Newman speaks to the issue of "Knowledge Viewed in Relation to Professional Skill."[80] First, he addresses the criticisms of liberal education made ironically by such persons as philosopher John Locke and the academics of Edinburgh. To their mind, liberal (or classical) education cultivates "imagination too much and other habits of mind too little."[81] It does not develop talent for speculation, original inquiry, or the habit of pushing things up to their first principles. In response, Newman says that if these latter are what the critics mean by "useful" education, then what they mean by "useful" is just what he means by "liberal."[82] In this broadened sense of "useful," even Newman supports useful education.

But second, and more importantly, Newman insists that a liberal education is useful though not professional. His point is essentially the one made above, that liberal education is the best preparation possible for the specific work of the professions. He draws a valuable analogy with bodily health. Bodily health is a good in itself, even if nothing comes of it, and is worth pursuing and protecting. The reason for this lies in Newman's Aristotelian assumptions about good arising from the fulfillment of purposes. Health is the purpose for which the body is intended. But of course health is also useful because it is the foundation on which the body may be devoted to particular manual labor. Newman bemoans the absence of an English word that captures the idea of intellectual perfection, such as "health" captures for physical nature and "virtue" does for moral nature.[83] But he believes the analogy holds. The cultivation of intellectual health (or "cultivation of the mind" as he calls it) is the business of liberal education. And that result, mental culture, like bodily health, is not only good in itself—the fulfillment of its purpose—but it is also good as an instrument. It enables the liberally educated person to do what those without such an education cannot, just as health enables the healthy person to do what the unhealthy cannot. The healthy person is strong, energetic, agile, and manually dexterous and has endurance for many tasks. By analogy, the liberally educated person can think, reason, compare, discriminate, analyze, and form judgments.[84] Such a person possesses a state of mind in which he or she can take up any one of the professions or vocations. Newman concludes, "In this sense then . . . mental culture is emphatically useful."[85]

> This then is how I should solve the fallacy, for so I must call it, by which Locke and his disciples would frighten us from cultivating the intellect, under the notion that no education is useful which does not teach us some temporal calling, or some mechanical art, or some physical secret. I say that a cultivated intellect, because it is a good in itself, brings with it a power and a grace to every work and occupation which it undertakes, and enables us to be more useful, and to a greater number.[86]

The instrumental value alluded to here is not only for the individual then but also for society at large. As Newman says, "Utility may be made the end of education in two respects: either as regards the individual educated, or the community."[87] This is true in part, of course, because the excellent exercise of the professions and vocations benefit all. "The training of the intellect which is best for the individual himself, best enables him to discharge his duties to society."[88]

Now the proximity of Newman to Cicero should be evident. Cicero acknowledged the value of knowledge for its own sake, though the chief end of education was preparation for citizenship. Newman acknowledged the usefulness of his "liberal knowledge," even to the point of recognizing its role in preparation for citizenship, though insisting that it is accidental or secondary compared with the chief value, which is intrinsic.

In conclusion, apparently the critical difference between the two historical traditions of the liberal arts has to do with which value is primary and which is secondary or, more practically speaking, which comes first and which second. Cicero implied that knowledge for its own sake comes after our "physical and political needs are supplied . . . and we are free from necessary duties and cares."[89] Newman insists that, like bodily health, liberal knowledge or mental culture ought to "precede" the specific profession or vocation to which one is called. The orators insist that rhetoric and oratio come first. The philosophers prefer dialectic and ratio.[90] While this disagreement of order may make a great difference in practical curricular issues, it is not the stuff of which Kimball's or McGill's radical incompatibility can be made.[91] It seems to be at most a tension of priority, not compatibility. In Newman's own words, "the Philosopher, indeed, and the man of the world [orator?], differ in their very notion, but the methods, by which they are respectively formed are pretty much the same."[92] In summary, while recognizing the fine line between marketing and prostitution, it should not be impossible to reconcile the intrinsic and instrumental values of a liberal arts education.

CHRISTIAN LIBERAL ARTS COMBINES BY GOING BEYOND BOTH

What does the Christian liberal arts college have to contribute to this long-standing debate about the value of education? Although the evidence from the liberal arts tradition seems to *permit* the reconciliation of intrinsic and instrumental values, I believe that Christian liberal arts show *how* that can be done. My view—and perhaps the central thesis of this book—is that when done right, Christian liberal arts combine the two historical traditions by going beyond both. Let me conclude this chapter by describing briefly *why* I believe Christian liberal arts can go beyond both traditions and then in the subsequent chapters begin to explain *how* I believe they can do this.[93]

Combining the Two Traditions: The Idea of Logos

In the closing pages of his book *Orators and Philosophers*, having argued persistently that these two traditions are irreconcilable and contradictory, Bruce Kimball begins to talk about the need to balance them. Whenever one form of liberal education has "become preeminent," it has brought along not only its strengths but its weaknesses. Kimball says, therefore, that a balance

must be preserved between reason and speech, *ratio* and *oratio.* These two
capacities, he says, have been considered the defining characteristics of
human nature—of what separates human beings from animals. It is interesting that Kimball goes on to point out that both capacities were combined for
the Greeks in the concept of *logos.*

> The balance between the two ideals [ratio and oratio] is difficult to maintain be-
> cause the distinction between reason and speech, though apparently sharp and
> clear, becomes obscure when analyzed closely, as shown by the fact that for the
> Greeks both capacities were denoted by the term logos.[94]

It seems that for the Greeks, each of the two ideals is a pole of *logos.* Thus
when Kimball calls for a restoration of balance between the educational traditions of the philosophers and the orators, it seems he is calling for something that can be captured in the concept of *logos.* "But this," he says, "is far
easier said than done."[95] In a sense, then, where Kimball ends is where I
want to begin.

Christians have long recognized the enigma of reconciling Hebrew and
Greek thinking in their faith. This problem has been the basis for councils,
charges of heresy, and even wars. I do not want to press the possibilities of
analogy between this problem and the tension of philosophers and orators
regarding intrinsic versus instrumental value in education. That I must leave
for another. But I do believe the words of the Gospel of John (1:1) provide
an obvious starting point for asking whether the Christian faith and Christian
liberal arts colleges may not have something unique to contribute to education. In that familiar passage, the author tells us that "in the beginning was
the *Logos,* and the *Logos* was with God and the *Logos* was God." Only a few
verses later the author makes the astounding claim that this *Logos* "became
flesh and dwelt among us." It is plain that his reference is to the person of
Jesus Christ. For Christians, the challenge is to discover the sense in which
the deliberate use of this word *logos* might open avenues for a distinctive
kind of education that will accomplish the balance of traditions which Kimball tells us is "easier said than done."

Combining the Two Traditions:
Becoming like Christ and Serving the World

The Christian faith includes reasons for doing what both the philosophers
and the orators have called for. Plato's overriding concern was to find Truth
that would liberate human thought from the shadowy world of mere opinion. He was not satisfied either with the individualistically created "truth" of
the sophists or the culturally created "truth" of the orators. Truth was objective. Likewise, the Christian is called to "know the Truth and the Truth shall

set you free."[96] But the Christian has a *reason* for seeking Truth that goes far beyond the limited human desire for understanding. For the Christian the entire focus of life is *to become like Christ*. Christ *is* the Way, the Truth, and the Life. "To live is Christ." This goal has intrinsic value. So the Christian has the greatest possible reason to know the Truth and thus the greatest possible reason to do what Plato asks of a liberal education.

On the other hand, Cicero's dominant concern was for duty to others in the community. He was not satisfied with the idea that knowledge could ever be separated from duty. He could not agree with Plato that to know the good was automatically to do it. There were too many examples to the contrary. Likewise, the Christian is called to "be doers of the Word and not hearers only" and reminded that often "we don't do what we want to do, and do what we don't want to do."[97] But the Christian has a reason for duty to society that goes far beyond the limited, often self-interested desire to help others or be part of community. For the Christian, the commanding example of Jesus Christ is plainly to serve. His radical, countercultural example is of servant leadership. For the Christian, the mission of Christ and his Body today is to serve others.

Thus the Christian's call combines the concerns of both Plato and Cicero. The call to become like Christ, who is the Truth, means following the model of Christ in *service* to others in the world around us. Knowing Christ is both intrinsically valuable and instrumentally valuable because it affects who we become and what we do.

Going Beyond the Two Traditions: Christian Liberal Arts

But these Christian reasons for combining what the philosophers and orators have called for point Christian liberal arts education to goals that are a step beyond both.

Christian liberal arts go beyond the philosophical tradition because for the Christian, knowing the Truth is more than merely an intellectual state of mind. This is because the Truth Himself is more than just a set of propositions. For the Christian knowledge is widened beyond cognition. While non-Christians may certainly pursue a liberal arts education, in no other tradition does the Truth become flesh. So to the Christian the call is to relationship. And in the end this unusual kind of knowledge amounts to becoming more like the Truth. To become like the Truth necessitates understanding Christ's character. Central to that character is His fundamental humility. "He humbled Himself."[98] A Christian liberal arts education is intrinsically valuable because it promotes the development of an attitude of humility toward our knowledge of all truth—what I call an attitude of critical commitment.

The Christian liberal arts also go beyond the oratorical tradition. For the Christian, "community" is larger than the "community" of shared interests. It is widened beyond that of mutual benefit based on social contract. The call to the Christian to serve the community is a call to serve all humanity. The Christian is "neighbor" to all humankind. That is what Christ taught and that is what He did. A Christian liberal arts education is instrumentally valuable because it is broadly integrative, directing students to address real-world problems. Again, other worldviews may, of course, commend service and even service to the widened community of humanity in general. But often the service is self-interested instead of self-sacrificial, even arising as a means of salvation. But in any case, it is my purpose only to show how Christian liberal arts combine and go beyond the classic traditions, not to argue that others cannot.

In this way the Christian liberal arts education brings together and goes beyond the best of both the oratorical and the philosophical traditions. The intrinsic value comes as Christian liberal arts education promotes the development of an attitude of critical commitment. The instrumental value is achieved as Christian liberal arts education addresses real-world problems. In parts I–II below, I develop the meaning of these two goals and in the final part how the Christian liberal arts college can accomplish them.

Part I

Christian Liberal Arts Means Becoming and Not Just Doing

*Critical Commitment: A Step Beyond
Both Dogmatism and Skepticism*

Part I

Christian Liberal Arts Means Becoming and Not Just Doing

Critical Commitment:
A Step Beyond Both Dogmatism and Skepticism

> The need is for liberal education dedicated "to a faith which will do away with both cynicism and bigotry."
>
> —Nathan Pusey, 1952[1]

> I do not give a fig for the simplicity on this side of complexity, but I would give my life for the simplicity on the other side of complexity.
>
> —Oliver Wendell Holmes[2]

In 1975, the president of the college at which I had taken my first full-time job took the new faculty to lunch. He had a heart-to-heart talk with us about what he believed made a Christian liberal arts college distinctive. The way he saw it, other Christian institutions of higher learning, including Bible colleges and even seminaries, gave their students answers to questions they had sometimes never even asked. On the other hand, secular institutions gave students all kinds of questions but no answers. The job of a Christian liberal arts college is more difficult in that it must provoke genuine questions and then go on to provide faculty who profess answers and support for students to find their own. In short, the Christian liberal arts college must *go beyond* other kinds of institutions.[3] It must facilitate students' development beyond what they would experience in other institutions. The Christian liberal arts college must care about who they are becoming.

Unfortunately, society at every level teaches us that our identity is found in what we do. Doing has superseded becoming. At work, at worship, even at leisure, we quickly try to establish where we stand in the "pecking order" of professional doers. Everyone wants to be busy because people who are busy doing things are "very important people." Unless you are occupied pursuing many kinds of diverse activities, including preferably a busy profession, you are not valuable. In all this doing, the question rarely arises, What kind of person are you becoming?

The same temptation arises in higher education. Students and parents alike ask, "What can you *do* with a college education?" In other words, "What is its instrumental value?" Far fewer people ask the equally important questions, "What kind of person does an education help you become?" "What is its intrinsic value?" The answers are the subject of this chapter.

But first I want to consider these preliminary questions. Why *should* an education be intended to help you become a certain kind of person? Why *should* it have intrinsic value? What exactly is the problem to which such an education is the solution?

Part of the answer is that the complex dilemmas facing society today require more than just knowledge of facts and more even than just skills in ethical decision making. As important as it is to know what others have done before and to have the thinking skills for applying principles, there are often no neat decision procedures or algorithms for resolving these dilemmas.[4] For example, there are no simple principles to guide the reconciliation of conflicting demands for economic development and equally legitimate concerns for environment and ecology. Or by what set of procedures does one consider the right to justice of both defendant and victim? And what about the tension between welfare entitlements and fiscal responsibility or parents' need to provide both self-esteem and constructive criticism to their children? When formal rules and decision procedures fail, the only recourse is to rely on the good judgment of persons of character. An education that promotes becoming a certain kind of person addresses this need.

Some may object that an education which promotes character development merely to equip graduates to address difficult problems is not really of intrinsic value. It is still only of instrumental value because its final end is to resolve pressing social dilemmas.[5]

So another part of the answer is that education should help students become a certain kind of person because that very development is intrinsically valuable. It may seem obvious, but it bears repeating that Christian and secular humanist alike agree that the goal of maturing to one's fullest potential needs no other justification. It is a legitimate end in itself. Students who do not become all they can become deny themselves and the world a great good. It is the loss of a lamp never lit or a horse never run.

Furthermore, those who do not become all they can become open themselves up to the risks—cognitive, moral, and spiritual—that go along with incomplete development. For example, the person who remains dogmatic without much reflection is vulnerable to manipulation by authoritarians.

Witness the cults, both religious and political. Those who remain skeptical and even cynical are often apathetic with little to offer others and even less to provide meaning in their own lives. These are among the specific problems to which education for character development is the answer.

Of course, life experience also produces such development; it too is a form of education. But a deliberate program can increase the likelihood that cognitive, moral, and spiritual becoming are not neglected. At least some institutions must make it their business to enhance development, build character, and promote becoming for its own sake.

It is not my purpose to focus on the reasons that make "education for character development" intrinsically valuable. In large measure, apart from the preceding brief comments, I assume that without argument. I take character development—becoming a certain kind of person—as a central distinctive of liberal arts and especially Christian liberal arts education. I want to talk about what that intrinsic value might be, why it is consistent with and even peculiarly suited to Christian liberal arts education, and how it can be achieved.

More specifically, in answering the first of these three questions, I want to examine what I will call "critical commitment." I believe that becoming a person of critical commitment should be the chief intrinsic value of Christian liberal arts. And I believe it represents a "step beyond" what usually results from other kinds of education. Second, I will look at why critical commitment is consistent with and even peculiarly suited to Christian liberal arts education Finally, I will describe briefly a few principles central to how a person or an institution can promote this kind of development.

3

What Is Critical Commitment?

Beyond Mere Answers and Beyond Mere Questions

It is hard to say which is the greater tragedy, unquestioned answers or unanswered questions.

On the one hand, Christian institutions are prone to provide a hothouse environment in which students are indoctrinated with "answers" to questions they have never asked! I say "hothouse" because the environment, too often, is artificial and because while the "answers" offered are usually good ones, they do not sink in because they do not address questions the student is really asking. Among these are questions about knowing, reality, values, and especially faith. But the questions extend into virtually every area of their lives.

> Is "seeing" the only dependable way to believing or is science only one limited way of knowing?
> Is the world really the way it seems?
> Is everybody's opinion as good as anyone else's?
> Is right and wrong really "up to" the individual—just a matter of personal preference or lifestyle?
> Is faith based only on family tradition or community?
> What about persons raised in other cultures or even in other denominations?
> Is Scripture literally true?
> Why does God allow evil?

Students emerge from high school with a penchant for neat answers, typically unacquainted with the blood, sweat, and tears of real questions. Such students are often passionately committed to "defending the Truth" and may be quite bold in their participation in important social and political issues. One well-known Christian writer-speaker has toured Christian colleges exhorting the students to "stand up" to their professors who may have "gone liberal," and student-led "witch hunts" are found on Christian campuses today. Their courage and involvement are commendable, but issues are presented and resolved in facile "black-and-white" categories. When Christian colleges cater to this, the graduates are dogmatic. Once students leave such a hothouse environment, the harsh realities of life often render the answers they have received seemingly irrelevant. They have only been inoculated with the answers, just enough to prevent them from ever really catching them. Answers that have been tested only against straw men are quickly forgotten or dismissed when real-world questions arise. Familiarity with those answers tends to breed contempt. The struggle that those answers originally occasioned in the crucible of their author's real life is never understood because the answers are given before students struggle with the questions. Merely giving answers is not enough.

On the other hand, in contrast to hothouses, secular universities too often provide "sterile," desertlike environments. Students are provoked to ask important real questions but are offered little help in finding answers! It is prone to be sterile because it appears that no one (including, ironically, the professors) is willing to profess anything except expressions of personal taste or preference. From an educator's point of view, it may be an improvement to have questions without answers rather than answers without questions, but it still falls short. Such students progress beyond simple "black-and-white" thinking but are abandoned in the multiplicity of relativism. Through the multifarious influence of professors and peers from a wide range of backgrounds they come to recognize the strengths and weaknesses of opposing points of view. This step is important and represents an improvement over uncritical dogmatism; life's issues are simply not black and white. But it can leave them paralyzed, noncommittal, and afraid to take a stand. Graduates of such institutions are often not dogmatic but are so skeptical of everything that they are cynical.[1] This also is not enough. What is needed is something that goes beyond both dogmatism and skepticism.[2] This is what I call critical commitment. But first a digression.

A DIGRESSION: POLITICAL CORRECTNESS—AN IRONIC REVERSAL

An interesting contemporary development has altered the secular campus in paradoxical ways and is probably changing its sterility. Academia has become dramatically politicized. Students can become infected with all kinds of "viruses" on secular campuses nowadays—including intellectual ones.

Exposure to such views is, I believe, a healthy step as I explain below in describing the benefits of dissonance as means to cognitive and moral development. To the extent that the myth of value neutrality is dying on American campuses today, students will all benefit and the legitimacy of Christian assumptions—long explicit on Christian campuses—should be affirmed (among others).[3]

The emergence of what is sometimes called the political correctness movement (PC) is producing an unusual mutation that fails to go beyond both dogmatism and cynicism and instead merely combines them in a way quite the opposite of critical commitment. This might be called dogmatic skepticism—a hybrid of dogmatism and skepticism based on a value system that self-destructs. Skepticism of all objective values reduces values to matters of personal or cultural taste and preference, lifestyles if you will. Value is reduced to a single quality: tolerance. Intolerance, not error, is the only remaining sin.[4]

But the movement's worship of tolerance does not extend to all world and life views at all.[5] On the contrary, only some are politically correct. There is an amazing intolerance and antipathy for traditional Christian "answers." Paradoxically, we see legions of activist authoritarian relativists—dogmatic skeptics. Having abandoned Truth, they are now bent and bound to conform everyone to their opinions. "Our university campuses are now islands of repression in a sea of freedom."[6] But when tolerance for the values of others does not include tolerance for those who disagree that values are only styles, there is contradiction. It is intolerant tolerance.[7] This paradox makes the movement an inherently unstable mutation.

Though paradoxical, the movement is not surprising.[8] Relativism leads to intellectual anarchy and, as Tocqueville observed long ago, that in turn tends toward tyranny.[9] Alasdair MacIntyre concluded that when values are seen as human creations, people affirm with Max Weber (or even Nietzsche) that there can be no rational way for authority to be legitimated. Consequently, everything reduces to power.[10] In short, the rejection of authority leads to authoritarianism.[11] This is the antithesis of liberal arts! Until this selective tolerance is done away with, the secular campus either will be as indoctrinating as the worst of religious institutions, producing dogmatists of a skeptical cynical kind, or will remain sterile as ever under the illusion of value neutrality.

CRITICAL COMMITMENT

The graduates of the Christian liberal arts college ought to be neither dogmatists nor cynics. To go beyond only dogmatism is mere reactionism. The genius of the Christian college is its aim to produce graduates who go beyond both; they are persons who embody critical commitment. They go beyond dogmatism in applying the best critical tools available to the real questions of life. They go beyond cynical skepticism in their willingness to be committed in spite of doubt. They recognize the limitations of human understanding and yet are prepared to take a stand and even stake their lives.

Critical commitment is the opposite of the dogmatic skepticism so au courant. Critical commitment is "committed" and not "skeptical" because it requires an affirmation of what is believed to be the Truth instead of insisting there is no Truth but only arbitrary relativistic belief. But critical commitment is "critical" and not "dogmatic" in the sense of an examining attitude open to new discoveries and changed belief, the way an experienced artisan looks over her work with a critical eye. It is not critical in the sense of an opposing or attacking dogmatic attitude intended to refute or turn back, as an envious opponent is critical. In short, those with critical commitment show an open attitude toward a firm belief. But those with dogmatic skepticism reveal a closed attitude that insists on open relativistic belief.[12] Because the difference here is largely a matter of attitude, it is subtle. To clarify this subtlety is the point of this chapter and to obtain it is a chief goal for Christian liberal arts.

This same goal can be expressed in terms of intellectual and moral liberty. An education that provides answers only and produces dogmatists is totalitarian. The totalitarian indoctrinator has ready-made answers for every question. "Liberty" actually means legalism, law. Those who succumb are brainwashed and become fearful dogmatists. On the other hand, an education that provides only questions and produces skeptics is anarchist. The anarchist libertine says no view is truer than any other. "Liberty" merely means license, freedom from interference. Those who agree become skeptical of all Truth and cynical. But the fact is that real social liberty flourishes under neither condition.[13] Real liberty goes beyond both. It is "freedom under law." It is no coincidence that the principles of liberal democratic forms of government have emerged from the tradition of liberal education. Thus for an education to be truly liberal, it must provide intellectual and moral liberty, which is "freedom under law." As Arthur Holmes has pointed out, these conditions can find a natural home in a Christian liberal arts college.

> Freedom is valuable only when there is a prior commitment to the truth. And commitment to the truth is fully worthwhile only when that truth exists in One who transcends both the relativity of human perspectives and the fears of human concern.[14]

Thus intellectual and moral liberty is the freedom to be critical and to question, combined with commitment to truth. This is critical commitment.

In this chapter I describe this kind of person, the graduate of the Christian liberal arts college, more fully, as someone who has become a person of critical commitment. Nathan Pusey, president of Harvard University in 1952, put it well in the report of the National Committee on Liberal Education cited at the heading of this chapter. He captured both elements well: the need to go beyond both mere answers and mere questions, beyond both dogmatism and skepticism, beyond legalism and license. The need, he said, is for liberal education dedicated "to a faith which will do away with *both* cynicism and bigotry." The Christian liberal college can do this. But the task will be twice as difficult as that of institutions which settle for either half.

DEVELOPMENTAL THEORY: A TOOL FOR UNDERSTANDING CRITICAL COMMITMENT

So the president was right that day at lunch. Christian liberal arts colleges must go beyond what other institutions do. What he might not have realized, however, is that his description matches closely the kind of human cognitive and moral development process that psychologists have uncovered. Because of that parallel, I believe their work can provide us with tools to facilitate the doubly difficult task of producing graduates who are critically committed. The Christian academic community has made too little use of these results. I believe careful attention to these results reveals that the goal of critical commitment is a step beyond both dogmatism and skepticism. This means that developmental theory can provide powerful direction in clarifying how Christian liberal arts colleges might achieve this distinctive goal.

Developmental psychology gives evidence that persons *become* who they are by developing through a number of identifiable stages or at least by passing through a number of identifiable positions. Studies of an empirical or quasi-empirical kind reveal these stages/positions in cognitive, moral, and even faith development. A great deal of attention has been paid to the "what" and "how" of human becoming—character development.[15]

The Theorists

It is always hard to pinpoint where a line of thinking (a "discipline") began. There are roots of human developmental thinking in Freud and Jung. But perhaps the clearest origins are found in the works of Erik Erikson and Jean Piaget. Each of them understood human development to be a kind of passage through stages or positions and attempted to identify those stages.

Erikson identified eight stages across the span of life, each concerned with resolution of a particular task. As each task or crisis was resolved, it laid the basis for movement to the next stage.[16] Piaget focused on cognitive and moral development, especially of young children.[17] He described this development in terms of transitions from heteronomy (externally based rules) to autonomy (internally based rules).[18] This transition occurred, he said, through a number of stages between the ages of six and twelve, proceeding from purely physical activities to concrete operations (ordering or organizing physical experience) and then to formal operations ("thinking about thinking").[19]

Perhaps the chief difference between Erikson and Piaget, and one that is crucial to us, was that Erikson believed the progression proceeded "automatically" and was based on biological maturation. People developed whether they were ready or not. On the other hand, Piaget took Kant's view seriously that knowledge is not just passive but active and that it is not just a matter of content but of structure. He believed that while biological development was a necessary condition, it was not a sufficient condition for cognitive and moral development.[20] Rather, he believed that development occurred, if it occurred and to whatever extent it occurred, by constructive interaction with the environment. For this reason, his views are sometimes called constructive-developmental models. My understanding of critical commitment falls into this Piagetian tradition. In other words, I believe the role of the educational institution *is* very important in the developmental journey of the student.

Lawrence Kohlberg built on the work of Piaget but focused more specifically on the question of how moral judgment develops. He identified six stages, two each at three levels—preconventional, conventional, and postconventional. In the preconventional stages, right and wrong, good and bad are determined by the immediate consequences to self. The first stage gives value to the avoidance of punishment and defers to power for its own sake, not because it represents underlying moral order. In the second stage, right is whatever satisfies one's own personal, hedonistic needs. Even "fairness" comes down to "you scratch my back and I'll scratch yours": an exchange of mutual pleasures. As the name suggests, the conventional stages make the expectations, rules, or "conventions" of one's family, group, or culture the highest standards of right and wrong. In stage three, the right thing to do is always to be a "good boy" or a "nice girl." This develops in stage four into a legalistic orientation toward authority and rules as means of maintaining social order. The final level Kohlberg calls "Postconventional, Autonomous, or Principled." Here there is an attempt to define moral values as principles that are valid independently of whatever person or group might happen to hold them. Stage five ("Law and Order") emphasizes a social contract whereby the rights of the individual are protected by laws that are created and modified by a rational procedure that considers social utility and not just rigid legalism, as in stage four. Some have identified this as the "official" morality of the U.S. government and Constitution.[21] Finally, according to Kohlberg, stage six ("Universal Ethical Principle Orientation") occurs when the individual defines right and wrong by decisions taken that apply ethical principles, which are in turn judged on their consistency, their universality, and their adequacy in dealing with the specific case dilemmas the individual meets.

Kohlberg's Stages of Moral Development

Preconventional
  Stage 1: Avoid punishment, obey power orientation
  Stage 2: "Scratch my back and I'll scratch yours"
Conventional
  Stage 3: "Good boy–nice girl" orientation
  Stage 4: Rigid law-and-order orientation
Postconventional, Autonomous, Principled
  Stage 5: Utilitarian social contract orientation
  Stage 6: Universal ethical principle orientation

Carol Gilligan has suggested that this scheme is distorted by the choice of subjects used in Kohlberg's research. She argues that Kohlberg's scheme is excessively individualistic, rationalistic, and justice oriented because the subjects were predominantly upper-class white males.[22] She asserts that this criticism can be made of Freud, Erikson, and Piaget as well.[23] Although Kohlberg claimed that the stages are universal, it is interesting, Gilligan points out, that when women are evaluated on the scheme, they consistently appear developmentally deficient. They seem to be fixed at Kohlberg's stage three, in which morality is defined in interpersonal terms and good is equated with helping and pleasing others. She says that if you begin with studies of women, a different "voice" emerges. From this perspective, moral problems are not couched in terms of competing rights requiring rules of justice to resolve, but in terms of conflicting responsibilities requiring care. She clarifies the difference between these two voices by using a story of a boy and girl at play. The girl wants to play "neighbors" but the boy wants to play "pirates." The boy's solution (Kohlberg) might be to propose that the "fair" solution would be to take turns, playing each game for an equal time, honoring each child's individual identity and rights. The girl's solution (Gilligan) might be to propose that the boy become the "pirate next door." This solution transforms *both* games; the neighborhood is changed by having a pirate around and the pirate by living in a community.[24]

Robert Sandin echoes Gilligan's criticism. Kohlberg's mature person is too rationalistic and justice oriented. Kohlberg's ideal moral agents will act reasonably to pursue their own highest good within the confines of justice. But this leaves no room for self-sacrifice. "Rational agents are fair, not saintly."[25]

James Fowler is a psychologist and theologian who has applied developmental psychology to religious faith. Building on the work of Erikson, Piaget, and Kohlberg, he describes six stages of faith development that follow closely the scheme of Piaget from preoperational to concrete operations to formal operations. The transition of greatest importance for our purposes is the one from assumed conventional faith (Fowler's stage 3) to critical self-aware faith (Fowler's stage 4).[26] This transition is characterized by a shift from dependence on the consensus of one's relevant community to a dependence on one's own reflective judgment in determining the shape of personal faith.[27]

Finally, there is the work of William G. Perry. His studies of cognitive and ethical development focused on the college years.[28] Because of this focus, his results are of particular use to us. He identified nine positions that can be roughly grouped by three successive characteristics: dualism, multiplicity, and commitment.[29]

Perry's Positions of Cognitive Development

Dualism
  Position 1: Basic duality
  Position 2: Multiplicity—prelegitimate
  Position 3: Multiplicity—subordinate
Multiplicity
  Position 4: Relativism subordinate/multiplicity correlate
  Position 5: Relativism (competing, correlate, or diffuse)
  Position 6: Commitment forseen
Commitment
  Position 7: Initial commitment
  Position 8: Orientation of commitment implications
  Position 9: Developing commitment

Perry himself was sensitive in listening and interpreting and scrupulously sought to avoid the temptation to reductionism. His often repeated axiom was "the person is always larger than the theory."[30] For this reason it is unfair to overly simplify his results. Even the threefold grouping above is troublesome as dualism, multiplicity, and commitment overlap considerably in the transitional positions.[31] But of course some simplification is necessary and fortunately Perry himself provides helpful summaries.

Position 1: "The student sees the world in polar terms of we-right-good vs. other-wrong-bad. Answers for everything exist in the Absolute, known to Authority whose role is to teach them."

Position 2: "The student perceives diversity of opinion and uncertainty and accounts for them as unwarranted confusion in poorly qualified Authorities or as mere exercises set by Authority 'so we can learn to find The Answer for ourselves.'"

Position 3: "The student accepts diversity and uncertainty as legitimate but still temporary in areas where Authority 'hasn't found The Answer yet.'" The student is puzzled by how teachers can assign grades.

Position 4: Depending on whether the student follows a path of adherence (assimilation) or opposition (accommodation) to Authority, either relativism becomes just a special case of "what they want" or a legitimate correlate domain alongside dualism, in which "anyone has a right his own opinion" and "no one can tell me I'm wrong."

Position 5: "The student perceives all knowledge and values, including authority's, as contextual and relativistic." They subordinate "dualistic right-wrong functions to the status of a special case" of relativism instead of the other way around as in position 4. A revolution has occurred.

Position 6: "The student apprehends the necessity of orienting himself in a relativistic world through some form of personal Commitment (as distinct from unquestioned or unconsidered commitment to simple belief in certainty)."

Position 7: "The student makes an initial Commitment in some area."

Position 8: "The student experiences the implications of Commitment and explores the . . . issues of responsibility."

Position 9: "The student experiences the affirmation of identity among multiple responsibilities and realizes Commitment as an ongoing, unfolding activity through which he expresses his life style."

Perry identifies positions 4, 5, and 6 as the critical ones during college years, and the transition from position 4 to 5 as perhaps the most crucial. Importantly, Perry's study allows for considerable change during the relatively short period of four years in college. He found that by the end of even their first year, when the first interviews occurred, freshmen took the outlook of positions 3, 4, or even 5 but described themselves upon arrival at college in decidedly dualistic terms (positions 1, 2, and 3). Seniors, however, were found to function in positions 6, 7, and 8 (75 percent had reached position 7 or 8), while position 9 was generally beyond what even a senior might be expected to reach. And interestingly, "the position at which a student was rated as a freshman was not predictive of the position at which he would be rated in his senior year."[32] All this provides some reason to be hopeful that four years is not too little time and that colleges can make a difference.

Finally, Perry allows that there are at least three obstacles to development. First, students may temporize, pausing for as long as a year without undermining their ability to move on at a later time. Second, students may escape at some middle position on the scale by detaching themselves and avoiding responsibility for growth. Forms of escape include a cynicism that uses multiplicity to defeat all value statements except, of course, affirmation of self as a nihilist. Or escape can mean using multiplicity to wash out self-identity completely, substituting either an attitude of "anything goes" or "intellectual game playing" with all commitment avoided.[33] Third, and finally, the student may retreat. Perry is uncertain whether retreat can occur back across the boundary of dualism and multiplicity; the implications of this will be of interest in discussing the place all this has for the Christian.[34] Variants of retreat include high anxiety reaction to multiplicity, "know it all" hate of multiplicity, negativism against authority without a cause of one's own, and dogmatic rebellion.

Working Assumptions in Developmental Theory

Although I will describe critical commitment chiefly in terms of Perry's scheme, let me begin by making some of my own assumptions clear. First, *developmental schemes are useful because humans are meaning makers*. The very mention of "developmental schemes" or "stages of development" is likely to raise the hackles or at least the eyebrows of some students of psychology. They object to any form of psychology that uses classification or typing. "People are more complex than that!" they insist. They rightly warn us to avoid the seduction of reductionism. It is always tempting to reduce complicated processes to simple, neat schemes. However, since Kant, I believe there is no avoiding the conclusion that people are at least partly meaning *makers*.[35] Unless we bring some structures to our inquiry, there will be nothing to know. Some may by temperament find developmental structures more objectionable while others find them useful. But that very statement may be objectionable to those who eschew such structures. My assumption will be that the notion of human development is a valuable tool in understanding and informing educational theory. Still, the warning against reductionism is well taken and we must be ever vigilant.

Second, *an interactionist developmental scheme is preferable to a maturationist or environmental developmental scheme*. Some may ask whether every theory of the educational process must start with the assumption that cognitive or moral or faith development is the aim of education. The answer, of course, is no; there are other possibilities. Kohlberg describes "three streams of educational ideology." He uses the word "ideology" because each rests on different assumptions about psychological development.

In the first stream, what Kohlberg calls the *romantic* stream, what comes from within the student is the most important part of education. The natural self is the starting point, and the educator's chief responsibility is to keep out of nature's way. The biological metaphors of health and growth provide models for education. The Aristotelian heritage here is plain. In terms of the categories described in the last chapter, one might also say that for the romantic, the chief value in education is intrinsic. The underlying assumption of psychological development is maturationist, that is, cognitive growth is the unfolding of prepatterned stages, at most nourished by the environment and at worst vulnerable to frustration and fixation.[36]

In contrast, Kohlberg describes a second stream, the cultural transmission view, which puts society and not the student at the center. The primary job of education is to transmit to present students a body of accumulated information and values from the past. The importance of this information and values is not intrinsic but derives from their place in the culture. In terms of the categories of the last chapter, on this view, the chief value of education is instrumental. The underlying assumption of psychological development here, says Kohlberg, is *environmental*. By this he seems to mean that the student is like a machine requiring carefully managed inputs in order to produce desirable behavior patterns as output, rather than something organic requiring nurture to mature. To this end, repetition, feedback, and other behavioristic methods are employed.[37]

Kohlberg aligns himself with the third educational ideology, which he calls the *cognitive-developmental* or *progressive* approach. Another name might be the *interactionist* theory of education because its goal is to stimulate the student's interaction with society and environment. On the romantic view, development is an unfolding of innate patterns promoted by educators who create an environment free of conflict.[38] In contrast, on this third view, development is hammering out progress on a pathway of invariant sequential stages. The process is active and is stimulated by what is problematic. The goal of the romantic view is healthy functioning at the student's present level while the goal of this approach is active changes in the structures and patterns of cognition, morality, and, we might add, faith. Development is "neither direct biological maturation nor direct learning but a reorganization of psychological structures" resulting from *dialectical* interaction with society and the environment.[39]

My assumption will be an interactionist or progressive one, of the kind and for the reasons described below. Kohlberg's interactionist approach to education with its underlying views of psychological development has several advantages.

In the first place, because it emphasizes the exchange between student and environment understood broadly, the interactionist view allows no isolating of cognitive development from moral, faith, or even emotional development. The interaction with experience is too complex for that. Instead,

> The progressive educator stresses the essential links between cognitive and moral development; he assumes that moral development is not purely affective, and that cognitive development is a necessary though not sufficient condition for moral development.[40]

Such an implication seems desirable at Christian institutions which, because of theological assumptions about the integrity of human nature, are committed to the education of whole persons.

Second, it seems that the interactionist view avoids ethical problems that undermine the other views. No educational enterprise can be value-free. The myth of value-neutral education overlooks the reality that educational theory must ultimately say something about what the student *ought* to become. That is why educational theories are actually "ideologies"; it is contradictory to claim to provide a "value-neutral prescription of educational goals."

So consider how the cultural transmission view addresses this challenge of prescribing educational goals. The solution is to appeal to the "values" of society, recognizing that these may be quite arbitrary because, of course, societies differ on what is right and wrong. But this kind of value relativism cannot provide a direction for education because it runs afoul of what philosophers call the naturalistic fallacy. The mere fact that cultural values differ does not by itself allow one to conclude that all values are relative unless one confuses facts and values, that is, unless one commits the naturalist fallacy. That fallacy states that one can never derive obligation from fact. From what merely "is" one can never determine what "ought" to be. The cultural transmission view seems to entail that the mere fact that society has promoted a set of values makes them right. But what makes *this* claim right? That question remains open. Some proponents of this view respond by saying that such values are good (obligatory) because they promote the survival of society. Behaviorists like Skinner fall into this group and are fond of talking about the value of reinforcement for survival while at the same time claiming value neutrality. But whether survival is really good remains an open question too. There is no escaping the dilemma.

Then consider how the romantic addresses the problem of prescribing educational goals. The romantic approach appears to oppose the cultural transmission view because the former advocates complete "freedom" to the student as the goal of education while the latter promulgates cultural "values." On the romantic view, whatever the student does is right. Whatever "feels good" must be educational. But the mere fact that, left to themselves, people *will* do what feels good does not at all entail that they *should* do what feels good. That is to confuse what philosophers call psychological egoism with ethical egoism and that confusion is just a variation of the naturalistic fallacy. As John Dewey put it, "growth is not enough; we must also specify the direction in which growth takes place, the end toward which it tends."[41] Some proponents of this view will respond by saying the direction is irrelevant: "We should tolerate all student views because values are relative." But *this* version of value relativity is problematic for two reasons. First, it is oddly contradictory for a value relativist to argue that one "should" do anything. Yet their affirmation of at least the value of tolerance is obvious. Second, it makes the educational enterprise self-defeating. Such educators could never even be justified in teaching their students the value of tolerance. They could not recommend the very value they themselves use to justify their own approach. In short, they could never really set even tolerance as a goal of education.[42]

Both the cultural transmission view and the romantic view struggle to provide a consistent value base for educational theory. Instead, their approach
to education is prone to elitism and manipulation. The cultural transmission
educator teaches the values to maintain a culture but not the values to create one. The romantic educator protects the student from all but happiness,
presumably assuming that a happy pig is better than an unhappy Socrates.
But by what right does she do this?[43]

In contrast, the interactionist view of development refuses to accept the
myth of value-free education and thereby can address the need to prescribe
educational goals while avoiding the ethical problems above. It avoids the
naturalistic fallacy by avoiding the kinds of ethical relativism that confuse
facts and values. Instead of relativism, the interactionist unapologetically affirms the universal value of rational principles.[44] In other words, rational ethical principles should arbitrate the goals of education, not the psychological
facts of the self *or* the cultural facts of parental or societal tradition.[45] Those
facts should, of course, inform the educational process; students, parents,
and society must be consulted. But they are not to be the determinants of
means or ends in education.[46]

Chief among these rational ethical principles is liberty. This is not the liberty of the romantic, which comes down merely to noninterference and is
only a means to self-expression. Instead, this liberty is an educational end as
well. In other words, it is a principle worth interfering in students' lives to
teach. It is a principle which requires not only that the educator respect the
students' self-expression (liberty as an educational means) but teaches the
students to respect themselves and others (liberty as an educational end).[47]
Viewed in this way, the rational ethical principle of liberty calls educators to
"talk their walk" and "preach what they practice." The educational aim is,
then, the construction of a strong, liberated character. This aim clearly agrees
with the idea that Christian liberal arts are interested in becoming and not
just in doing.

But the critic is eager to object. Whether the romantic or cultural transmission
views successfully avoid them or not, the ethical problems with value-free education arose from its attempt to avoid the dangers of indoctrination. In contrast, the interactionist approach to development has jumped from the frying
pan into the fire. The interactionist seems to be indoctrinating students into a
particular set of values. Part of the answer available to the interactionist is that
promoting cognitive and moral development is not indoctrination because developmental stages are said to be transcultural and sequential.[48] Stimulating natural development is not indoctrination.[49] More importantly, the "values" taught
are not so much formulae or ready-made behaviors grounded in authority as
they are principles or tools for shaping one's own thinking and judging. But

most importantly, the interactionist avoids indoctrination by involving the student in the teaching/learning process. As Kohlberg puts it,

> It is impossible for the teachers not to engage in value-judgments and decisions. A concern for the liberty of the [student] does not create a school in which the teacher is value-neutral. . . . But it can create a school in which the teacher's value-judgments and decisions involve the students democratically.[50]

Such a school might be called a dialectical community founded on liberty. We will return to that idea in chapter 8, where I undertake to discuss *how* critical commitment can be taught.

My third assumption is that *I adopt no particular interactionist developmental scheme*. Even among those who would call themselves interactionists there will be objections to the particular names or nuances of the typology. Still others disagree with claims about the irreversibility of such development. So although I have already sided with Piaget and Kohlberg against Erikson and Skinner (interactionist vs. maturationist or environmental development), it is not my intention to defend any particular interactionist scheme of cognitive, moral, or faith development in detail. At the very least, I want to call those involved in Christian liberal arts education to pay attention to the reality of student cognitive, moral, and faith development in general. But more than that, I also believe there is considerable agreement about the process of development and even about some broad characteristics of the highest stages.

It appears that the process of development itself has some general features. First, stage development seems to be sequential and invariant. This means that apparently cognitive, moral, or faith development occurs in a particular order that cannot be significantly altered. We cannot function at "later" stages until we have first functioned at the "earlier" ones. In other words, we cannot "leap" into cognitive, moral, or faith maturity. Instead it is a process of growth. Second, while developing, people cannot comprehend the characteristics of any level more than the one immediately beyond where they are presently functioning. For example, the child who judges right and wrong in terms of unquestioned obedience to authority or avoidance of punishment (Kohlberg stage 1) *may* understand the idea of doing something good for someone so that he or she will do something good for you (Kohlberg stage 2) but will not even understand, much less accept, the possibility that something might be good because "it is what good girls do" or because it will preserve social order (Kohlberg stage 3). Third, because we do understand them, the characteristics and operations of cognition, morality, or faith at one level beyond one's own are attractive, even though it might be attractive only as something dangerous or risky. Like the simultaneous fear and fascination we sense about fire or the unknown, we all find ourselves intrigued by those who function at the next stage of development beyond our own. Finally, it appears that movement through the stages—whether cognitive, moral, or faith—is effected at least in part when disequilibrium is present. This means that development seems to follow when our current way of coping becomes inadequate. When problems surface that cannot be resolved from the perspective of one's current state of development, the stage is set for movement to the next stage. This feature of almost all developmental schemes offers a clue to the methods that must be considered below (chapter 5 and part III) in asking how the Christian liberal arts college can help students *become* critically committed.[51]

But beyond agreement about these features of the developmental process, there is also considerable agreement among interactionists about the broad characteristics of the highest stages of development from scheme to scheme. This agreement will become apparent in the discussion of critical commitment.

Critical Commitment: A Developmental View

I referred to critical commitment at the beginning of this chapter. Let us now examine it in the light of developmental theory.

Critical Commitment Goes Beyond: Two Critical Transitions

I have described critical commitment as a kind of becoming that goes beyond mere answers or mere questions, beyond both dogmatism and skepticism, bigotry and cynicism, and beyond both legalism and license. In the language of Perry, what I am calling critical commitment goes beyond both the positions of dualism (1–3 or 4) and the positions of multiplicity (5 and 6). This suggests that there can be two critical transitions for the college student, the first from authority-bound dualism to multiplicity and then from multiplicity to commitment.

Dualism to Relativism

Most students arrive as freshmen well established in black-and-white thinking. Having functioned as "seniors" in high school, they are confident that their patterns of structuring experience are working fine and are largely complete, although they do not have all the answers yet. Questions typically have only one answer and it seems unavoidable that each new college freshman class will once again try the patience of its professors by interrupting loquacious soliloquies with questions like "but which is the correct view?" or "will this be on the test?" There is usually very little tolerance for ambiguity. The unavoidable diversity among their peers, pluralism of views to which they are exposed, and multiplicity in the curriculum, both formal and informal, make them uneasy. A common reaction is to hate "interpretations." Perry says that the very idea of "interpretation" does not make sense to many because it requires the presupposition of uncertainty.[52] Classes in the humanities, such as philosophy or English, often take abuse because they "never solve anything" or "always read between the lines." It is enough to make professors in these classes more than just a little paranoid. The natural sciences and to a lesser extent the social sciences still seem to have answers, but before long, students discover that the authorities in these areas do not seem to have answers either; at least not yet. This is a blow for the students, however, because the criteria for evaluation of their work will be different from what they have thought. They worry the teacher is grading arbitrarily or on "style alone" and begin to pay much greater attention to "what the teachers want." Depending on whether they still trust the authorities, they either will learn to "play the game" or will see authorities as "cowardly or incompetent." But in both cases, a fissure has appeared in their way of understanding truth and value. Students who trust the authorities discover that "what they want" is a "way of thinking" that recognizes alternative starting points and emphasizes the comparison of alternate patterns of thought and the need for reasons. This "way of thinking" and the Truth seem to pull students in opposite directions. Those who are not so sure about the authorities create a split between the world of authorities, in which right and wrong still prevail, and the world of multiplicity, in which "everyone has a right to their opinion." This is a kind of dual dualism, and the student can use it for a new rebellion.

The pressure of this growing fissure may cause some to temporize and put the whole issue on a back burner. Others retreat to earlier positions, becoming very negative and reactionary. Sometimes this is the conservative student, more common on Christian campuses today than twenty years ago, who challenges the professors and even the institution as a whole for having abandoned Truth to become liberal. They may even do it with the backing of family, pastors, and well-known Christian leaders. Still others escape the challenge altogether by largely abandoning "intellectualism" or by practicing it cynically as a game while maintaining their largely authority-based black-and-white categories.

For the large majority, however, the pressure results in a transition to some kind of relativism. It is a revolution. Instead of relativism as a special case of absolutes, absolutes become special cases in a new relativistic context. Relativism is perceived as the common characteristic of all thought.

> The revolution is the "most violent accommodation of structure in the entire development, yet it is the most quiet. It involves a complete transposition between part and whole . . . yet almost no student in our sample referred to it as a conscious event, a discrete experience, a 'realization.'"[53]

As in the philosophy of science, little work has been done to describe the features of such transitions themselves. Thomas Kuhn talks about revolutions in scientific paradigms, and there can be little doubt that this transition is similar.[54] How long do these transitions take? Do they, like a gestalt shift, occur in a moment? Are they deliberate or spontaneous? Do religious students experience this revolution in fundamentally different ways than those who are not religious? In particular, do religious persons actually abandon, however temporarily, their anchorage until it reemerges in the position of commitment?[55] Perry's experimental group included religious students and I will turn to his few comments about them below, but much more work could be done here.[56]

For the most part, those who make the transition to positions of multiplicity learn to "play the game well." These students become sophisticated in their ability to pick apart the claims of others whether they are just opinions of friends, news editorials, or the edifices of traditional institutions. They have advanced beyond the stage of "answers only." Now they are experts at asking questions. They have moved beyond the dogmatism of earlier dualism and now embrace tolerance. Instead of the intolerance for ambiguity associated with dualism, students now rejoice in their sense of new-found freedom.

> When you get in a narrow shell or something you sort of just can't break out, you're just, just looking around. It's like being in a room with all the windows down and all of a sudden you're let out. . . . Ah, I think college has opened the shell for me, let me out. I can see things that I've never seen before and think about things I never really thought about or thought were important.[57]

The relativistic way of thinking spreads to other areas and becomes a habit. The old dualistic self is scorned.

Relativism to Commitment

But, as with dualism, problems begin to arise here too. Students may cope for a while saying, "You have your way, I have mine; what counts is sincerity." But the cost in emotion and energy to maintain such a position takes its toll. As Perry's subject put it,

> Soon I may begin to miss those tablets in the sky. . . . I apprehend all too poignantly now that in the most fateful decisions of my life I will be the only person with a first-hand view of the really relevant data, and only part of it at that. Who will save me then from that "wrong decision" I have been told not to make lest I "regret-it-all-my-life"? Will no one tell me if I am right? Can I never be sure? Am I alone?[58]

And as Sharon Parks has pointed out, "Doubt is deepened when someone points out that both Martin Luther King Jr. and devotees of Adolf Hitler were in a sense 'sincere.'"[59]

As before, the failure of the current cognitive and moral structure to deal adequately with experience may prompt another change, the second critical transition. Under the threat of loss of identity, students begin to look for a place to stand. This brings us to commitment, not in the narrow sense referring to the object of commitment but to the very act, ongoing activity, or, better still, the attitude of commitment. The person becomes agent and invests energy, care, and identity in various aspects of life. Perry pointed out that this emerges first as only an inkling that commitment will be the way to avoid the problems of relativism without actually adopting that strategy. It is important to recognize, however, that not all students come to this point. In fact, some may never reach it. The relevance of education is plain. The student has, for a second time, moved "beyond," this time not only beyond the stage of "answers only" but now also beyond the stage of "questions only."

In his study of faith development, James Fowler echoed Perry's conclusions about this stage "beyond" both dualism and multiplicity. He said that a crucial transition of faith typical for the young adult in college years is from conventional, assumed faith to critical, self-aware faith. Conventional faith (Fowler's stage 3) is characterized by forms of cognition corresponding to Perry's dualism bound to authority (positions 1-3). In both cases the individual's patterns for structuring experiences (religious, cognitive, and moral) are rooted in authority. Critical, self-aware faith, on the other hand (Fowler's stage 4), is characterized by forms of cognition associated with Perry's commitment (positions 7 and beyond). In both cases the individual's ways of structuring experiences involve assuming personal responsibility and go beyond uncommitted criticism as well as uncritical commitment.[60] What is interesting is that Fowler characterized adult faith as a critical faith that "goes beyond."

Sharon Parks elaborates on Fowler's approach in a wonderful metaphor. She suggests that the journey of faith is like that of the people of Israel who left Egypt, the land of authority, to go beyond into the wilderness of uncertainty but eventually beyond even that into the Promised Land.[61] She adds, however, that Perry's scheme may be inadequate in describing the full extent to which commitment takes us beyond. The highest stages of Perry's scheme are described in terms of commitment in relativism. Yet Fowler believes there is a stage of faith beyond even that of commitment in relativism. It is the faith of the mature adult and may be rare or even impossible for the college-age student. Parks wants to call it convictional commitment.[62] It may provide the means to avoid what seem to be the purely subjectivist and even existentialist implications of Perry's scheme. I discuss below what critical commitment means to a Christian who continues to affirm the reality of absolutes. But it certainly reinforces the present point that critical commitment takes one beyond both uncritical commitment and uncommitted criticism.

As these complicated-sounding expressions suggest and as we will see in the next section, the distinction between uncritical and critical commitment may not be obvious to the observer. But the difference is profound. Justice Holmes put this much better, I think, in the quotation cited at the beginning of this chapter: "I do not give a fig for the simplicity on this side of complexity, but I would give my life for the simplicity on the other side of complexity."[63] It is in this sense that I believe liberal arts education in general and Christian liberal arts education in particular must take students a step beyond.

Critical Commitment Is a Tension   Critical commitment is characterized by tension in the sense of equilibrium and balance. Consider some of Perry's own characterizations of commitment.[64]

The committed person balances narrowness and breadth. Commitment means giving up certain potentials. To the student who has only recently experienced the "opening up" of multiplicity, this can bring a sense of loss or even regression. Commitment also means a tension of stability and flexibility. This is really the same tension as that of narrowness and breadth but spread out along the axis of time. And commitment means balancing sureness and tentativeness. The world generally prefers and even rewards those who are sure, and thus institutions that seek to produce students who are critically committed will face opposition from the culture. This is hardly news to those committed to liberal arts! Commitment embodies a tension of analysis and synthesis too. Analysis was the preferred mode of transition into multiplicity. The student's professors all cultivated this "skill" with zeal in the early years of their education. But now the time has come to go beyond mere analysis to "some form of synthesis from which action is possible." Finally, according to Perry, commitment also calls the student to balance detachment and involvement, that is, breaking with the past and continuity with one's origins.

Carol Gilligan expressed this latter set of balances most eloquently in her important work *In a Different Voice*. The heart of her work is to take issue with Kohlberg's scheme as too individualistic and principle oriented. When women are included in a study, the highest levels of moral development embody an ethic of care and not just justice. She voices her objection in terms of separation (individuation) and attachment (mutuality).[65] Development, she says, is too much associated with separation and individuation. Separation should lead on to attachment and individuation to mutuality.[66] "Though the truth of separation is acknowledged in most developmental texts, the reality of continuing connection is lost."[67] Her "vision of maturity" is one in which both "voices" are needed. Separation is important for the empowerment of self—for the discovery of the freedom and right to choose and act. But attachment is also important because it brings the responsibility to actually choose and act. The mature person merges identity (derived from separation) with intimacy (derived from attachment). Maturity is the complementarity of two moralities, that of rights and that of care.[68] The genius of what Gilligan adds, and something I have affirmed above, is the idea that the vision of real adult maturity goes beyond either voice alone and embodies a tension of affirming oneself as separate and individual with rights but at the same time as attached to others in relationship and mutually involved in responsibilities.

Perry elsewhere described the tension characteristic of critical commitment as coming to peace with complexity, which means a balance between "tentativeness and wholeheartedness."[69] In relativism, the "certainties" of dualism have been lost, and with them much of the intellectual confidence and passion they brought along. A person in this place "must affirm his own position from within himself in full awareness that reason can never completely justify him or assure him."[70] Gordon Allport echoed Perry when he wrote that "a person can be half-sure without being half-hearted."[71]

Finally, and perhaps most painfully, critical commitment embodies a tension between ambiguity and action. The complexity of a world with diverse opinions and value systems yet with practical expectations to choose and act "demands a capacity to tolerate paradox in the midst of responsible action." It is characteristic of dualism to find action easy because right and wrong are plain. It is equally characteristic of multiplicity to be paralyzed by alternatives, unable to reach any conclusion at all. The freshman crusades, the sophomore debates topic after topic to exhaustion, and the senior tries to act in the face of ambiguity.

In summary, the tension characteristic of critical commitment looks a lot like the *methodological dogmatism* characteristic of good science or the *methodological skepticism* characteristic of good philosophy. They are really two sides of the same coin. According to historian of science Thomas Kuhn, dogmatism has an essential place in the practice of science. It functions as a methodological principle that drives the working scientist to persevere in defense of the prevailing theory. Without this kind of dogmatic allegiance, premature abandonment of a theory will never allow it to receive the thorough testing it needs. The idea is that procedural errors and even theoretical flaws will show up more quickly if the scientist is reluctant to give up current thinking.[72] *In other words, the scientist practices commitment in order to be effectively critical.* By contrast, Descartes advocated methodological skepticism. In an age of substantial uncertainty, Descartes's concern for certainty led him to believe the best approach was to doubt everything. Descartes took the most basic assumptions about God, the world, and even self and imagined that they were false in order to see if they could be established as true. The idea is that flaws in one's reasons for belief will show up more quickly if the beliefs are challenged. *In other words, the philosopher practices criticism in order to be justifiably committed.* Both scientist and philosopher understand the tension of critical commitment.

Critical Commitment Is an Attitude   It is impossible to reduce critical commitment to a formula, and it is difficult to even describe it. But its most important feature (and perhaps the most important assertion I make in this volume) is that critical commitment is an attitude and not just knowledge or skill. Like the attitudes of dogmatism and cynicism it supersedes, critical commitment is an attitude that pervades character and shapes both thought and deed. I believe that an important part of the ongoing task of those involved in the liberal arts is to uncover its features more fully. But I believe an important key lies in the neighborhood of "epistemological humility." One of my colleagues described epistemological humility some time ago in one of those classic hallway conversations. He said, "How we hold truth is as important as what we hold to be truth."[73]

I say humility, but meekness would be more appropriate were it not for the fact it is so commonly misunderstood and viewed almost as a weakness: evidence of compromise. Critical commitment does not go beyond or embody tension in the sense of compromise. The Greeks understood the strength of humility. "Prautees" was disciplined, controlled power. One preacher illustrated this idea by contrasting the difference between the mighty Zambezi River along the border of Zambia and Zimbabwe before and after it was dammed to form one the world's largest lakes and to produce electricity for two nations. Untamed, it had roared and crashed through deep gorges in a furious display of energy and action. But the energy was dissipated and was largely show. Once channeled, the mighty river seemed unexciting. Yet its power remains, actually reinforced by accumulation and control, and becomes "responsible" by its use. The same preacher went on to point out that the man God singled out to describe as the "meekest man on earth" was anything but a compromiser. Moses did not compromise with Pharaoh, nor with his own people. Instead he brought them out of authoritarian Egypt, through the wilderness of skepticism, and into the Promised Land.[74] The same might be said of those who model critical commitment.

Arthur Holmes's description of liberty or academic freedom captures much of the attitude I have in mind. He has suggested that liberty goes beyond both legalism and license and beyond both totalitarianism and anarchy, just as I have said that critical commitment goes beyond both dogmatism and cynical skepticism. This liberty means "exploring the truth in a responsible fashion," thinking, making mistakes, correcting them, teaching others to do the same, and "equipping them carefully for its exacting demands."

> The qualifying words "responsible" and "carefully" require emphasis. . . . [It] implies a responsible motive, neither selfish nor narrowly partisan, but first a love for the truth and then a concern for the common good of the community to which one belongs. It implies care about attitudes, lest one grow heady and opinionated and cease to bow in humility and awe.[75]

Epistemological humility means holding commitments with a gentleness that is tolerant.[76] It should be open-minded and self-critical. It should manifest itself in a listening spirit, slow to draw conclusions and patient with complications and alternative points of view.

Without abandoning the centered authority of the self and a disciplined fidelity to truth, [it] has a new capacity to hear the truth of another. [It] resists forced syntheses or reductionist interpretations and is prepared to live with ambiguity, mystery, wonder, and apparent irrationalities.[77]

Yet, as "meekness," it must be passionate, not half-hearted, commitment. It must be courageous commitment; courageous like Tillich's "courage to be in the face of the fear of nonbeing." It is the courage of fear and trembling. It is a willingness to choose and act in spite of ambiguity. It is the courage of Abraham binding Isaac on the slopes of Mt. Moriah.[78]

The attitude in question is almost childlike in its questioning and believing spirit. It goes beyond the credulity of the dualism and yet also beyond the incredulity of multiplicity. It should be, as Paul Ricoeur put it, a kind of "second naivete."[79]

Critical Commitment Is a Virtue   Critical commitment requires cognitive, moral, and even faith development. These components have been distinguished in some of the schema already mentioned, but in reality they are largely inseparable. They usually come together in the development of character. Desirable character traits are virtues, and, in the final analysis, critical commitment is a virtue; liberal arts education thus aims at helping students become virtuous.

J. H. Newman drew an explicit connection between liberal education and this notion of virtue, saying that professors of this liberal education "have ever been attempting to make men virtuous."[80] He bemoaned the fact that all too often they have failed, but their purposes are clear. Elton Trueblood also believes that liberal education should aim at virtue. "Nothing is more important than the development of character in such a way that better and better choices are made."[81]

Contemporary ethical theory has rediscovered virtue ethics after generations of attention to what might be called cognitive or formalistic ethics. Cognitive ethics takes the narrow view that knowledge is enough. "To know the good," Plato said, "is to do it." So the focus of ethical discourse in too much modern philosophy has been on the elucidation of principles by which persons might know in particular cases what is right or wrong. By contrast, virtue ethics says there is more to morality than just knowing what is good or bad, right or wrong.

Here Kohlberg's developmental scheme becomes inadequate. He rejects ethical relativism and from his empirical research concludes that there are universal stages and invariant sequences of development that constitute objective values.[82] And he does affirm the attitude I called liberty in the previous section. Kohlberg insists that education is not indoctrination because it is a rational dialectic in which the student's freedom (liberty) to choose is central.[83]

Yet, as Robert Sandin has pointed out, Kohlberg's ethics are too formalistic.[84] This means that for Kohlberg it is the method used in making moral judgments, not the conclusions, that determine their morality. In Sandin's view Kohlberg places too much confidence in the ability to resolve moral dilemmas by appeal to rational principles alone: "Kohlberg has seriously underestimated the intractability of conflicts among moral principles. . . . there are conflicts among competing duties that remain stubbornly unresolved."[85]

Formalism overemphasizes "What ought I to do?" and fails to make a place for "What is good?"[86] In short, Kohlberg neglects virtue. But what is virtue? Aristotle defined it as "a state of character concerned with choice, lying in a mean . . . this being determined by a rational principle, and by that principle by which the man of practical principle would determine it."[87]

To paraphrase Sandin, it is a state of being that frees the human mind for thinking about the dilemmas of cognitive, moral, and spiritual decision making.[88] As we saw in the previous section, it is more than performance—it is an attitude. Here, in contrast to Kohlberg's model of maturity, it is also more than a skill; it is a state, a property not of action but of character. It is a disposition, which means it is a tendency, actually, to do the good. The virtuous person is the one who has both knowledge and willingness to do the good. That disposition is another crucial part of what it means to be critically committed.

Which state, which disposition is critical commitment? It is the cognitive and moral and faith state I have described that is beyond dualism and multiplicity, beyond both uncritical commitment and uncommitted criticism. It is the state of living in peace with cognitive, moral, and faith tension. It is the attitude of epistemological humility.

Critical Commitment Is Habitual   Aristotle said that virtues keep us from being swayed by distracting passions from what is good.[89] These virtues are acquired in large measure, as we will see, by habituation. But that means the attitudes of critical commitment must be habitually expressed. The virtue unexpressed is dead. Just as relativistic thinking becomes automatic and ceases to be self-consciousness for those who have moved beyond dualism, the attitudes of those who move beyond multiplicity must also become automatic and habitual.[90] John Newman defined liberal education as "a habit of mind"[91] and insisted that the virtue that comes from liberal education

> is not a mere extrinsic or accidental advantage, which is ours today and another's tomorrow, which may be got up from a book, and easily forgotten again, which we can borrow for the occasion, carry about in our hand, and take into the market; it is an acquired illumination, it is a habit, a personal possession, and an inward endowment. And this is the reason, why it is more correct . . . to speak of a University as a place of education, than of instruction. . . . Education is a higher word; it implies action upon our mental nature and the formation of character; it is something individual and permanent, and is commonly spoken of in connexion with religion and virtue.[92]

But mere habit is not virtue. In fact, routine mechanical behavior is evidence of the lack of virtue. It is how these behaviors are habitually done that makes them virtuous. Critically committed people will regularly believe and act in certain ways. But not just any person who believes and acts in these ways will be critically committed, only those who believe and act as the critically committed person would.[93]

4

Why Is Critical Commitment Christian?

In chapter 3, I described critical commitment. But is it Christian? To put the question differently, Why should Christians be especially interested in critical commitment or why should Christian institutions be suited to produce it?

Christians certainly do not have a monopoly on this virtue. It can arise in educational institutions that are not Christian. But it is central to my view that Christian liberal arts colleges are in an unusually good position to teach this virtue and ought to make it a chief distinctive.

CRITICAL COMMITMENT IS EASILY
CONFUSED WITH OTHER POSITIONS

One obstacle to convincing anyone that critical commitment ought to be a chief goal for a Christian liberal arts college has nothing to do with whether the college is Christian or not. It is simply that critical commitment is very difficult to understand.

Depending on whether a person is functioning from a dualistic or relativistic stage of cognitive development, she may find critical commitment misguided for quite different and almost opposite reasons. To the dualist, it embodies everything that is wrong with relativism because it maintains a self-critical, open attitude toward whatever is believed. To the relativist, it is a regression to stages of dogmatic dualism that only recently have been outgrown.

Critical commitment can be difficult to differentiate from both dualism and relativism because it combines elements from both. Sharon Parks says it is "paradoxical,"[1] and Perry illustrates how easily dualism and commitment can be confused: "In a curious way, [the senior in commitment] may startlingly resemble himself as a freshman. . . . Ironically enough, these seniors have forced us to consider what the difference may be between their kind of outwardness and that of the most hard-shelled anti-intellectual [dualist]. The difference defines liberal education."[2]

I am reminded of a public mass demonstration on abortion. The demonstrators included dogmatically committed dualists as well as those who were critically committed. They shared the conviction to act but were worlds apart in their thinking. Among those missing on the street were sophisticates and intellectuals who saw so many sides of the issue that they were paralyzed. They may have found it difficult to differentiate among those different kinds of commitment represented on the street.

But critical commitment may also be confused with relativism. To many beginning students, philosophy is a useless exercise. I sometimes perversely confirm their worst suspicions by telling them philosophy begins in befuddlement and often ends there too. "What's the use?" they ask. In philosophy they believe they lose answers and are condemned to float forever in a sea of uncertainty. That is true to the extent that a liberal education to critical commitment will forever alter the kind of certainty that can be acquired. However, it overlooks the fact that one must progress through the uncertainty of a kind of relativism before finding critical commitment.

Although critical commitment may be difficult to understand, the transition to the stages of commitment, according to Perry, is the "the most crucial moment in higher education."[3] The student discovers that the "old hope for certainty" characteristic of the dualist "has just gone underground, and in his senior year he has the whole job to do over again."[4] If the student balks, if the intellectual energy required to make these commitment is not available, paralysis or escape may occur. Students have the "tools" to compare and analyze and to contextualize data but may respond by saying,

> No one can ever be sure. It's all up to the individual in the end. . . . So why bother. If it's all a matter of opinion in the end, why not in the beginning? Why bother with all the intellectual effort? This is retreat to . . . everyone has a right to his own opinion. It says that unexamined opinion is as good as examined opinion. *It is the moral defeat of the "educated" man.*[5]

Confusing critical commitment with other positions stands in the way of making it a chief goal for the Christian liberal arts college or for any liberal arts college. Only a deliberate program of education can overcome this obstacle for those who are considering higher education. Critical commitment must be described more clearly and shown as the natural outcome of healthy human development. All those concerned must understand this and see the whole process, not just the risky stages of multiplicity. Both

Christian and non-Christian liberal arts colleges need to reaffirm with Socrates that the unexamined life is not good enough.

CRITICAL COMMITMENT IS RELIGIOUSLY THREATENING

I once received a phone call from a mother who was concerned that her daughter (a senior student) was about to take my course in Christian apologetics. She said her daughter had already had to withdraw from one course in the Religious Studies Department because the professor had "presented alternatives without clearly identifying the truth." In the same class a different senior student confessed near the end of the term that he had had doubts about taking the class because he was sure it would be dogmatic indoctrination.

In both cases the educational process was religiously threatening. For the parent, it was threatening because it might destroy her daughter's faith. For the second student, it was threatening because it might indoctrinate or "brainwash" him. The first kind of threat sometimes provokes a defensive reaction, what Arthur Holmes has called an "attack from the right." The second kind of threat also sometimes provokes a defensive reaction, an "attack from the left."[6]

Responding to the Attack from the Right

The first kind of threat is the one that makes many people wonder if the liberal arts and especially this goal of critical commitment are really consistent with Christian faith at all. This reaction often comes from the very persons a Christian liberal arts college seeks to serve. The problem is made worse in several ways.[7] Parents, often without the benefit of a liberal arts education themselves, are justifiably concerned about faculty who will be shaping their children's thoughts and habits. Hardheaded businessmen and businesswomen of the "real" world question the usefulness of the "eternal questioning" associated with the developmental process leading to critical commitment. Pastors too, in this post-Christian age, may be defensive and prone to a kind of anti-intellectualism. They justifiably wonder if the liberal arts may not be just another "liberal" influence to draw their students away. And the trustees of Christian liberal arts colleges may not understand the goal of critical commitment much better than the students, the parents, the businesspeople, and the pastors described above. Yet they may play a crucial role in setting direction in curriculum and personnel. Finally, no Christian college faculty is perfect. Faculty and administrators themselves may not understand this goal or may see it only in part. For this reason, some of the fears felt by those on the right may be justified. So it is crucial to respond and to explain why critical commitment is a Christian virtue.

A few years ago one of my Introduction to Philosophy students from an underrepresented ethnic group began the semester enthusiastically. She was pleased that the method of the course was to challenge the usual ways of thinking. She seemed delighted when other members of the class had their views challenged about such things as whether persons are free or determined and whether there is a world external to mind or not. Perhaps she was pleased to see majority perspectives challenged the way hers had so often been challenged. But when the course turned to religious matters, including the existence of God and the problem of evil, the same questioning methodology became threatening. Gradually I saw her disengage and withdraw. When I talked to her about what I saw happening, she reported that her mind "just didn't work that way" and then added that over a weekend at home she had discussed the class with her family and had shown them the textbook. They had been puzzled, wondering why such questions as these were being raised in a Christian college. Despite further conversations she never reengaged.

The process of moving toward critical commitment is painful. No wonder it is threatening. The students begin to "miss those tablets in the sky" and ask, "Will no one tell me if I am right? Can I never be sure? Am I alone?"[8] As Sharon Parks has pointed out, the transformation of a person's sense of truth involves "threat, bewilderment, confusion, frustration, fear, loss. . . . There is an element of 'shipwreck.'"[9]

But of course the point here is that to understand the threat is to transform it into something that strengthens and does not threaten faith. Let me explain this first in terms of Perry's developmental model, then in more specifically religious language, and finally in philosophical language.

Response from a Developmental Perspective

In Perry's language, our question, Why is critical commitment Christian? might take the form, Can Christians go through the stages of multiplicity without losing their faith? Students who are justifiably uncomfortable with the intermediate developmental stages of multiplicity (Perry's positions 4, 5, 6) may wonder if moving beyond that stage can possibly improve matters.

But Perry points out that this going beyond multiplicity is precisely what makes one's faith one's own. It is a faith that does not come out of what others have told you but out of something that you truly believe yourself. One of Perry's subjects, a Radcliffe student, had always taken it for granted that she would go into Christian ministry. Her development beyond multiplicity did not alter that direction. But it did alter the way she saw her religious commitment. She described "the transition from the old unexamined commitment to the prospect of a new."

The thing is, when you have a bunch of beliefs sort of handed to you, you don't really do that much thinking. I mean I was never even concerned with philosophy, I never read a single thing, I didn't have to. I mean, I accepted the Christian faith because my parents were Christians and I believed that, well, you know I never even thought, well, maybe there isn't any God. I mean it doesn't enter your mind. . . . I didn't know what I was really gonna do with my life. . . . I never really thought about what is my, you know, place in the universe. . . . But the thing is, it really hasn't been unsettling, because . . . I mean starting to think about these things, because . . . well, I don't know, now I feel . . . more honest about, about my beliefs, now that I'm sort of getting them on my own. So I'm very happy.[10]

Another of Perry's student subjects reported in this way on the effect this development had on religious faith.

The four years [in college] have contributed doubt, certainly. One thing I heard someone say about religion at Harvard was that people who came here, religiously committed, went out more confirmed in their attitudes than they came in. The impact of Harvard had been to cause them to rethink and reshuffle and reformulate, but that they came out as strongly committed in a different sense somehow as they had come in.[11]

The common theme running through Perry's reports of this new kind of faith, this faith beyond multiplicity, is the changed attitude it brings along with it toward others of differing beliefs and faith. It brings an attitude of tolerance rather than contempt, an attitude that

represents the point of critical division between "belief" and the possibility of "faith." Belief requires no investment by the person. To become faith it must first be doubted. Only in the face of doubt is the person called upon for that act of Commitment that is his contribution, his faith.[12]

The attitude that distinguishes this faith in an Absolute from mere belief is respect. Perry wrote that "in one sense they 'must' be wrong, but in another sense, no more so than oneself." This attitude is paradoxical and there again lies the mystery, the tension, the difficulty in understanding the goal of liberal arts education.

Response from a Theological Perspective

"To be faith it must first be doubted." That statement provides another opening to answering the question, Why is critical commitment a Christian virtue?

What is Christian faith? When one finally reaches the limits of human reason, faith is all that remains. This is not to say that faith is irrational but only that reason is not enough.[13] Such faith requires *courage*.[14] Theologian Paul Tillich made this plain when he described faith as a courage "in spite of" ambiguity or, as we might say, "in spite of multiplicity."[15] Sharon Parks echoed Tillich's approach when she described the person moving beyond multiplicity as someone "looking for a place to stand."[16] If this is the kind of faith that characterizes Christianity, then it is easy to see how critical commitment is a Christian virtue—an appropriate goal for Christian liberal arts education. Certainly defenders of Christian liberal arts want students to have the kind faith that stands courageously in spite of the alternatives. Such faith requires courage not because the alternatives are internally weak and are just propped up by social or political power. It requires courage because the alternatives have been examined and have internal strengths that make them attractive. "Faith in spite of this attractiveness" is real faith. Until those alternatives have been examined, this kind of faith is impossible. This kind of faith is critical commitment.

Besides courage, Christian faith requires humility. Elton Trueblood made this attitude explicit: "In the face of Truth, only humility can truly result."[17] As Arthur Holmes described it, "faith is NOT a way of knowing OR a source of knowledge but is an attitude of openness to God's self-revelation."[18] In Sharon Parks's analogy between Christian faith and the journey of God's people from authority-bound bondage in Egypt through the wilderness of doubt and beyond into the Promised Land, the Promised Land is not a static state. It was not enough for God's people merely to be in the right place. Their spirit—their attitude—was critical. Repeatedly they fell short. The attitude of openness essential to Christian faith is expressed in the following model of faith.

> Our greatest truths are but half-truths. Think not to settle down forever in any truth, but use it as a tent in which to pass a summer's night, but build no house for it or it will become your tomb. When you first become aware of its insufficiency, and descry some counter-truth looming up in the distance, then weep not, but rejoice: it is the voice of the Christ saying, "Take up your bed and walk."[19]

Such openness is a distinguishing mark of critical commitment. So once again we can see how critical commitment is an appropriate goal for Christian liberal arts education.

Of course Christian faith is much, much more than just courage and humility. It is certainly not my intention to limit the definition in that way. Many other "faiths" show these features. But unless these essential characteristics are recognized, what is offered as faith will be a cheap counterfeit more akin to dogmatism.

Like critical commitment, Christian faith as openness is paradoxical. The warning not to "settle down forever in any truth" may seem quite heretical. It is not that liberal arts students are to be urged to move beyond Truth but only to show the attitude that carefully considers the limitations of human truths about

that Truth. "Our greatest truths are but half-truths." When that attitude is cultivated, the student can often maintain the same beliefs while dramatically
changing in faith. How we hold truth is as important as what we hold true. This
is the paradox of Christian faith that makes it like critical commitment.

Response from a Philosophical Perspective

In more distinctly philosophical language, our question, Why is critical commitment Christian? can be put another way: Is Christian faith logically consistent with commitment in relativism? Can one consistently choose (an action apparently dependent on self) a value system that is objective
(something independent of self)? Does not the fact that critical commitment
involves a choice among multiple alternatives make it really merely a form
of subjectivism? If that were true, then critical commitment would be inconsistent with a Christian faith that affirms the objectivity of values and Truth.

There is another way of expressing this threat, which critical commitment
might appear to present to Christian faith. Some may object that what I have
called critical commitment is really nothing more than a thinly disguised
form of existentialism. If critical commitment consists merely in choosing arbitrarily in a world that is fundamentally relativistic, then choosing creates
meaning, or, as existentialists might put it, then "existence precedes
essence." The criticism is all the more pointed because critical commitment
is modeled after Perry's positions 7, 8, and especially 9. Perry himself acknowledged his allegiance to existentialism, calling his own view "contextualist," "pragmatic," and "existential." And he said that reasoning is "circular
by ultimate necessity."[20]

It seems to me that two different responses are possible here. The first
is to show that Perry's positions do not entail radical subjectivism at all.
The second is to acknowledge that Perry's positions do indeed culminate
in a kind of commitment that is overly subjectivist and thus incompatible
with Christian liberal arts but then to distinguish critical commitment
from Perry.

Taking the first approach, it seems that Perry at least does not view commitment as inconsistent with religious belief in Absolutes. He says there is no inconsistency in making a commitment to values that are objective so long as it is
done from the context of already having discovered the contextualism and relativism that are endemic to the human epistemological situation.

> For example, a student at an advanced position of development in our
> scheme might commit himself to a faith in a religion which includes a faith in
> an absolute order manifest in human affairs in Natural Law. Even if we our-
> selves disagreed at concrete levels, we would still be free to honor his values,
> since, in our context, he has elected them in a world which he has learned to
> consider, from another point of view, as relativistic. . . . his Commitment to

an absolute represents, for us not a failure of logic (or a regression to earlier forms) but a considered and courageous acceptance of an unavoidable stress.[21]

Theistic objectivists might reply that even if this is not existentialism, it still boils down to nothing more than a thinly disguised form of fideism. On balance I think that this reply is valid and that Perry's commitment is probably inconsistent with most orthodox Christian understandings of faith. It would appear to reduce faith in an objectivist worldview to a purely arbitrary subjective preference, indistinguishable from others.

Yet a final word might be said in Perry's defense. Some who criticize him along these lines could be interpreting Perry too narrowly. They seem to assume that Perry would not allow rational considerations to make any contribution whatsoever to the choice of commitment. Referring to Perry's stage of commitment, Robert Sandin wrote,

At the farthest reaches of inquiry, reason leaves the thinker with no way of choosing from among equally legitimate perspectives. . . . The commitments of maturity emerge not from critical examination of the rational foundations of belief, but from the affirmations of selfhood in an incomprehensible world."[22]

I find this an unnecessarily subjectivistic interpretation of Perry. I find nothing in Perry that would prohibit the examination of alternative beliefs among those recognized in multiplicity. Perry would not prohibit the rejection of views that are internally inconsistent or, for that matter, views that are inadequate to make sense of major features of human experience. Even Sandin was equivocal in his criticism. In one sentence he reported Perry as saying, "Unexamined and unjustified commitments . . . are the stuff of our common life." Yet in the previous sentence he criticized Perry by asserting that "reason can never *completely* justify him or assure him" (emphasis added).[23] It would be one thing for Perry to claim reason cannot completely justify faith but quite another to say that commitments cannot be examined at all. If Perry is merely reporting the insufficiency of reason for faith, then surely his understanding of commitment would not be as radically subjectivist as it might appear. Criticism to this effect is therefore overstated, even if in the main still correct.

The second approach switches from defending Perry to reinterpreting him. This is the approach I take and that both Parks and Fowler seem to take as well. They describe stages of faith development that appear to go beyond Perry's positions in cognitive and ethical development. Parks talks about "convictional commitment" as "another form of knowing on the other side of commitment in relativism" as if this went beyond what Perry described.[24] She also indicates elsewhere that she understands "convictional commitment" to be a modification and extension of Perry's positions.[25]

But of course the issue is not whether what we call critical commitment is identical with Perry or even whether Parks and Fowler have correctly understood Perry. The real issue is whether having once recognized the presuppositional character of all human inquiry (Perry's positions of multiplicity) a person can ever again believe in absolutes. In other words, can critical commitment be meaningfully distinguished from the kind of radical subjectivist (existentialist) commitment that would be inconsistent with a traditional Christian worldview and hence unacceptable as a chief goal for Christian liberal arts?

I firmly believe the answer here is yes. I believe critical commitment does not entail that values and truth are relative, only that human access to them is. These are completely different matters often confused. The former has to do with whether essence precedes existence—whether meaning is purely a human creation. The latter has to do with whether humanity has a neutral, assumptionless access to eternal Truth. The former has to do with whether there *is* Truth, the latter with whether humanity can ever fully grasp it. It is far too easy to assume that because our modes of representing Truth are so subjective and relative that Truth itself is subjective and relative. But that is to throw the baby out with the bath water.

Here I think the distinction between the existentialism of Kierkegaard and that of Sartre is helpful. For Sartre, meaning was just the result of arbitrary human choices. If this were what someone meant by critical commitment, then it would surely be inconsistent with Christian faith. But for Kierkegaard, there is a Reality independent of human decisions that can only be found by choices that are made "in spite of" ambiguity and paradox. Although it is not necessary to say that such choices are irrational, they surely do go beyond reason.[26] Since this is what I take critical commitment to be, there is plainly no inconsistency with faith. Although there is certainly more to faith than just critical commitment (e.g., the work of the Holy Spirit), as Fowler would certainly agree, such commitment is a central and even necessary part of mature faith.

On this issue there is an honest epistemological parting of the ways among Christians. To some, virtually any element of subjectivism in one's epistemology precludes the possibility of an objectivist theory of truth and value. But as I have noted above, to my mind this sounds like a false dilemma. It seems to suggest that either one adopts a subjectivist epistemology *and* a subjectivist view of truth and value ("knowledge" is uncertain and truth is relative) *or* one must adopt a foundationalist epistemology *and* an objectivist view of truth and value (knowledge is certain and Truth is universal).

For example, these seem to be the only alternatives Robert Sandin allows. One way Sandin expresses this is in his criticism of Perry:

> Knowledge is not for Perry the discovery of truth. The knowledge that it is the
> business of the university to share consists of the meanings human minds have

made as they view a complex and many-sided world. Truth is the meaning we construct out of the world we see. . . . The truth we find in the world . . . is a meaning we create."[27]

I have already suggested that it may be an overly subjectivistic interpretation of Perry to say that he believes knowledge is merely "made," in some arbitrary, nonrational way. But the reference in this passage to the "discovery of truth" also suggests that Sandin's own epistemology is decidedly foundationalist and thus represents only one side of the "parting of the ways" I suggested above.

Foundationalism says faith is warranted because it rests on traditional forms of properly basic beliefs, which require no evidence.[28] But contemporary Christian philosophers of religion indicate that traditional foundationalism is not the only rational warrant for faith. One can be within one's epistemic rights to believe without evidence, so long as that belief is coherent with one's noetic structure. This is not the place to discuss Alvin Plantinga and William Alston on this subject. But it seems to me that such views recognize at least the legitimacy, if not the inevitability, of a subjective element in the epistemology even of those who profess an objectivist view of knowledge and value. Since Kant, understanding of the human epistemological condition has been changed, and it oversimplifies things to suppose that Kant's insight must inevitably drive one to subjectivist extremes.

Perhaps the plainest illustration of this parting of the ways has to do with the attitude one adopts toward the knowledge and the faith one claims to have. And because I take the attitudinal component of critical commitment to be the crucial one for educational purposes, this is where I part company with Robert Sandin, despite our obvious mutual agreement on the objectivity of Truth and Value. What I take to be of value in Perry, and in Kierkegaard too, is the need to commit in spite of ambiguity. Sandin believes commitments must be "affirmations *wrested* out of ambiguity" (emphasis added).[29] He says this faith is wrested from ambiguity "by the Thinker, who has resolved the conflicts and dilemmas presented by an incomplete experience . . . grounded in an intellectual synthesis that reconciles the previous tensions in moral outlook."

This contrasts to what Sandin finds objectionable (and I find valuable) in Perry. According to Sandin, for Perry,

Commitments . . . require "the courage of responsibility" and realistic acceptance of our human limits, including the limits of reason. Maturity is the capacity for commitment when one is not in possession of truth. . . . If he is still to honor reason, he must reach some kind of affirmation in full awareness that reason can never completely justify him or assure him. . . . [Students] would be helped, says Perry, by an education that showed them how to embrace dialectical tension without resolving it."[30]

The attitudes Perry expresses here are exactly the ones I believe should characterize the critically committed faith of educated Christians who recognize the limitations of reason and the human epistemological situation.

In summary, critical commitment is religiously threatening. That threat provokes an attack from the right, which fears that critical commitment will result in the loss of faith. But when we look carefully at what critical commitment means from a developmental and a philosophical perspective and when we look at what Christian faith also really means from a theological perspective, we discover that there is no threat. Not only are Christian faith and critical commitment logically consistent, but critical commitment is an essential part of real faith. It is an appropriate goal for Christian liberal arts education.

Responding to the Attack from the Left

There is a second kind of threat occasioned by Christian liberal arts education. It is threatening to those who say it is mere indoctrination. This threat may be felt by non-Christians as well as by Christians like the second student in my apologetics class, who, having escaped the dogmatism of dualistic thinking, now fear that Christian education will drive them backward instead of beyond. The result in either case is an attack on the goals and methods of Christian liberal arts that can be said to come from the left.

The attack goes something like this. Because Christian liberal arts education is obviously committed to certain objective truths, it obviously cannot be objective (sic!). By this is usually meant that because it affirms that some things are true regardless of whether anyone happens to believe them, Christian liberal arts education cannot be neutral (i.e., free of bias) in both ideology and method. It is assumed these are hallmarks of good science and thus of good education. Consequently, Christian liberal arts are not respectable.

The basic flaw in this line of reasoning is that the kind of objectivity it refers to is a myth. This kind of neutrality is impossible. One need not read any farther than the first critics of positivistic philosophy of science to discover the bankruptcy of such thinking. For years, the unity of science movement assumed that good scientific method could be appraised syntactically, that is, that method was theory neutral. The assumption was that observations and theories could be easily distinguished. With a suitable base of observational data ("protocols") one could complete Hume's program of tying every theory unambiguously to observation. Then with appropriate logic (either induction or deduction in the form of falsificationism) one could construct a system that adequately accounted for the physical world. Choosing truth was unencumbered by ideology or bias. The ideal scientist was free of all prejudice and bias and followed truth wherever it led.

But beginning in the mid-1960s this mythological view of science died the death of a thousand qualifications. In the first place, the idea that observations or "facts" were really theory neutral was laid to rest by developments in the psychology of perception.[31] "Facts" do *not* speak for themselves but often are merely the conclusions of more deeply entrenched theoretical inferences. The same sense experiences can constitute different "facts." Most of us take what we see in a telescope or microscope to be plainly fact. But that is only because we accept the theories of optics taken for granted in the use of these instruments as theories that are more reliable than the theories of planets or cells we are using these instruments to test. Of course it was not always so, as the critics of Galileo illustrate. To them the telescope was black magic. Today, the philosophy of science recognizes the role of convention in determining which "lower level theories" will be held unproblematic (deemed "fact") in order to test higher level theories of interest.[32] But of course, "conventions" are working assumptions that show science is not theory neutral.

In the second place, logical problems arose which showed that even if such theory-neutral observations were actually available as "fulcra," the methodological "lever" of empirical science was faulty. The logic whereby such "facts" might be used to confirm or refute a particular theory is not free of assumptions. Traditional appeals to the logic of induction stumbled on Hume's own criticisms. For induction to be justified, one must make assumptions about the uniformity of nature. Or if one chooses to make induction a basic kind of inference requiring no justification, then that in itself is an assumption. Others attempted to avoid the appeal to induction and tried to show that science could proceed using the power of deduction found in the method of falsification. True theories could not be verified, but false ones could be falsified. Unfortunately, even this solution stumbles. The logic involved is ambiguous because scientific theories are complex, not simple. They usually consist of a whole constellation of assumptions. A negative experimental result in practice only rarely causes scientists to reject their theories. Instead they usually tinker with auxiliary hypotheses to make things come out right. But of course, adding and modifying to these auxiliary hypotheses reveals once again that science is not methodologically neutral.

The fact (sic!) is that all human inquiry is essentially presuppositional. We all make assumptions. Not even science is neutral. The feature that makes any case of human inquiry reliable, "objective," is whether the process is really open in recognizing and examining the assumptions it inevitably makes. In short, this comes down to an attitude of honesty. From this conclusion it is a fairly easy step to see the answer Christian liberal arts can provide to the attack from the left. The goal of critical commitment is just exactly to take students beyond the dogmatic dualism in which assumptions are unconscious. Furthermore, critical commitment takes students beyond the multiplicity in which assumptions are made explicit but none is embraced. Critical commitment seeks to take students to a stage of development in which commitments are made with assumptions in full view. Critical commitment is essentially characterized by open honesty and humility. By adopting these attitudes toward its own assumptions, the liberal arts model good science and, not incidentally, provide a hospitable environment for good empirical science as well as for humanities. Christian liberal arts is no exception merely because its assumptions happen to be those of the Christian worldview.

Unlike mere multiplicity, critical commitment does more than just recognize its assumptions. It takes them for granted and takes the risk to build on them. In this sense, when it makes critical commitment its goal, liberal arts in general and Christian liberal arts in particular are actually a better environment for genuine inquiry than pseudoneutral environments that are unwilling to recognize the assumptions they make. Students who are afraid Christian liberal arts will "brainwash" them ought to be more afraid of the brainwashing that goes on in supposedly "neutral" institutions that cling to the myth of "objectivity."[33] As Roberta Hestenes put it, "The worst bias is the one that claims there is no bias."[34]

This defense of Christian liberal arts to the attack from the left is especially powerful in the age of political correctness. David Winter, president of Westmont College, suggests that as secular universities are politicized, they gradually become aware of the myth of objectivity and are forced to come to terms with their assumptions. This indirectly sheds a new light on the legitimacy of Christian liberal arts colleges, where assumptions have always been explicit. As Winter points out,

> the recognition by the public that the personal values of professors are communicated in the teaching process may be a virtual breakthrough in American education. . . . Christian colleges have been up front about [their] beliefs . . . but . . . state schools have not been expected to let students . . . know of their religious commitments. . . . The result has been the impression . . . that at Christian schools there is less academic freedom. . . . No, it has been the pretense of neutrality, objectivity, that has been a danger in American higher education.[35]

5

How Is Critical Commitment Produced?

DISSONANCE

Arthur Holmes provides a wonderful metaphor that bridges the gap between our discussions in previous chapters of the what and the why of liberal arts to the first central principle of how liberal arts are implemented.[1] He says a good education is a kind of intellectual gestation and the role of teachers and colleges is like that of the Socratic midwife. It is a "calculated risk," already seen in the transition from dualism through multiplicity toward critical commitment. There are always dangers of escape and regression. "Education is not like training: most children can be successfully trained, but not all babies are successfully delivered." The "incidence of miscarriages" is not reduced by crippling the attendant midwife or doctor with restrictions but, as we have also seen, by encouraging the greatest use of honesty and critical technique possible. In the end, Holmes says, "intellectual gestation, while unavoidably necessary and delightfully rewarding, can still be a dangerous and painful process."[2] As mothers and athletes know, "no pain, no gain." While I do not want to quibble about whether this principle is universally true or whether pain is "evil," I do believe it holds true as an important guideline for liberal arts education.

Athletes know that if they do not stretch the appropriate muscles just a little beyond what they are accustomed to, then there is no growth, only maintenance. Too much pain can be crippling, but without any pain the chances are small that strength is increasing. Why should educational development be any different? The interactionist recognizes that age by itself will not lead to new stages of development, regardless of experience. According to Perry, this means that

> as applied to educational intervention, the [interactionist] theory holds that facilitating the child's movement to the next step of development involves *exposure* to the next higher level of thought and *conflict* requiring the active application of the current level of thought to problematic situations.[3]

In short, this means that the educational experience must include conflict, dissonance, or what we have called "pain." I want to pursue Perry's notion of "exposure" in the discussion of habits and community below, but first the role of conflict. According to Duska and Whelan,

> to create cognitive stimulation . . . is to upset the equilibrium of the individual by setting up a situation where [they] experience sufficient conflict in resolving a problem to realize that [their] reasoning structures are too limited to include the new perspectives the conflict is intended to present.[4]

Fowler says that "in most cases, stage transition involves pain."[5] And Wolterstorff agrees.

> Everyone wants to eliminate "cognitive dissonance" (in other words attain "cognitive equilibrium"). . . . When the dissonance between one's environment and stage of reasoning becomes sufficiently severe, one moves on to a higher stage in order to attain equilibrium. . . . This goal of advancing the student in the form of his or her reasoning is accomplished by producing dissonance between the environment of [students] and that particular stage within which they find themselves.[6]

Obviously this entails (1) paying attention to the student's modes of thought, judgment, and faith (i.e., to their stage or position) and (2) matching the stimulation (conflict, dissonance) to their position. The evidence is they will not be attracted to lower stages and cannot even understand stages more than one level higher than their own.[7] Only under these conditions will the induced conflict produce growth.[8]

This dissonance can occur in many different contexts, as discussed in part III. But of central importance are discussions among peers, as Sharon Parks points out, when "one professor's point of view seriously conflicts with another professor's."[9] Perry illustrates with an example to which we will return below. In making the transition from dualism to multiplicity, he says, students are often shaken when they realize that their professors are uncertain too. "Here was this great professor, and he was groping *too!*"[10] Perry goes on to say this provides faculty with excellent opportunities to provoke dissonance and promote growth. When students realize that their work is evaluated not according to some standard cut in stone but by the judgment of faculty, which varies from professor to professor, they are bewildered. "What do they want!?" When teachers capitalize on this bewilderment with the appropriate encouragement, they promote development using dissonance. Because students are often at different stages in their development, this usually requires different procedures for different groups. We will discuss the more practical implications of this below. But Perry concludes from empirical studies that "the introduction of *calculated incongruities* was required to instigate movement in a [student] group . . . toward the next developmental stage."[11]

In the study by David G. Winter described in chapter 2, there is further empirical evidence of the central role of dissonance in development. The study concluded that graduates of liberal arts institutions do, in fact, make more progress in achieving the aims of autonomy, critical thinking, leadership, and so on, which had been identified as goals of the liberal arts. What is interesting here is that there seemed to be a direct correlation between the level of frustration (dissonance) experienced by freshmen and the degree to which they increased in measures of critical thinking and leadership.

> Those students who found Ivy College more frustrating as freshmen later showed significantly larger increases in critical thinking . . . and in the leadership motive pattern. . . . Whatever the sources of this initial frustration, it does seem to spur the development of both conceptual ability or critical thinking and leadership concerns in all students.[12]

This principle of promoting growth by provoking dissonance has characterized the education of leaders since Plato. He argued that young people intended for leadership should be taken from the comfortable context of their families and challenged in order to grow. British schooling in the nineteenth century sent future colonial rulers to boarding schools characterized by rigor and frustration.[13]

But of course, there are risks. Some students do not respond well to such dissonance. Like an athlete pushed too far, they can be injured, some temporarily, others for much longer. It seems obvious that a Christian liberal arts college should not be a hothouse where answers are given to questions students have never asked. But when Sam Keen restates this, it seems much more threatening. "The whole notion of teaching young people to be saints before they are sinners is ridiculous. . . . They try to teach wisdom before folly has been tasted."[14]

Apparently one must actually fall into sin and folly before one can progress developmentally. It sounds exactly like what Christian parents and students fear most. It sounds like the very lapse they try to *avoid* by choosing a Christian college.

Because the risk of intellectual, emotional, and spiritual damage is so serious, the responsibility of faculty "coaches" is enormous. In part III we consider some practical ways to minimize these risks. Even more important than selecting which techniques to use in promoting dissonance, we must recognize that although this calculated strategy may be a necessary condition for development toward critical commitment, it is most certainly *not* a sufficient condition. We consider other necessary conditions in the next sections. I do not believe that actual moral and faith failure is necessary for development. And in the section below on community I will show that even Sam Keen agrees.[15] But if Holmes is right and education is more like intellectual gestation than training, then the risks are unavoidable. "[It] can still be a dangerous and painful process."[16]

HABITUATION

I have argued above that there is more to a liberal arts education than just achieving the ability to think or form judgments in a developmentally advanced way. Critical commitment means actually thinking that way and forming judgments that way. Plato believed that knowing the good meant doing the good, so he might have been surprised by experiments showing that the link between concept and deed is not strong. "Cognitions concerning charity [for example] are not sufficient to affect the behavior."[17] In other words, it is not enough to have the tools to make critical commitments. The liberally educated person must tend to use those tools to make such commitments more regularly than those who are not. But this tendency or disposition reflects an altered condition of the student's character.[18] In short, it means that critical commitment is—as I have argued above—a virtue. In Aristotle's words, "With regard to virtue, then, it is not enough to know, but we must try to have and use it."[19] More than a form of reasoning, it is an attitude and even an affective state.[20] But this brings us to a second principle of how critical commitment is produced. Virtues are the result of habituation.

Perry says that when an individual begins to see how more developed modes of reasoning and judging work, they begin to apply them more broadly. "This expansion, at first conscious, deepens the tendency of the activity to become habitual."[21] Cardinal Newman also called it a habit, "a habit of mind is formed which lasts through life," and said it was the work of discipline.[22]

Both Plato and Aristotle had a lot to say about how one acquires virtues. Plato seemed to want to distinguish knowledge from virtue and concluded in the *Meno* that virtue could not be taught. It was a divine gift, the result of nature.[23] Aristotle also distinguished knowledge (intellectual virtue) from virtue (moral virtue) and said the former could be acquired by teaching but the latter only by habituation.[24] "Virtue, then, being of two kinds, intellectual and moral, intellectual virtue in the main owes both its birth and its growth to teaching . . . while moral virtue comes about as the result of habit."[25]

In Aristotle's terminology, critical commitment is both an intellectual and a moral virtue. Consequently, in addition to teaching, habituation must play an essential part in its acquisition. "We learn by doing. . . . Thus in one word, states of character arise out of like activities. . . . It makes no small difference, then, whether we form habits of one kind or of another from our very youth; it makes a very great difference, or rather, all the difference."[26]

Christian liberal arts institutions that wish to inculcate the virtue of critical commitment will find that it happens not with teaching and instruction alone but only as students are provided opportunities to learn by doing—opportunities to actually develop the habit of exercising the cognitive, moral, and affective elements of critical commitment.

Developing habits requires discipline. So it should be unsurprising that empirical studies of the effectiveness of liberal arts institutions in producing graduates who embody critical thinking, independence of thought, leadership, and personal maturity show that some of the greatest correlations occurred with activities that involved discipline, including "systematic and disciplined practice involving conceptual diagnosis" and, interestingly, varsity sports.[27]

The point here is, of course, that the aims of liberal education go beyond knowledge or the acquisition of a certain skill. They include the inculcation of virtue. This follows naturally and even obviously from the Christian view of humanity. Christians, and in fact the Judeo-Christian tradition, insist that persons are more than just minds. They are wholes comprising minds, hearts, and bodies. An education must address them all. It's not enough to teach students how to make sophisticated intellectual and moral judgments; they must be aided in becoming persons who actually do make such judgments. Failure, or sin, is not chiefly from ignorance, a lack of knowledge, but from a lack of virtue. It is a flaw of character, not intellect. For this reason, it is obvious why habituation as a means of virtue education should be central to Christian liberal arts.

MODELING

Of course, not all habits are good. As Nicholas Wolterstorff points out, "Some of our tendencies must be stifled."[28] Here, of course, those who hold maturationist theories of education will part company. Their purpose is to promote whatever potential is within the student on the assumption that humanity is basically good. But Christians disagree, so the question arises *which* virtues will be inculcated. This brings us to a third principle of how critical commitment is produced. Virtuous habits are most effectively engendered by modeling.

Most agree that modeling works. Advertising amply demonstrates the powerful influence models have. The fact that modeling is used so widely on Madison Avenue and is attacked so vehemently by those who would protect children shows how powerful it is taken to be. Education is no exception and theorists across the spectrum agree. As Bruce Wilshire describes it, education is a "setting in which elders have a responsibility for demonstrating already achieved forms of humanness, and for working with the young so that we all can make sense of the inevitable stages of our lives."[29]

William Perry's studies make it plain that the wholistic character of developmental education places an enormous responsibility on the educator. "The exigency of [the] developmental crisis seems to us to impose a profound responsibility on the educator, a responsibility which is no longer a separable task like 'building character' which was once somehow 'tacked on' to regular teaching."[30]

He says this demands that educators become models. This is true at all positions of Perry's developmental scheme. At lower positions (3-4), they model the independent thinking characteristic of multiplicity. Paradoxically, students begin to think independently because "it was the way They want you to think."[31] At higher positions (8-9), educators must show "a certain openness—a visibility in their thinking, groping, doubts, and styles of Commitment. Most of our students seemed to have found one or more models of this kind."[32]

Kohlberg also confirms the principle of modeling in the same place he underscores the role of dissonance. He says that "facilitating the child's movement to the next step of development involves exposure to the next higher level of thought and conflict requiring the active application of the current level of thought to problematic situations."[33] The "conflict" is the dissonance I spoke of as the first principle of teaching critical commitment. "Exposure" requires that there be persons who can model the higher level for students.

When R. J. Schenkat describes a liberal arts–oriented teacher education program, he agrees. "Educators must make evident their readiness to risk, and especially to risk making their own thinking visible. Students should be able to see how instructors analyze, synthesize, and generalize new material, and especially how they grope for new possibilities, handle doubts, and figure things out."[34]

When William Bennett says he believes faculty must engage their students "not dispassionately,"[35] I believe he is speaking of modeling. Faculty must get past the myth of objectivity and be honest. Professors must begin to profess something!

There has been considerable study of the way in which modeling works. The results are profound and even disquieting. The effect of preaching and practice on the moral behavior of children was examined in a number of experiments conducted about twenty years ago. In one experiment, children were asked to "test" a new bowling game. The purpose was to determine how a model would affect the generosity of the children. In six variations, models either practiced charity or greed and preached charity, greed, or were neutral. Unsurprisingly, behavioral example (practice) was more effective in producing generosity than verbal exhortation.[36] This was true (as shown in other experiments) even when the behavioral example (model) was portrayed symbolically (in film rather than in person) and even when the model had neither power nor status over the subject.[37] One can imagine how much more effective the modeling would be in the classroom, where the faculty model is live and usually has both power over the subjects as well as respect in their eyes.

What was more surprising, and even unsettling, was that negative models (those who practiced greed) were significantly more effective in producing greedy behavior than positive models (those who practiced generosity) were in producing generous behavior. In cases where the model did not preach any particular standard, leaving the child to speculate about what the model actually believed, an example of greed was copied almost twice as frequently as an example of charity.[38] Nicholas Wolterstorff remarks on this relatively greater effect of the negative role model in a chapter entitled "Cultivating Tendencies by Modeling" of his book *Educating for Responsible Action*. He draws on a comparable study by A. H. Stein and says, "Apparently modeling may *weaken* one's resistance to temptation, but it is not effective in *building up* resistance."[39]

In another experiment, children were again asked to "test" a new bowling game. The purpose was to examine how effectively different kinds of models would cause children to internalize a standard of scoring. In four variations, the models were either consistently strict, consistently lenient, inconsistent in favoring the child (child-indulgent), or inconsistent in favoring themselves (self-indulgent). The children's scores were controlled and they were allowed first to play alongside a model and then later by themselves. The experiment confirmed the greater effect of the negative model and showed that the worst situation is that of a self-indulgent model who holds the child to a higher standard than the model holds himself. Such inconsistency produced the greatest number of violations of norms, which in the experimental situation amounted to theft. It also produced the fewest number of children who internalized whatever standard the model had been preaching. The same experiment also showed that the greatest success in inculcating the highest standards was found in cases in which the model consistently preached and practiced those high standards for himself and for the subjects.[40] In describing this same experiment, Wolterstorff concludes that "the decisive determinant of how the children would act was always the *action* of the model. The children tended to practice as the model practiced and preach *as the model preached!*"[41]

Of course, the effect of modeling is not limited to children. There is empirical evidence of its effect on the moral behavior of college-age and adult subjects.[42] But empirical evidence of the effect of modeling is also not limited to

moral development. "Just as behavior modeling involves more than just showing behavior, cognitive modeling involves more than just describing knowledge
or techniques. . . . it means making covert mental processes observable."[43]

Although everyone will agree that modeling works, there will be some
who will try to restrict it to modeling the *forms* of cognitive or moral reasoning. But doing so overlooks the fact that critical commitment as I have described it is a virtue and goes far beyond just the forms of reasoning.

Others who hold to a strong liberal arts ideal may agree that the goals
of liberal education, call it critical commitment or not, are virtues and do
require that modeling go beyond modeling the forms of cognitive and
moral reasoning to include modeling behaviors and attitudes. But these
same people may nevertheless try to encourage a kind of modeling that
remains "content free" or neutral. I do not believe this is possible. The
form and passions of cognitive and moral thinking cannot be separated
from the content.

Genuine liberal arts, and Christian liberal arts in particular, must be careful that students are not fed an artificial substitute for genuine critical commitment. Like the infant at Christmas, they might get the idea the wrapping
is the present. Like actors or sophists, they can get the idea that passion or
technique are just ornaments to be "put on" rather than being the fruit of the
struggle of cognitive and moral development. Models should be real people
modeling real commitments. Professors should profess.[44] For Christian liberal arts this means there should be models who make visible not only the
forms of thinking and judging characteristic of higher stages of development
and the attitudes and passions of those stages but, most importantly, the content of those beliefs and judgments. At the appropriate times and places in
the curriculum—dependent on the developmental progress of the students
involved—faculty and staff at Christian liberal arts colleges should express
their real conclusions about important issues running the gamut from preferences of lifestyle to social issues and theological commitments. Models
should make visible the way in which Christian principles of love and justice
are translated into particular forms of thinking, particular passions, and particular conclusions. Christian faculty should visibly exemplify and clearly articulate not only the *forms* of thinking and moral reasoning but also the distinctively Christian *content* of the conclusions they have reached. Unless
they model the distinctive differences in content arising from adopting a
Christian worldview in their thinking, we may have good liberal arts but not
Christian liberal arts.

It is here that the biggest difference between Christian faculty at secular
universities or even good liberal arts colleges and those at enlightened
Christian liberal arts colleges emerges. For over twenty-five years, I have
engaged in an ongoing friendly disagreement about this with a dear friend
and former mentor from college InterVarsity Christian Fellowship days.

Every five years or so we sit down and have another go at it. He has insisted that if I wanted to make a difference in the lives of students, my efforts would be better invested teaching in a secular university than in a Christian college. There, he argues, students are asking real questions and the Christian faculty member will be in the right place at the right time to provide answers.

My answer, and the theme of this whole book, is that the Christian liberal arts college should go *beyond* the secular institution; to do *more,* not *less.* If Christian colleges do not ask real questions, if they are just intellectual hothouses providing pat answers to unasked questions, then my friend is right. But I am not yet so pessimistic. This is why I am so concerned that Christian colleges recognize their distinctive genius. I believe that faculty at non-Christian institutions may be limited in how explicitly they can model the content of their distinctively Christian scholarship. This can be true either because of actual policy restrictions on what can be said or merely because of the informal pressure brought to bear on them by peers or by a promotion and tenure system that does not reward scholarship which might be judged as parochial or sectarian. But it is the special opportunity and privilege of faculty at Christian colleges to be at the cutting edge, at the point of distinctively Christian reflection and commitment about the thorniest problems of the human condition in general and contemporary issues in particular. As they model and articulate the content of these distinctively and explicitly Christian conclusions, they go *beyond* what is generally possible on the secular campus. This is one aspect of Christian scholarship as integration discussed in part II.

But the idea that faculty should model content as well as form brings us to a thorny issue. Those who wish to restrict modeling to form or form and attitude do so for a perfectly understandable reason. They are justifiably worried that there is a fine line between modeling and indoctrination. How can Christian liberal arts institutions allow faculty and staff to not only model the forms and attitudes of higher cognitive and moral development but also profess boldly their own particular beliefs? Won't this brainwash the students? Won't these models unduly influence them as the experimental evidence discussed above suggests? Some kind of check is needed, and this brings us to the fourth and final principle of how critical commitment is produced.[45] Modeling must occur in a community.

COMMUNITY

I have set out critical commitment as a chief intrinsic value of liberal arts education. It goes beyond both dogmatic dualism and cynical multiplicity. It means more than just knowing certain facts; that is why dissonance is an important principle in its production. It means more than just reasoning or judging according to more developed cognitive and moral forms. It is a virtue, which means it includes important attitudes and passions; that is why habituation is also needed. Yet forms of reasoning and judging and attitudes and passions cannot be empty, generic. Critical commitment must have content; that is why modeling of real concrete examples is another principle in how it is produced. But finally, critical commitment is not indoctrination; that is why community is essential.

Those who wish to avoid the excesses of indoctrination can take at least two approaches. One is to block expressions of opinion altogether in an effort to remain neutral. The other is to encourage the wide expression of strong belief.

The approach that tries to be neutral not only misunderstands that such neutrality is a myth but often demeans and patronizes the student. It assumes they cannot decide for themselves. Unless they see real live role models of genuine belief, students stagnate in multiplicity, become cynical, and view the alternatives they may have studied as just so many "styles" in what amounts to nothing more than an intellectual game. While this avoids the risk of believing the "wrong things," it also loses the opportunity to believe "what is right." To paraphrase William James, such people are more afraid of making a mistake than of losing the truth.

In contrast, I believe indoctrination can better be avoided by exposing appropriately developed students to a plurality of strongly held beliefs.[46] This affirms the value of their choice and development. The people around them who serve as role models of belief challenge them to make commitments themselves. But the differences of opinion among those role models balance the risk of indoctrination *so long as those persons remain in community.* In short, development is enhanced and indoctrination is avoided when diversity is affirmed in the context of community.

The problem, of course, is in the very expression "diversity in community." What does it mean? Like the word "multiculturalism," it is almost a contradiction. To the extent that diversity is emphasized, community is usually sacrificed. To the extent that community is emphasized, diversity is usually reduced. But if modeling real live critical commitment is to avoid the danger of indoctrination in Christian liberal arts colleges, community must embrace diversity.

"Diversity" is au courant, almost a buzzword. Ours is an age of diversity. Predictably, the result is often the loss of community. This is true not only of American society generally—litigious, fractious, and rights oriented—but also of academe. And Christian academe is no exception. In part II, I will describe the effect of professional fragmentation on the Christian college campus in more detail. But my point here is that with such emphasis on diversity, attempts to affirm community are often neglected, which means that modeling occurs out of context and runs the risk of becoming indoctrination. That effect can be seen on politically correct campuses where factions arise around the most visible models who express their commitments most loudly. The appropriate check-and-balance is genuine community.

Consider what several advocates of cognitive, moral, and faith development have to say about community. Perry says community is essential. Dissonance will be ineffective in promoting development if it is perceived as coming from *outside* the individual's community.

> Where the pressure comes from sources the person can perceive only as "other," his tightening of his boundaries in rejection or combat will be the same whether he is acting from "intolerance" or simple "integrity." The issue will be clear only where the pressure for change comes from a source perceivable as within his own community, or where his resistance to the pressure would itself involve him in activities contrary to the values he already shares in that community.[47]

He says that modeling is *not* enough. Development will occur only if the student identifies with the role models in community.

> The educational community may do much to nourish the probability of a favorable outcome by acquitting its own responsibilities to the student in addition to that of training him in intellectual expertise. These responsibilities would seem to involve more than the provision of models for emulation; we infer from our students' reports that the most urgent requirement may be that of providing the student with recognition and confirmation of his community with these models, a community earned not only through his expertise but through his courage in the face of doubt.[48]

Community balances the "loneliness" of critical commitment. "The larger community also includes those who think differently, and one must both believe in one's own commitments and somehow acknowledge others' even when they contravene one's own principles."[49]

It is, in Tillich's words, the need to balance the "courage to be as oneself" with the "courage to be as a part." Perry says that the relevant kind of community is not just a shared set of "worthwhile things to care about" nor even the "expectation that the student *will* care" but rather a shared "sense of community *in the risks of caring.*" "The educator's efforts would be, then, to increase the student's experience of recognition and confirmation as a member of the community by virtue of the courage with which he undertakes the risks of care."[50] For the Christian liberal arts college this might mean that our sense of community must go beyond any shared set of worthwhile beliefs or even expected attitudes. It should include the mutual recognition that faith in Jesus Christ is a "risk": an act of courage and submission in which all members share.

Duska and Whelan echo this insistence on the role of community. In describing the means for best promoting moral development, they make it plain that dissonance is not enough. Empathy must be added to make the dissonance effective. And empathy occurs in community, whether this is in "moral education groups" or family.[51]

Sam Keen, in dialogue with James Fowler, describes moral and faith development using terminology first used by William James. He says persons can be "unborn," "once-born," or "multi-born." The unborn person does not really develop at all but remains fixated in a childlike understanding of herself and her faith. The once-born "makes a gentle rise throughout their lives. . . . They don't have revolutions. . . . They grow and they continue." The multi-born "lives in up and down movement. There are crisis points."[52]

> In a society that was functioning right . . . there would be fewer patterns of the twice-born variety and there would be more once-born journeys. I fault education for this. . . . In a healthy society more once-born journeys would be possible there and twice-born people would have better techniques to make their way in the world too.[53]

I believe the kind of society Keen is describing would be a genuine community.

Sharon Parks is among the strongest advocates of the view that community is essential to cognitive, moral, and faith development. With Piaget she is convinced that "human becoming absolutely depends upon the quality of interaction between the person and his or her environment."[54] She explains that dependency on community is often discouraged because the mark of psychological adulthood is seen as "autonomy" and maturity is measured in terms of "individuation."[55] The characteristics Parks ascribes to community include the paradoxical "convictional commitment" I have called critical commitment, along with interdependency and openness to others.[56] Dissonance provokes conflict in the mind of the student. But that conflict must occur in community to be sustained and transformed into the development and commitment that are its goal. "The conflict must be held in a 'context of rapport,' which is to say, held in community, in communion, in trust. Teachers must have staying power. The conflict is creative only if one is not left alone with it, overwhelmed by it."[57] Each professor has the potential to become a "spiritual guide," each syllabus the potential to become a "confession of faith."

> Educators introduce appropriate conflict, dissonance, and wonder so as to awaken the learner. . . . But this is also a moment of discipline. The educator must do more than raise issues and heighten curiosity. It is part of the educator's task to initiate the learner into a discipline of definition and critique.[58]

To ensure that this does not become mere indoctrination, the community must initiate the student into a conversation—"a self-conscious participation in the dialectic toward truth."[59] Such a community contrasts with the positivistic community that dichotomizes subjective and objective and searches for the value-neutral fact. Such a community, says Parks, equally rejects "both uncritical conventional dogmatism and unqualified relativism" because

[it] recognizes that every perspective is rooted in and, therefore, relative to particular personal, social, and cultural conditions. Yet because each incomplete perspective is, nevertheless, an attempt to comprehend the one reality there is, it is possible to make judgments about their measure of validity as multiple perspectives mutually inform and correct each other.[60]

Finally, I have already cited Kohlberg's agreement that community is essential and is the key to avoiding indoctrination. "It is impossible for teachers not to engage in value-judgments and decisions. A concern for the liberty of the [student] does not create a school in which the teacher is value-neutral and any pretense of it creates 'the hidden curriculum.' But it can create a school in which the teacher's value-judgments and decisions involve the student democratically."[61] According to Kohlberg, only this kind of community resolves the "problem of indoctrination."[62]

The community described is democratic and dialectical *if* it respects the liberty of all those who participate. It is dialectical *if* it deliberately values the diversity and dissonance that promotes ongoing discussion and criticism. Robert Sandin adds his support.

Indoctrination in values-related education is the inculcation of particular beliefs, doctrines, or standards of worth on persons without respecting their capacity for free inquiry and critical judgment. . . . Education on the other hand is always dialectical, being based on a method of criticism. Education fosters human freedom; indoctrination tends to restrict it.[63]

The community is also a "dialectical community" *if* it seeks to go beyond the artificial disconnection between empirical truth and questions of meaning, value, and truth. From Kant onward the academy has been "tyrannized," says Parks, by the view that only the phenomenal, the empirical, could properly be known. All other matters were merely for practical reason and not legitimate concerns of the university. The dialectical community refuses that sharp separation and strives to take students beyond both stages of development that arise from it. It goes beyond dogmatism, which puts all truth on one side of the dichotomy as if it were like empirical fact, *and* beyond relativism, which puts all truth on the other side of the dichotomy as if it were purely subjective.

Dissonance, habituation, models, and community: four principles that I believe enable students to acquire critical commitment. We will return to them later when I describe the Christian liberal arts college which makes that intrinsic value a chief goal for students.

CONCLUSION TO PART I

In part I, I have been concerned with the intrinsic value of a liberal arts education. It is not just what students can do with their education that counts. It is also who they have become. I have said I believe that critical commitment is among the chief characteristics of a liberal arts education. In three chapters, I have tried to describe what that is, why it is consistent with Christian faith, and how an institution might begin to accomplish it. The underlying assumptions have been openly developmental and post-Kantian (post-positivist). In part II, I explore the question of the instrumental value of a liberal arts education. But first a concluding comment.

Some may feel that I have not said enough about *Christian* liberal arts. In fact, almost everything here is as applicable to non-Christian liberal arts as to Christian liberal arts. That assessment is essentially right. Although I have tried to explain in the second section why my vision of the liberal arts is especially consistent with a Christian worldview, I do not deny that this vision may also be consistent with others. This vision, however, does presuppose an objectivist theory of truth and values. Thus some who espouse allegiance to liberal arts could not pursue what I have called critical commitment. Finally, I have explained in several places why I think the Christian liberal arts college is especially suited to accomplish this task, for example, because of emphases on modeling and community. This fact, more than even the character of critical commitment, makes this vision one that I believe could become the distinctive intrinsic value of Christian liberal arts education.

Part II

Christian Liberal Arts Means Tackling Real-World Problems

Integration: A Step Beyond Both
Dabbling and Overspecialization

Part II

Christian Liberal Arts Means Tackling Real-World Problems

Integration: A Step Beyond
Both Dabbling and Overspecialization

> Because of the equivocal echo-nature of language, even identities or ho-
> mophones sound on: the sound of Sa is knotted with that of ça, as if the text
> were signaling its intention to bring Hegel, Saussure, and Freud together. Ça
> corresponds to the Freudian Id ("Es"); and it may be that our only "savoir
> absolu" is that of a ça structured like the Sa-significant: a bacchic or Lacan-
> ian "primal process" where only signifier-signifying signifiers exist.[1]

For two years I taught in the Philosophy Department at the University of
Zimbabwe. Throughout Easter week 1988 I lectured to my graduate students
on the topic of alternative theories in the philosophy of time. On Good Fri-
day afternoon I found myself bumping and swerving along the deserted pot-
holed, two-lane highway stretching from the Zimbabwean border deep into
the interior of war-torn Mozambique. Mozambique was at the bottom of lists
of the poorest, most oppressed countries in the world. Millions had been
killed and displaced in a sixteen-year-old guerrilla war. The atrocities were
unspeakable. Famine, fear, and disease were rampant because the government and infrastructure were largely nonexistent or ineffective. Over the
next seventy-two hours that weekend, I saw dedicated Christians using the
simplest of skills bring tangible relief and comfort to victims. I saw a Japan-
ese student who had left law school in Japan, unable to speak either Por-
tuguese, the Mozambican national language, or the local dialect, rise early
each morning to bake hundreds of small bread rolls to distribute in the holding camps nearby where those dislocated by war in other parts of the country had fled for a somewhat safer haven. I saw an ex-convict deported from
both the United Kingdom and his own country, Zimbabwe, huddle every
night to the sound of automatic weapons fire with fifteen war orphans in an

eight-foot wooden box on the streets of Gondola. By day he would transport them twenty-five miles in a truck to a farm too dangerous to occupy by night, where he could bathe, clothe, and teach them. I saw a Zimbabwean doctor and nurse stand by helplessly as a tiny baby died of measles and malnutrition. I was frustrated to learn that the small band of naked refugees I saw emerge from weeks of fleeing in the bush could not be clothed with donated clothing stacked in rooms nearby because no one had the time and skill to sort the clothing by size and gender. The contrast with my seminar room only two hundred miles away in Harare was unsettling. It was easy to conclude that what the world needed was a little less skill in graduate philosophy and a little more skill and willingness to sort used clothing.

In part I, I referred to a perennial question asked by my philosophy students: "What will an education in philosophy or in the liberal arts do *for* me?" My answer was to suggest the student is asking the wrong question. Instead, a student should ask, "What can philosophy do *to* me?" In preceding chapters, I have argued that this intrinsic value of liberal arts is crucial but neglected. It has to do with becoming—with character development. It is the virtue of critical commitment. But my complete answer to the student question is that *both* questions are important. They should ask both "who can I become with liberal arts?" and "what can I do with liberal arts?" Although the intrinsic value is the one more often overlooked, a liberal arts education also has powerful instrumental values.

In part I, I pointed out that the liberal arts are useful because they develop skills in thinking and communicating and prepare students for graduate study and research, for more rapid advancement in jobs of all kinds, and for the exercise of good citizenship. No parent, prospective student, or institution should overlook these instrumental values, especially in evaluating and promoting the liberal arts.

But there is a use that is of even greater value. This is the preparation liberal arts provides for tackling real-world problems. Part of the genius of a liberal arts education, and a Christian liberal arts education in particular, is to equip students to address the particularly complex, thorny issues people face today. The distinctive ability of liberal arts graduates to deal with real-world problems arises from more than their acquisition of transferable skills. It arises from the integrative character of their education. But because integration is a hackneyed and abused concept, especially in Christian liberal arts circles, I undertake its rehabilitation with some fear of being misunderstood.

I will look first at *what* integration is. This requires a brief look at the development of education in America and, for contrast, at the alternative understandings of scholarship in many Christian liberal arts colleges today. Second, I will examine *why* integration is not only consistent with but also necessary for Christian education. Finally, as in part I, I will suggest principles central to *how* an institution can promote this kind of integration.

6

What Is Integration?

Beyond Dabbling and beyond Overspecialization

TRANSITIONS IN THE MISSION OF
AMERICAN HIGHER EDUCATION

The picture of what an American institution of higher education should try to accomplish has changed dramatically over its two-hundred-year history. To clarify my use of the term "integration," it is particularly important to understand two historical transitions. First, academia shifted emphasis from general education to disciplinary specialization and second, from teaching to research. Almost everyone in higher education today acknowledges both of these transitions. It is not necessary to document the history of American higher education, but some historical understanding of these changes is necessary to explain why calling for integration is so difficult.[1]

Specialization: Colonial Colleges to Land Grant Universities

Institutions of higher education in colonial America were primarily religious in character. They combined the purpose of British collegiate life—to build character and prepare students for citizenship—with the goal of preparing graduates for ministry. Moral and spiritual growth was at least as important as intellectual growth. Historian Theodore Benditt wrote that "professors were hired not for their scholarly ability or achievement but for their religious commitment. Scholarly achievement was not a high priority, either for professors or students."[2]

But before long, a more instrumental side of higher education began to emerge. Institutions like Rensselaer Polytechnic Institute, founded in 1824,

95

brought a different, more specialized purpose to higher education. By 1846 Yale had created a professorship in "agricultural chemistry and animal and vegetable husbandry." No doubt the biggest boost to this transition was the Morrill Act of 1862, later called the Land Grant College Act. Federal land was given to states, the proceeds from the sale of which supported the creation of a new kind of institution of higher education. These institutions were devoted to the liberal arts but also to training in practical skills, which would be needed to support the westward expansion of the nation. The new colleges became the foundation for the agricultural and mechanical revolutions of that day.[3] The dimension of service began to challenge moral, spiritual, and intellectual growth as the hallmarks of higher education.

This turn to service automatically meant a turn from general education to specialization. As Bruce Wilshire described it, "The trend to greater specialization was not limited to the sciences. A secular ethos of proficiency and expertise created a tidal force that carried the humanities with it. In the 1870s and 80s two hundred learned societies were formed in addition to teacher's groups. Every university divided itself into departments according to the divisions of these academic professional associations. Authority was now vested with master knowers in specialized areas as these knowers were recognized within that sector nationwide."[4]

Francis Bacon's assumption that knowledge is power encouraged this specialization. Liberal learning with its general studies was viewed by many in frontier land grant colleges as a luxury. Specialization brought with it a shift in loyalty from the local institution to the professional guild. "Professional groupings began to shoulder aside local communities. Individual advancement within professions tended to supplant civic duty."[5] Today faculty members' loyalty is to their career rather than their institution.[6]

The turn to specialization led naturally to the second major shift in American higher education. Once professors must look beyond their own institution for specialized evaluation and review, their agenda and their rewards also come from outside. This means that emphasis shifts from teaching to research.

Research: English College to German University

The early tradition of American higher education, which made teaching the first priority for faculty, also followed the model of British schools. The teacher was expected to be an educational mentor and a model in the broadest sense. On that model, as George Douglas has described it,

> learning is accumulated slowly over time by people who come together in a kinship of learning. . . . I mean that people must be able to talk to one another regularly and intimately; that they must be on the same wavelength. . . . In the intimate dining halls or reading rooms of Oxford or Cambridge an eighteen

year old might not be aware that he or she is sitting next to a Nobel prize winner. . . . A college is not a collection of specialized departments but a community of individuals. . . . These "colleges" were all first and foremost human communities. If they also housed "experts," all to the good, but that little accretion trailed along afterward.[7]

As late as 1869, even as the turn from general studies to specialization was well under way, Charles Elliot, president of Harvard, declared, "the prime business of American professors . . . must be regular and assiduous class teaching."[8]

But the addition of service, especially in land grant institutions, made applied research an acceptable alternative. And the move toward specialization complemented this tendency toward research as the vitality of professional societies came to depend on the lifeblood of shared research publication. Basic research had not played a large role in American higher education but by the mid-nineteenth century, with confidence in science particularly strong, the research orientation characteristic of German universities found its way to America. The Massachusetts Institute of Technology was founded in 1864, and in 1876, the Johns Hopkins University became the first American institution of higher education deliberately based on the assumption that knowledge was best advanced by research. Its founding has been described as "perhaps the single most decisive event in the history of learning in the Western Hemisphere."[9] Ernest Boyer reports that by 1895, the president of the newly formed University of Chicago could require all new faculty to sign an agreement that their promotions in rank and salary would depend chiefly upon their research productivity.[10]

George Douglas concludes that the shift from the British to the Germanic model, from teaching to research, left only a "trickle down" for undergraduates. "No idea that has ever taken hold in the American university has been more harmful and destructive than this one."[11]

THE RESULTANT TRENDS TODAY

The effects of these two transitions, from general studies to specialization and from teaching to research, are obvious in contemporary American higher education. What is perhaps even more interesting is that these effects are part of considerable controversy about the state of higher education both in the popular media and in academe. The 1983 Department of Education report on education in America, *A Nation at Risk*, was seminal. It found a "rising tide of mediocrity" in American education generally. The next year, 1984, brought two harsh sequels that focused on problems in higher education: the National Institute of Education's *Involvement in Learning* and the National Endowment for

the Humanities' report *To Reclaim a Legacy*. The next year, 1985, brought the
Newman Report of the Carnegie Foundation for the Advancement of Teaching.
In 1989, Carnegie conducted an extensive survey of faculty that was followed
by another independent survey the next year. In 1990, the Carnegie Foundation
released its results and Boyer's *Scholarship Reconsidered*. Even Canadian
higher education was criticized in a 1991 report by Stuart Smith. And there have
been numerous individual critiques, like the ones of Allan Bloom, Bruce
Wilshire, Dinesh D'Souza, and George Douglas.[12] In my judgment there is a
common thread in all of these criticisms. They point out problems wrought in
large measure by the transitions from general to specialized education and from
teaching to research.[13]

Overspecialization

American colleges and universities have become overly specialized. The NIE
report asserted that "specialization may be a virtue for some students. But as
ever more narrow programs are created, they become isolated from each
other, and students end up with fragmented and limited knowledge. . . . To
a large extent, our recommendations seek to reverse the trend implied by
these indicators and to restore liberal education to its central role in undergraduate education."[14]

The report recommended that "all bachelor's degree recipients should
have at least two full years of liberal education."[15] "What should distinguish the baccalaureate degree from more specialized credentials is the
broad learning that lies behind it."[16] And it said, "College officials should
both define scholarship broadly and demand that faculty demonstrate that
scholarship."[17] It concluded, "We value strongly breadth and integration in
higher education."[18]

The NEH report issued the same year was even stronger. "Undergraduate
teaching has been damaged by . . . narrow specialization in the graduate
schools." The report cites John Sawyer, president of the Andrew Mellon
Foundation, who stated that graduate education which prepares college
teachers is characterized by "hyperspecialization and self-isolating vocabu-
laries."[19] And according to the 1990 Carnegie report, "Specifically, at many of
the nation's four-year institutions, the focus had moved . . . from general to
specialized education."[20]

The problem with specialization is sometimes taken to be the loss of
some particular content of general education. For example, Francis Oakley, president at Williams, has taken this line against critics of overspecialization.[21] He claims that for these critics, in general education "it is
content, above all, that matters."[22] To illustrate, he quotes William Bennett:
"Merely being exposed to a variety of subjects and points of view is not
enough. Learning to think critically and skeptically is not enough. . . .

[What is crucial is that students be called upon to] master an explicit body of knowledge . . . become participants in a common culture."[23]

I agree with Bennett that education needs to go beyond mere exposure to points of view and the ability to think critically. It must go beyond multiplicity to critical commitment. It must include the modeling of virtues. However, this is *not* my argument with overspecialization. The real problem with overspecialization is not that it undermines allegiance to particular truths and canon but the effect it has in preventing scholars from addressing real-world problems.

Excessive Research Orientation

Disciplinary specialization has contributed to a research and publication orientation. Sixty years ago, A. N. Whitehead was already warning against overemphasis on written expressions of the professorial task. "It would be a great mistake to estimate the value of each member of the faculty by the printed work signed with his name . . . there is at the present day some tendency to fall into this error; and an emphatic protest is necessary."[24]

Jencks and Riesman put it this way in 1969: "College instructors have become less and less preoccupied with educating young people, more and more preoccupied with educating one another by doing scholarly research which advances their discipline."[25]

The NIE report complained that "many of our colleges and universities overemphasize research and minimize quality teaching in personnel decisions, and this tradition has potentially damaging effects on student learning and development."[26]

In the 1984 NEH report, William Bennett said that "unless graduate schools reexamine their priorities, much of our teaching will remain mediocre."[27] In 1990 Ernest Boyer agreed, citing evidence from as far back as 1958 that while faculty are often hired as teachers, they are evaluated as researchers.[28] More recent evidence is even clearer. In the Carnegie Foundation survey of faculty in 1969, 21 percent strongly agreed that it was difficult to obtain tenure without publishing. By 1989, that number had doubled.[29] Even though 70 percent of the faculty surveyed indicated that their primary interest was in teaching, 77 percent felt compelled to conduct research to earn tenure.[30]

In retiring as president of Harvard University, Derek Bok cautioned that "the quality of education and teaching are at risk in a research university because the rewards of society are so powerful in the direction of research. . . . Society is voting heavily in favor of research rather than education in which it is putting its money all of the prizes, the visibility, the excitement, and consulting. . . . We have to be more imaginative in figuring out how to develop incentives that will ensure greater attention to teaching."[31]

This trend has not left liberal arts colleges unaffected. The 1989 Carnegie survey showed that 43 percent of faculty at comprehensive colleges strongly agreed that tenure was difficult to obtain without publishing, whereas only 6 percent had said so in 1969. Even at liberal arts colleges, the number strongly agreeing had quadrupled from 6 percent to 24 percent.[32]

In My Department It Is Difficult for a Person
to Achieve Tenure If He or She Does Not Publish
(*Percentage Saying "Strongly Agree"*)

	1969	1989
All respondents	21	42
Research institutions	44	83
Doctorate granting	27	71
Comprehensive	6	43
Liberal arts	6	24
Two-year	3	4

The good news is that at liberal arts colleges so far, only 22 percent of faculty believe the pressure to publish reduces the quality of teaching. Without comparative data it is hard to document the trend. However, at comprehensive colleges, 41 percent say it reduces quality and at doctorate and research institutions, over 50 percent say this.[33] The fear is that even as research universities begin to reemphasize teaching, institutions that have always emphasized teaching will, paradoxically, move in the opposite direction because of the momentum of emulating their more prestigious competitors.[34]

Sadly, increased emphasis on research seems to mean reduced attention to teaching. If teaching load is any indication, the commitment to teaching seems to be weakening, as loads have decreased over the past twenty years. At many institutions, senior faculty prefer to work with graduate students and not teach undergraduate courses.[35] Stanley Wolpert, professor of history at UCLA, says, "I think most everyone realizes that the undergraduate education doesn't get nearly enough attention here. The faculty will tell you that their research is their top priority. But the university has never insisted that teaching be given at least equal value."[36]

A 1991 survey of over 23,000 faculty, but limited to research universities, indicates that "teaching can hurt you, but it can't help you. . . . Although administrators might speak about the importance of teaching, their behavior in personnel actions, in allocation of . . . resources, and in the criteria used in the promotion and tenure system tend to convince faculty otherwise."[37]

What is worse, the trend toward research to the detriment of teaching is found even in colleges traditionally best known for their teaching. There has always been research at good liberal arts colleges like Carleton, Beloit, Macalester, Smith, and Wellesley. But increased pressures on faculty at such institutions have threatened to change the campus climate in dramatic ways. Faculty now see research as a way of furthering their career and administrators see it as enhancing the reputation of their institution. New faculty with recent Ph.D.s assume that pursuit of their often narrow graduate interests is the way to get ahead. Consider what faculty at such institutions are saying:

> In barely definable ways, the campus is different. . . . There's a sense of loss that the faculty is feeling for the values . . . embodied in the past. . . . You cut out all the contemplative stuff. . . . You find yourself teaching hysterically and doing research hysterically.

> What I'm worried about . . . is younger faculty spending the first six years here tending to their careers, whereas I think that part of their responsibility is tending to the joys and charms of teaching.

> It's quite possible to take an excellent teaching college and turn it into a mediocre research institution.[38]

One professor jokes that "the best evidence that professors are doing more research is that campus parking lots are empty on Tuesdays and Thursdays because many faculty members work at home those days. . . . The more that research is openly rewarded, the more pressure is put on young faculty to publish, the less likely you are to attract faculty who want to spend the bulk of their time teaching."[39]

Even students are beginning to complain about the way faculty and institutional emphasis on research is undermining the quality of their education. A *Los Angeles Times* article reported that seventy-five seniors at the University of California Los Angeles complained that "most classes are large and impersonal, that professors seem far more interested in research than teaching, and that the 19,000 undergraduates believe they are ignored. . . . Teaching is just not valued here."[40] In an article in the *Chronicle of Higher Education,* students at the University of Texas complained that "with the professors, their research comes first and then their attention goes to graduate students. The undergraduates come last."[41]

And the complaints are not coming solely from students at large research institutions. Even Wellesley students complained they could not complete degree requirements within the traditional time frame because not enough courses were offered.[42]

There is no doubt that even the most research-oriented liberal arts colleges still emphasize teaching more than large research universities. But the problem is the *trend.* Faculty do not have unlimited energy and time. Faculty loads have been cut at places like Grinnell and Wellesley and reductions are under consideration at many others. Interdisciplinary courses go begging for staff because younger faculty judge them to be digressions from their research interests.[43] When something is added, something is lost. The fear is that teaching suffers. Faculty either cut back on teaching or if that is impossible they are strained to keep up quality and give adequate attention to other aspects of their personal lives. Bruce Wilshire says that "many professors are driven by anxiety to publish perpetually, and find no time for personal growth, for commemoration of personal or communal sources, for family or general citizenship; teaching easily becomes a chore."[44]

Francis Oakley has taken issue with those who charge that faculty are fleeing from teaching to research and with the view that research comes at the expense of teaching. He says the Carnegie Foundation data show no such thing. He cites the 1975 analyses by Trow and Fulton of the 1969 Carnegie data.[45] They reported that "judged by the staff's self-conceptions, the American academic system as a whole is *primarily* a teaching system. Any notion that teaching generally takes second place to research is certainly not borne out."[46]

In one sense Oakley is right. Even the 1989 data clearly support the view that faculty across the board report they are primarily interested in teaching, not research. At two-year colleges, 93 percent feel this way, but surprisingly, 55 percent at doctorate-granting institutions say the same thing; almost startlingly, 33 percent at research institutions agree.

What Oakley notes but fails to address is the incongruity between these self-reports expressing preference for teaching and equally startling data about research expectations to which they are being held. These same respondents indicated that teaching effectiveness rather than research should be the primary criterion for promotion (60 percent) and that in their department it is difficult to achieve tenure if they do not publish (54 percent). Yet another survey in 1990 and 1991 reinforces this conclusion. Peter Gray, Robert Froh, and Robert Diamond surveyed 23,300 faculty and administrators from forty-seven campuses. "Perhaps one of the best kept secrets in higher education is that most faculty and administrators [even] at research universities disagree with the present emphasis on research as opposed to teaching."[47]

What is going on here? Why are faculty being held to standards that are inconsistent with their own priorities? Don't faculty generally shape those standards? Are promotion committees dominated by a minority of research-oriented faculty? Are they dominated by administrators with skewed ideas about how publication will enhance the public relations image of their institutions? Or are faculty just wrong about the expectations placed on them to do research?[48]

Whatever the explanation, Oakley should not be so quick to dismiss criticisms about the rise of emphasis on research, particularly because the trend is clear in data he did not cite. The results of a different 1990 survey show that 26 percent of all faculty believe the shift at their institutions in recent years has been overwhelmingly away from teaching and toward research, while only 17 percent believe it has been the other direction.[49] Gray, Froh, and Diamond confirm this. Their results show that faculty and administrators alike believe the university is moving in the direction of increased emphasis on research, despite the fact that they agreed that already "the emphasis was too great and needed to be modified."[50]

The Result: Loss of Concern for Real-World Issues

The combination of increasing specialization and greater emphasis on published research can result in faculty unconcerned with real-world problems and with real-world students who must address these problems. Faculty ability to address the questions of society or even the dormitory is severely restricted.[51]

"What should I do?"
"What am I going to make of myself?"
"How can the world balance justice and mercy?"
"How does one accommodate economic development and ecology?"
"How can I survive, much less support my family, when famine and war have devastated my country?"
"How can one cope with violence in the home, on the street, and in the media?"
"Can families survive the increased pace of life?"
"Is technology improving or undermining the quality of life?"
"How should the Church respond to changing notions of gender roles and sexual orientation?"

People on the street and people in the pew are asking these questions every day. They are the stuff of newsmagazine features and editorials. They are complex, multifaceted human problems. They are real human problems for real live people. Derek Bok, former president of Harvard University, warned that American universities are failing to provide the scholarship and leadership needed to solve society's most pressing problems. "If you take some of the basic problems facing our society . . . and then make a list of all the things that a university could contribute . . . and ask yourself how do all these things rank in the list of priorities of the modern university, one is struck by how low they rank."[52]

But not only do faculty hardly speak to issues of students and society, they often can hardly speak to one another because their research has become excruciatingly narrow.

The epigraph at the beginning of part II shows only the tip of an embarrassing iceberg. Skimming the program of almost any professional association meeting or glancing at the index of any major disciplinary abstract would reveal more evidence. In every discipline, disciplinary jargon has made scholarly research so esoteric it excludes all but experts in each subspecialty.

Page Smith condemns the "publish or perish" research syndrome. He writes that the "routine and pedestrian far outweigh the brilliant and original; that routine and pedestrian research is not merely a very expensive nullity but a moral and spiritual drag on the institutions in which it takes place and a serious distortion of the nature of both the intellectual and the scholarly life."[53]

Smith concludes that "aside from the enormous amount of time such research takes away from teaching, it falsifies human experience and the true nature of research. If bad research (not technically 'bad' or methodologically bad but unimportant and largely irrelevant research) does not drive out good, it constantly threatens to bury the good in a vast pile of mediocrity."[54]

The problem even becomes a matter of satire, for example, the title of Pablo Parrish's article "Seven Ways to Lengthen a Publication List without Doing Anything Very Original."[55] And consider the following list of scholarly papers:

"Aspects of Iconicity in Some Indiana Hydronyms"
"Victorian Underwear and Representations of the Female Body"
"The Polygenesis of Long Vowels in North Italian Dialects: An Autosegmental Analysis"
"Self-Consuming Fictions: The Dialectics of Cannibalism in Recent Caribbean Narratives"
"Gross Feeders and Flowing Cups: Is Naked Ministering Pornographic in Book 5 of *Paradise Lost?*"
"Assume the Position: Pluralist Ideology and Gynocriticism"
"Retrospective Participant Observation on Driving and Car Ownership in Nigeria"
"Effects of Pitressin On Cochlear Microphonics Modified By Sodium Chloride Crystals Administered on the Round Window Membrane."[56]

Objections and Replies

It might be objected that I am dismissing all narrow disciplinary research. But that is not my intention. In the first place, some of it has intrinsic value. I have argued in the preceding part that the liberal arts are an expression of the belief that disciplined thought is valuable in itself and for Christians can even become a form of worship. Liberal arts institutions must affirm the intrinsic value of such work. Second, some of this research also has instrumental value in producing cognitive, communicative, and experimental skills in those who conduct it. The research itself may not be useful but the competence acquired in doing it may later produce results that are useful. And, finally, some of this research, especially in the sciences, may be directly useful. It may be precisely the link needed to produce technology that will revolutionize human life.

It might be objected that I am making teaching and research incompatible when in fact they are complementary. First, however, I am not interested in whether faculty can teach and conduct research at the same time. Setting aside problems of time, of course they can. I am concerned with the relative priority they receive and the dangerous trend I see at colleges and universities that, unlike private research institutions, claim to have educational purposes.

Second, while it is not my point to say teaching and research are incompatible, it does not follow that they are complementary if that means that one automatically promotes the other. I am skeptical of claims regarding the connection between good research and good teaching. It is true that at least one study shows that "liberal arts colleges which involve students in faculty research produce a disproportionate share of American students entering Ph.D. programs in the sciences."[57] But that statistic is probably not an adequate measure of teaching success, at least not for liberal arts colleges.

More directly to the point, studies contradict the supposed correlation between good teaching and good research.[58] Page Smith cites these studies and writes that "the first fact to be established is that there is no direct relationship between research and teaching. The notion that research enhances teaching, although thoroughly discredited by experience and by research, is one that lingers on and is often trotted out by the ill-informed as a justification for the publish or perish policy."[59]

Third, and finally, the question of whether research complements teaching clearly depends on what is meant by "research." My concern is with the usually narrow disciplinary research driven by the agenda of professional guilds rather than by institutional or pedagogical priorities. Although it is no substitute for focus on teaching, research understood more broadly can vitalize teaching. It is surely critical that to be good teachers, faculty must remain intellectually active and curious. With this understanding, the objection is well taken and the contrast between teaching and research becomes a false dichotomy.

Reversing the Trends

How then can the trend toward overspecialization and excessive research be addressed? What can be done?

The first step, I believe, is that each educational institution must clarify its distinctive mission. This will lay the foundation for setting relative priorities on research and teaching and on the kind of research that will be encouraged. In places where the priority on research is most deliberate perhaps undergraduate education should be eliminated. Some such institutions or unusually research-oriented departments might better become research institutes.[60]

In those institutions that retain the mission of education, especially undergraduate education, the second step is to reverse the trend and reaffirm the value of teaching. This should entail a radical reorientation of curriculum and personnel policy, some of which I discuss in part III. Stanford has taken this direction. In 1990 former Stanford president Donald Kennedy said that teaching must be reaffirmed as the primary task of the university and that scholarship should be redefined in such a way that it gives greater dignity to undergraduate teaching.[61] By the next year, Stanford had begun to implement a comprehensive plan to put teaching back at the center of university life.[62]

The third step, and the one I want to develop below, is to define research scholarship in a way that matches the institution's distinctive mission. Specifically, the question is, How do specialization and research figure into the mission of liberal arts colleges, especially Christian liberal arts colleges? These institutions too must identify—or in some cases unashamedly reclaim—their distinctive mission. They must abandon the myth that there is only one standard of what counts as excellence in higher education and in scholarship.

BEYOND BOTH DABBLING AND OVERSPECIALIZATION

As I have already said, I believe that the crucial instrumental value of a liberal arts education, including a Christian liberal arts education, is its ability to tackle real-world problems. But the trend seems to be that these institutions are adopting the agenda of specialization and research and are becoming clones of major research institutions. So what is the answer?

Liberal arts colleges must identify and aggressively pursue a kind of scholarship that is distinctively, even uniquely, suited to liberal arts faculty. It must be consistent with the intrinsic value of critical commitment and aimed squarely at the distinctive instrumental value of tackling real-world problems. It is quite different in some ways from the scholarship pursued by universities and especially research-oriented universities. Liberal arts colleges should do something they alone excel at doing instead of competing, often at a disadvantage, using someone else's rules. This kind of scholarship is what I call "integrative scholarship."[63]

Overcoming Old Stereotypes

Unfortunately, the word "integration" has become a cliché at many liberal arts colleges. This is especially true at Christian liberal arts colleges. In the past when many small liberal arts colleges could not afford to attract faculty with advanced degrees from prestigious universities, integration came to be associated with a mediocre kind of interdisciplinary general studies. Faculty sometimes had limited postgraduate training and often had heavy course loads and wide-ranging assignments because of staff shortages. So faculty were constrained to limit their teaching and their scholarship to general studies at a fairly basic level. Many at Christian liberal arts colleges today know the stories of self-sacrificial faculty who, during the early years of their institution, taught courses outside their disciplines.

But as noble as it was, this "integration" has come to be viewed as unnecessary because the academic marketplace has made it much easier for smaller institutions to attract specialists with advanced degrees, sometimes even from prestigious universities.[64] More importantly, this "integration" is also often seen as inadequate. It may have consisted of a respected member of the science faculty dabbling in theology or the professors of Bible teaching philosophy, or the chemists teaching biology or mathematics. It might better have been called "preintegration" because it often involved persons not quite current with the state of their own discipline and usually even less acquainted with the other disciplines on which they pronounced. In short, it often consisted in "half-baked" dabbling or dilettantism.

Small wonder this concept of integration is rejected as a model of scholarship by liberal arts and Christian liberal arts colleges today. Its limitations are now all the more glaring because many new faculty adopt the agenda of specialization and research from their graduate experience and impose it on the institutions at which they teach. Christian liberal arts scholarship must go beyond dabbling.[65]

The obvious problem is that in reacting to the inadequacy of this preintegrative model of scholarship, faculty who adopt the agenda of specialization and research err on the side of scholarship that is too narrow. Instead of dabbling they promote overspecialized esotericism. This trend of academic culture entraps them. It sets them up for failure as they compete with graduate universities on terms for which resources of time (because of teaching responsibilities) and finance (because of limited size) are usually unavailable. Meanwhile, their institutions suffer loss of distinctive.

But when faculty see the choice as one between narrow specialization and integration understood as mediocre interdisciplinary general studies, the former has more integrity. Better to know a little well than a lot "half-baked." It is tough to convince such faculty that there could be a good kind of integration.

Integration Reconsidered: Addressing Real-World Problems Requires Integration in a New Sense

What is needed is a new understanding of integration.[66] In order to prepare liberal arts students to achieve the distinctive instrumental goal of tackling real-world problems, they must be given an education that is authentically integrative. This means the institution must be characterized from top to bottom by authentically integrative scholarship. I believe authentic integration is integrative in three important ways. It is integrative first of disciplines, second of theory and practice, and third of values and learning.

Integrative of Disciplines

Real-world problems rarely submit to the confines of a single discipline. As Richard Cummings puts it, "we must never lose sight of the fact that disciplines are convenient but artificial constructs; academia may be divided into disciplines but the world is not."[67]

So if addressing real-world problems is a central instrumental value of liberal arts education, then it should be obvious to faculty and students alike that disciplinary studies will not be enough. Liberal arts institutions cannot neglect interdisciplinary studies.

Yet interdisciplinary studies remain second-class citizens in academe. Ironically, this may be more true in selective liberal arts colleges (Christian or otherwise) than in major universities, in which interdisciplinary studies may be experiencing some resurgence.[68] Some of these liberal arts institutions hope to escape the odor of mediocre dabbling by fleeing from interdisciplinary studies and embracing the research agenda of the larger, more prestigious schools. It becomes almost impossible to interest faculty at such places in staffing or creating interdisciplinary courses, much less in doing interdisciplinary research. They continue to be haunted by the ghost of the old view of mediocre integration. It is seen as a digression from their real work, which is to pursue the more narrow agenda of their own professional guild. That is the scholarship which is rewarded not only by their guild but increasingly by the promotion and tenure policies of their own institutions. Without reflecting on whether it suits the mission of their own institutions, administrators at such colleges have adopted wholesale the trends in academe toward specialization and research as their own. Then when the institutional distinctive is lost and morale drops, there is bafflement about what has happened.

Interdisciplinary studies are *general studies*. They begin with problems and focus on them instead of on the theories that may or may not already be available within a particular discipline. They try to avoid the limitation of seeing issues from the conceptual framework of only one discipline. This is the limitation that made Karl Marx see everything in terms of class struggle and Sigmund Freud see everything in terms of sexual development. When a disciplinarian has only a hammer to work with, everything too easily looks like a nail. Instead, interdisciplinary studies draw on the perspectives of multiple disciplines in addressing real problems.[69] Leo Marx, professor at MIT, says that interdisciplinary studies are contextual. Their necessity arises from our growing awareness that "when we try to establish the meaning of any datum, event, or experience, [we must of necessity] consider the larger real-world context in which we conceive it."[70]

Interdisciplinary studies are also *bridge studies*. Some problems are improved by examining them from multiple perspectives, but other problems cannot even be framed without the benefit of several disciplines. Sociological, psychological, and biological perspectives can be complementary in accounting for juvenile delinquency. Both physiological and philosophical perspectives are probably essential even for framing the problem of human freedom. And both mathematical and aesthetic considerations may be needed to understand the question of whether elegance is a reliable guide for solving problems. Finally, consider the infamous Hancock Tower in Boston. Windows exploded like shrapnel because calculations of wind pressure and metallurgical stress were not reconciled with the aesthetic vision of the architect.

I believe this bridge quality applies to interdisciplinary studies however one chooses to define "disciplines." The word "discipline" comes from the Latin meaning "instruction" or "training." By the fourteenth century it was used to refer to a "branch of learning," and the traditional disciplines were distinguished by *content*. The Trivium comprised grammar, rhetoric, and logic and the Quadrivium, arithmetic, geometry, astronomy, and music. But it can also be used to distinguish differences of *methodology*. Hence studies traditionally lumped together in a single discipline like clinical psychology and experimental psychology might actually be more different as disciplines than others traditionally thought to be on opposite sides of even C. P. Snow's major divide, for example, philosophical logic and mathematics.

Interdisciplinary studies try to avoid but often expose the "turfism" that dominates academia. Richard Cummings has facetiously suggested there are the "Ruling" disciplines and the "Drooling" disciplines.[71] In general, the sciences still "rule," as C. P. Snow pointed out thirty years ago. And in general, the other disciplines either "drool" at the privilege granted the sciences or strive assiduously to become more scientific themselves. Sometimes even names are changed to facilitate this striving. For example, physical education becomes "sport science" or "kinesiology," and psychology becomes "cognitive and brain science." But instead of this turfism, interdisciplinary studies calls for a willingness to make connections whenever and wherever it is profitable.

Interdisciplinary studies are *advanced studies*. The usual assumption about interdisciplinary studies parallels the thinking about integration generally, namely, that it is low-level, mediocre, or second-rate. While it is true that there is a place for introductory courses that expose students to the complexity of real problems primarily as a motivation for concentrating their studies in one or more of the disciplines most crucial to solving those problems, this does not go far enough. The idea of "advanced general studies" is almost an oxymoron for many in academe today. Their vision is shortsighted and one-dimensional, limited to a simplistic choice between only two pairs: interdisciplinary and low-level or specialized and advanced. But with expanded two-dimensional vision (see figure), interdisciplinary studies, in the

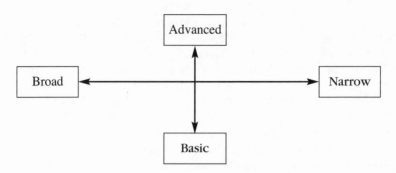

form of advanced general studies, can be the most sophisticated studies a student will ever do. Sadly, for lack of opportunity or because faculty themselves are unprepared to undertake such studies, students are sometimes never confronted with the kinds of issues that they will face the day they graduate. This brings me to the last characteristic I want to mention about interdisciplinary studies.

Interdisciplinary studies are not a form of integration that comes before disciplinary competence but one that presupposes it. In keeping with our theme, it is something that goes beyond both dabbling and overspecialization. In order to avoid the scandal of what I have called a half-baked kind of preintegration, interdisciplinary studies require faculty who are competent and current in a particular discipline. The tragedy of interdisciplinary studies for students of the liberal arts is that faculty have not taught it directly. Instead, we have offered a smorgasbord of various disciplinary tidbits and then exhorted the students to use their critical skills to bring it all together. But to be effective, interdisciplinary teaching must change. Faculty themselves must do the hard work of going beyond their disciplinary expertise and actually address real-world problems by asking how other disciplines might see the same issue.

If faculty address real-world problems without first mastering the current state of theory in a discipline and polishing its tools, they are guilty of mere preintegration. They are dabblers. But unless faculty go beyond those disciplines, actually modeling for students how to reconcile their disciplinary perspective with that of other disciplines on the same real problem, they are guilty of esotericism and irrelevance. Such education would be largely irrelevant to the concerns of contemporary society, and its graduates would confirm the worst cultural suspicions of the impracticality of liberal arts.

Recently Zimbabwe experienced a serious drought, which compounded an economic crisis and led to political turmoil. The economic crisis was brought on by an aggressive program to follow International Monetary Fund guidelines in moving from a socialist to a market economy as well as eliminating artificial currency controls and crippling import taxes. The drought destroyed 75 percent of crops, and what was normally a food-exporting nation desperately needed relief. Zimbabwe has protected its wildlife population far better than most other African countries, boasting large herds of elephants and more rhino than anywhere else. Under normal circumstances, for example, elephants herds are culled annually, but now even plentiful species faced decimation. With herds elsewhere now virtually gone, poachers from adjoining countries have slaughtered elephant and rhino for the precious tusks and horns, reducing herds by over 50 percent during a five-year period. AIDS is rampant. Some say over 50 percent of the Zimbabwean military is HIV positive. The demographic group hardest hit is the young, educated urbanite, who forms the backbone of the industrial and commercial hope. In all this, the previously popular president struggles for the first time to control dramatic political opposition by his former fellow guerrilla combatants, students at the national university, and a tiny minority of white farmers who produce 80 percent of the country's food supplies, now outraged by a new land appropriation bill to endow landless peasants. War in neighboring Mozambique threatened landlocked Zimbabwe's commercial access to the sea. Zimbabwean troops invited by the Mozambican government protected a crucial corridor to the sea. Meanwhile, the struggle against apartheid accelerated toward crisis in adjacent South Africa.

Should the government kill elephants and use them to feed starving subsistence farmers? Should rangers dehorn the rhinos to protect them from poaching? Should Zimbabwe pull its troops from Mozambique in order to speed the peace process, thereby crippling trade and even the supply of food relief for its own people? Should Zimbabwe provide moral and political support for black nationalists in South Africa, many of whom supported the Zimbabweans in their drive for independence only ten years before by imposing trade sanctions on the South African government? Or should they maximize trade in order to facilitate food importation and the survival of their own economy? Should farmers' lands be purchased on a willing buyer–willing seller basis? What is "fair market value" for postcolonial property? Should AIDS statistics be widely disseminated in order to reinforce educational efforts or will that induce panic in the population?

Closer to home, the citizens of a small seaside community in southern California face increasing racial tension. Population has exploded in the past few years, in large measure because of immigrants coming, sometimes illegally, from Mexico. They find ready employment that few whites would take in fields and nurseries as well as at other low-paying tasks without prestige. They work hard, often for a pittance, rising with the sun and shouldering several jobs. Rental costs are high, so often they live in overcrowded conditions. By culture, for lack of adequate living space, and because they walk for lack of vehicles, they are highly visible on the streets.

On weekends, again in part by culture, beer flows and loud Mexican music permeates neighborhoods unaccustomed to the sounds of Tijuana. Soccer games fill the parks. Old cars clog the streets at night. Shopping carts lie on street corners. City services are "taxed" to the limit and often the new residents are not. Schools are bursting so quality drops. Hospitals are overwhelmed so costs skyrocket. Some landlords tell new residents they must not rent from anyone else or they will be turned in to "La Migre" (U.S. Immigration). Unaware of their rights, they submit to extortionate rents. Local employers, like the entire state of California, build their business on the backs of such workers but often shun obligations to provide housing or seasonal accommodation for them.

Should the city council impose restrictions on the number of persons living in a home or an apartment? Does this violate rights of association? Would it reduce crime, known to correlate with crowding? Should the council enforce statutes long on the books regarding the number of vehicles parked in driveways and on streets to preserve aesthetic values and protect property values? Should bilingual education be encouraged? Or will it undermine community in the long run by eliminating the one thread that may tie America's cultural diversity together? Do schools have the right to require proof of legal residence before providing instruction? Should the law be changed that presently makes it easy for illegal residents with only driver's licenses to vote? Should employers who circumvent social security and tax liabilities be actively prosecuted for greedily perpetuating a cash-based informal economy at the expense of their fellow residents?

Such real-world problems obviously do not submit to the confines of a single discipline. The issues are economic, agricultural, political, medical, ethical, and ecological; and the list goes on. What these situations need are persons with virtue, including the virtue of critical commitment, who are able and willing to tackle these very real-world problems.

Integrative of Theory and Practice

Derek Bok condemned American education for failing to take the leadership needed to solve America's most pressing problems.[72] "Armed with the security of tenure and the time to study the world with care, professors would appear to have a unique opportunity to act as society's scouts to signal impending problems long before they are visible to others. Yet rarely have members of the academy succeeded in discovering the emerging issues and bringing them vividly to the attention of the public."[73]

This suggests that the job of the university is not only to *think* about these issues and train its students to *think* about them, but actually to *do* something about them or at least produce graduates who actually will. Nicholas Wolterstorff calls for Christian education that leads to "responsible action."[74] Like faith that without works is dead, an education that remains only theoretical is of little value. One need not travel to Mozambique to see the need for practical applications of the best theory available. Liberal arts education must be integrative in this second way. It must integrate theory and practice.

It is not uncommon for us to compartmentalize our lives along the lines of theory and practice as much as along the lines of disciplinary frameworks. We are all too familiar with the religious hypocrite who preaches one thing and practices quite another, or the politician who promises one thing and delivers another. These examples make it plain that at its worst, an education that does not translate into practice is deceitful. It is a living lie.

Too often in the liberal arts we introduce students to broad perspectives, strong principles, and clear thinking, but deny them the means by which to use what we teach them. We urge them to go out into the world and "make a difference." Yet we expect them to do all the work of figuring out how what we have given them can actually be connected to specific behaviors. As a result, when it comes to making specific choices, they are forced to begin theorizing from scratch. They often cannot even recognize the concrete choices they face as cases of the elegant theories they have been taught.

For example, I always include a section on the problem of free will and determinism in my introductory philosophy courses. Most students find the idea of human determinism disagreeable or offensive. Yet many of these same students advocate a strong theory of operant conditioning when it comes to education of young people. They do not see any connection between using M&M candies to alter children's behavior and theoretical assumptions about human determinism. Nor do they automatically see the connection between determinism and state policies regarding the purposes of criminal incarceration. Of course one does not have to be a determinist to use Skinnerian behavioral modification techniques. But it is important to see the connection between the theoretical discussion of determinism and the practical choices about how to alter behavior.

Or to give another example, sometimes these same students will advocate only a rehabilitative form of criminal punishment even though they have strongly defended a radical view of libertarianism that says persons can always, anywhere, and under any circumstance overthrow their hereditary and environmental conditioning. If true, such power would render rehabilitation largely pointless. The idea that somehow the principles of determinism discussed in theory in a classroom will entail specific implications for choices they must make or even votes they must cast on practical behavioral questions often escapes them. The integration of theory and practice has not been done.

Students of economics are sometimes baffled when someone points out that capitalism *might* be said to make assumptions about the rights of human property that are inconsistent with Christian theory (theology) of persons as mere stewards of God's creation. Or they are surprised when it is suggested that capitalism *might* work only if people act first out of self-interest and not so well if they are unselfish. When the theoretical similarities between practical socialism and Christianity are pointed out, they seem anguished. And this is so *even though* they have become reasonably expert in their economic theory and are quite sincere about their faith. While part of this is merely a developmental limitation that has to do with the ability to think logically about implications, another part, I believe, has to do with the failure in the liberal arts to integrate theory with practice.

But helping them recognize instances of the application of theories we have taught them is only part of what it means to integrate theory and practice. More importantly still, they must be taught how to translate their own theoretical conclusions into practice. This again means modeling (discussed in chapter 5). They must see examples of faculty whose very lives reflect decisions taken from the theoretical frameworks they profess. It also means opportunities, even requirements, to take such steps themselves. The "arts" in liberal arts means skill and not just knowledge. As Garrett Bauman puts it, "Let them *live* life while at college, not merely study it. Let them become self-sufficient in living, not in attending college. This is the truest interdisciplinary education, where study most closely approximates life as lived."[75] Bauman goes on in this connection to advocate a component of "self-reliance" courses as a part of the liberal arts curriculum. I address the "how" of integration below and in part III.

Integrative of Values and Learning

Finally, I believe that authentic integration brings together learning and values. For Christians, of course, this means an integration of faith and learning. For others in the liberal arts tradition, it means recognizing that knowledge not only *can* affect our behavior and attitudes but, depending on our values, it *must* do so. A liberal arts education will be not only descriptive but prescriptive. In a chapter entitled "The Demise and Rebirth of Moral Education," Derek Bok writes that, between the Civil War and the Second World War, "intellect and technical proficiency" triumphed over character as "pre-eminent goals of the professoriate." And with regard to students, "For the first time, the training of the mind and character was separated and placed in different hands."[76]

My wife once remarked that life was a whole lot easier when she did not know what she now knows. Ignorance does indeed have its blissful side. Once we know how being systematically oppressed by sexist language makes a woman feel, there is obligation to act differently. Once we understand how institutions can embody racist and religious prejudice, we are forever accountable. Education will banish the politician's favorite hiding place:

deniability. Once we know, we are obliged. A liberal arts education must deliberately set out to produce graduates whose lives are no more dichotomized by a separation of their values and their knowledge than by a separation of theory and practice or of disciplinary perspectives.

But of course to live out our values is not a heavy burden. In fact, it is also the most liberating and human thing we can do. If the liberal arts are indeed to liberate us, it will be *from* narrowness of perspective and *to* the possibility of critical commitment. Those commitments express *our* values. To the extent they constitute who we are, their expression becomes the most significant thing we can do. To separate our values from our learning is to become intellectually schizophrenic.

The integration of values and learning overlaps with the integration of theory and practice because, of course, some of the theories we hold will embody our values. For a biologist to investigate whether "deep ecology" and "eco-feminism" have different implications for the use of Brazilian rain forests illustrates the integration of theory and practice. For the biologist to investigate how to accommodate "stewardship" in her ecology because her personal Christian faith requires it illustrates the integration of values (faith) and learning. For a historian to investigate how current affairs illustrate patterns seen in previous ages shows integration of theory and practice. For the historian to inquire whether his personal Christian faith requires him to reject a cyclical view of historical events illustrates the integration of values (faith) and learning. For a physicist to train students to apply basic mechanics to calculate the forces exerted along beams in a house illustrates the integration of theory and practice. For the physicist to choose among the several possible interpretations of Heisenberg's Principle of Uncertainty on the basis of which is more consistent with her view of whether humans are free is perhaps an illustration of integration of disciplines, of theory and practice, and perhaps of values and learning. For a Christian social scientist to create workshops for the training of Christian missionaries illustrates the integration of theory and practice. For him to articulate a theory of third world development based on the need to balance justice and mercy because he believes those are the two primary principles of Christian ethics illustrates the integration of values and learning as well as perhaps the integration of theory and practice.

But to integrate values and learning does not mean merely enhancing students' knowledge of moral principles or merely honing their skills of moral analysis. Derek Bok complains that in 1945, the *Report of the Harvard Committee* concluded that "the college will have to confine itself to providing a proper discrimination of values (through the study of the humanities, social sciences, and sciences) and will trust to the Socratic *dictum* that the knowledge of the good will lead to a commitment to the good." Bok concludes, "There is scant evidence those expectations were ever fulfilled."[77]

There is a movement in education that advocates reintroducing values into the curriculum. Sometimes this is described in the language of "values clarification." While it represents an important first step for students to be able to recognize what they actually believe, this does not go far enough. It seeks to help students become more positive, enthusiastic, purposeful, and proud.[78] The assumption is that while one's values are hidden or implicit, one will not be fulfilled. By facilitating the process of making one's values explicit, values clarification will improve that fulfillment. It is essential to the process that the teacher avoids recommending or condemning any particular values lest the student be indoctrinated.

The view of "value" that this movement adopts makes values only "the goals that person has in fact adopted for action, not the goals that ought to be adopted."[79] Values are private and entirely relative to the individual.[80] There is no "should" involved since, had the person adopted other even contradictory values or were she to do so later, those values would be just as acceptable. In other words, the program is entirely descriptive, not prescriptive. Nicholas Wolterstorff says it might be more accurate to call this program one of "goals clarification" rather than "values clarification" because such descriptions are not what most people mean by "values." For most people values prescribe and proscribe, that is, condone and condemn. In other words, for most people values are obligatory and normative.

But as Wolterstorff makes plain, values clarification, as usually practiced, involves profound contradiction. Having adopted a strictly descriptive view of values, values clarification *recommends* (prescribes) the adoption of its program and *condemns* (proscribes) teachers who might recommend or condemn certain values the student considers. The contradiction here is apparent.[81]

But if "values clarification" is faulty, one might ask, how then does the integration of values and knowledge avoid the criticism of indoctrination? How can liberal arts institutions holding to varying value systems all accomplish this kind of integration?

The answer comes back to the myth of value neutrality. One cannot teach students how to be critically committed by refraining from making commitments. One cannot teach students how their values will require them to accept or reject alternative theoretical frameworks merely by presenting many such frameworks and then expecting them to choose. One cannot teach students to understand that values entail obligations, that values are normative, that values are prescriptive, without prescribing certain values. Unless at least one particular value is modeled, obligation is not modeled at all. In short, one cannot teach students how to integrate values and learning without actually applying real values to real learning.

This will not be indoctrination so long as critical commitment remains a chief intrinsic goal of the institution. Without this goal, one of two alternatives will be attempted: neutrality or mere pluralism. The fact that neutrality is myth makes it *impossible* for an institution to integrate values and learning if its faculty takes no position whatsoever. There are no examples of integration to be seen. On the other hand, the mere presence of multiple diverse points of view is *ineffective*. They provide examples of strongly held values, but they are proselytizers, not models. Faced with competing ideologies, students will be victimized by the most outspoken and persuasive. The politics and will to power on some politically correct campuses today illustrate this alternative well. Instead, by regular and deliberate exposure to a consistent set of values balanced with focused attention to inculcating the virtue of critical commitment, the student is taught to hold to values but not uncritically and to examine their learning but not cynically. The epistemological humility this virtue engenders and the respect it affirms for free moral judgment is crucial. In this way indoctrination can be avoided.[82]

The Distinctive Scholarship of Christian Liberal Arts Colleges

I have suggested that the distinctive instrumental value of liberal arts colleges, including especially Christian liberal arts colleges, is their ability to produce students who can address real problems. As I have elaborated, to accomplish that means their education should be integrative of disciplines, of theory and practice, and of values and learning. This integration goes *beyond* the dabbling of faculty who are no longer or not yet competent in their disciplines. Such "preintegration" has given authentic integration a bad name and made it hard for faculty at liberal arts colleges to find a worthy and challenging direction for their scholarship. They often turn to narrow research agendas set by their professional guilds. But authentic integration also goes *beyond* this esotericism as well. Faculty who are "up to speed" in their disciplines must go beyond their narrow specialization, not back to basic general studies but ahead to advanced general studies. They must go ahead and beyond to tackle issues at the intersections of disciplines, ahead and beyond to tackle problems requiring actual decisions affecting behavior, ahead and beyond to make plain how their own critically held value commitments are consistent with and even determinative of their disciplinary conclusions. This is where real-world problems are found. There are a number of practical reasons why neither the faculty at vocational and professionally oriented institutions nor the faculty at large research-oriented institutions may be as well suited to accomplish this task as effectively. (See part III.)

If faculty at liberal arts colleges could recognize this distinctive form of scholarship, if they could see this as their distinctive niche in academia, if they could recognize that this is something they are unusually if not uniquely suited to accomplish, it would restore a sense of mission and purpose. They would no longer feel like second-class citizens.

There is evidence that some already do understand this. In an article entitled "The Distinctive Scholarship of the Selective Liberal Arts College," Kenneth Ruscio uses data from a 1985 Carnegie faculty survey to point out differences in attitudes and priorities between faculty at research universities and selective liberal arts colleges. Although the survey and Ruscio's discussion were limited to research rather than scholarship more broadly construed to include teaching and institutional curriculum, I believe the findings provide wider insight into thinking on these campuses. He concludes that "faculty at selective liberal arts colleges accept the norm of research, but reject the way it is practiced at the leading research universities."[83] I believe this is good news and bodes well for the future of liberal arts institutions that will affirm this distinctive.

One primary finding ties in closely with what we have called the integration of disciplines:

> Faculty in liberal arts colleges are critical of the work in their disciplines. They perceive their fields to be preoccupied with narrow, specialized topics and marginal, incremental contributions to an arcane literature. They blame this on the counterproductive pressure to publish which compels those in research universities to conduct professionally safe, risk-free research. . . . Scholarly work has a high priority but the boundaries of specializations and the taxonomies of the disciplines are considered artificial and constraining. Transcending these boundaries is not only tolerated but encouraged.

Ruscio also confirms what we have said about the difference between preintegration and authentic integration:

> But neither are these professors out of touch with their disciplines. They attend national professional meetings almost as frequently as their university counterparts. And they have a credible record of publication. . . . Most faculty in selective liberal arts colleges are deeply engaged in scholarship, but they feel less compelled to contribute to the discipline in the conventional manner, to be "taxonomically upstanding." . . . They were not dilettantes . . . but the grip of research was looser than in research universities.[84]

Supporting yet another point I have made about the advantage of liberal arts faculty in educating in this interdisciplinary way (a point to be developed more below), Ruscio reports that such faculty believe they are unusually well suited to do it. He describes one molecular biologist as saying that "a scientist might have to perform 'horizontal research'—research that crosses over into neighboring subfields or even neighboring disciplines—instead of the 'vertical' research found in a university setting. . . . I am better prepared to ask interesting questions about membrane biochemistry because I am forced to keep up with a pretty wide area."[85]

Apparently these faculty value knowledge of other subjects. Over 70 percent believe "undergraduate education would be improved if there were less emphasis on specialized training and more on broad liberal arts."[86] The Carnegie data support the "ease with which faculty crossed disciplinary boundaries."[87]

But the evidence also suggests that integration of values and learning is more important to faculty at selective liberal arts colleges than elsewhere. Five times as many said they believed their institutions were doing an excellent job in teaching values.[88] There is even support for my claim that integration of values and learning overlaps with integration of disciplines and of theory and practice. "Responses from the professors suggest that the topics [of their research] will reflect the values of the institution."[89] Ruscio concludes that for these faculty, "values have a place in education."[90]

Ruscio believes, as I do, that liberal arts colleges must make the most of their distinctives. He says he believes economic realities and the need to lay claim on limited public resources will make it more and more important for liberal arts colleges to articulate their distinctives.[91] He says these differences will slowly increase and "variations" will emerge on the research university model of scholarship, which are more appropriate in other sectors.[92] I hope he is right.

7

Why Pursue Integration?

Liberal arts colleges must articulate more clearly their distinctive scholarship in order to survive economically, but mere survival is not enough. Integration in all three senses (described in chapter 6) is crucial if the liberal arts are to be instrumentally valuable in addressing real-world problems. But why should "real-world problems" be a priority, and are there further reasons apart from this one why integration has value?

REASONS TO ADDRESS REAL-WORLD PROBLEMS

Addressing Real-World Problems Is the Natural Extension of Personal Development

First, Christian liberal arts should address real problems because doing so is consistent with the developmental assumptions that have been made. Action is the natural extension of the developmental process. William Perry says that decisive action is the only escape from the paralysis that often characterizes the intermediate stages he calls multiplicity. "Action itself, when it is not simply a 'flight into reality,' seems to provide in the end the most workable focus for sanity."[1] One student reported that endless discussions of basic questions like "are we free or determined?" and "can you have objective morality?" gave way by his senior year to problems of a technical and administrative type. "And when you reach that level it seems to me you've had a more profitable educational experience."[2] The transition from multiplicity to commitment creates the need to *do* something. It is a transition from contemplation to action.

Richard Marstin, in his book *Beyond Our Tribal Gods*, builds on the work of James Fowler and unapologetically affirms that each successive stage of development is not just different from but better than the previous one.[3] It is a process of moving toward both truth and justice. The latter demands action. The advance to critical awareness is not enough if the individual shows less concern for others and remains exclusively within a selective community. In short, critical commitment, the chief intrinsic value of liberal arts, naturally leads into action, which is to address real problems.

Addressing Real-World Problems Is Essential to the Mission of the Church

Second, and most importantly, *Christian* liberal arts colleges should educate students to address real-world problems because that is the mission of God's people. The prophet Micah asks, "What should humanity do?" The answer is to "love justice, to show mercy, and to walk humbly before God."[4] I have described critical commitment, the intrinsic value of liberal arts education, as a virtue—an attitude with a central element of humility. But the further charge in Micah to love justice and show mercy goes beyond attitude to action. It demands that Christians address real-world problems.

Jesus tells his disciples that to offer even a cup of cold water in his name will be remembered in eternity. To provide clothing and food to those in need is part of the work of the present Kingdom of God on earth. "Inasmuch as ye have done these unto the least of these my brethren, ye have done them unto me."[5] His own ministry did not neglect the physical and emotional needs of the people. He fed the crowds. He healed the sick. He comforted the sorrowful. His work was to give sight to the blind and to proclaim liberty to the captives.[6] He washed the feet of his own disciples. There can be no doubt that Jesus called his disciples then and today to serve.

The call to service is clear in the example of the early church. The need of widows and orphans was mentioned often. Believers were called to "share one another's burdens." St. Paul reminds us that Christians are to humble themselves and become as servants, even as Christ humbled Himself by taking on the form of a man.[7]

But there is no need to rehearse all this. There can be no doubt that any institution calling itself "Christian" must take seriously Christ's call to serve. And surely that means addressing real-world problems. If it does not, then what else could service mean? And if it does, then for a Christian educational institution, integration can be a chief tool. Neither vocational training nor narrow disciplinary education will suffice because real-world problems are just not like that.

On the one hand, narrow disciplinary education usually falls short. First, real problems are usually multidisciplinary, not circumscribed by the categories of a single discipline. Second, addressing those problems requires passionate commitments to values not necessarily cultivated in an educational environment that does not integrate values and learning. But third, and most seriously, the study of narrow disciplinary theory is not helpful for service so long as it remains isolated from practice.

On the other hand, vocational/professional training may seem more practical and more service oriented than even integrative liberal arts. But in the end, the complexity of real problems requires more than a technical solution. Of course this is not to say that technical training is unimportant. Without it, generations of missionaries, ministers, and laypeople would not have been able to accomplish what they have done in Christ's name. Who could argue with the service of the medical missionary or the jungle pilot. But such training without the benefit of an authentically integrative framework may miss the complexity of the real problem and offer only incomplete solutions. The nurse must understand cultural differences regarding hygiene. The urban planner must know the history of local ethnic groups. The businessperson must understand the values expressed in their advertising.

I believe that an integrative approach to education is more likely to prepare students to face real-world problems. So I believe that Christian academics have an unusual responsibility to consider this approach and a strong reason to provide it.

FURTHER REASONS FOR INTEGRATIVE SCHOLARSHIP

Integrative Scholarship Is Superior for Intellectual, Pedagogical, and Social Reasons

There are three arguments for the interdisciplinary component of integrative scholarship that are not limited to Christian liberal arts colleges. The first is one we have already touched on in describing "what" integration means. Jerry Gaff calls it an "intellectual argument."

> Ideas from any field are enriched by theories, concepts, and knowledge from other fields. Problems of the world are not organized according to the categories of scholars. . . . solutions . . . require knowledge and perspective from other disciplines.[8]

The second argument is pedagogical. "Students learn better when knowledge is organized into meaningful wholes rather than isolated bits."[9] Disciplinary approaches often fragment the curriculum by offering at best a smorgasbord, or cafeteria, approach to integration. I have likened it to giving students injections of various introductory studies and then praying that it all gets "integrated" in their heads. The third argument is social. As Gaff puts it, "Learning is an individual but not solitary activity; it is more effective when it takes place within a supportive community of learning."[10] Such community emerges naturally when interdisciplinary studies draw faculty and students from multiple disciplines into common projects.[11] Taken together, these arguments make a strong case that even secular institutions should emphasize interdisciplinary studies. But there are other arguments that apply specifically to Christian liberal arts colleges.

Integrative Scholarship Facilitates the Distinctive Role of Christian Liberal Arts Colleges in the Institutional Church

Christian liberal arts colleges should be at the cutting edge of solving the world's real problems. They should be places in which Christian students are educated for a willingness and an ability to address such problems. But they should also be important resources for the institutional Church as it seeks to be salt and light in the world. Unfortunately, the record is not very good. When pastors and parishioners today face pressing problems, they do not turn as often as they might to Christian liberal arts colleges. Abortion, sexuality, cults, budget management, stress, new age, community relations, parenting, media influence, military service, and war are just a few examples of real-world problems that scholars at Christian liberal arts colleges could help pastors and parishioners address.

Christian colleges should take the lead here. Even before the issues arise in popular culture, Christian faculty should be considering such matters. If scholars at Christian colleges have not thought about them, how likely is it that others in the Church will have done so? To borrow a metaphor from Derek Bok, who used it for the role all universities should play for society, Christian colleges should be "scouts" for the Church, "signaling impending problems long before they are visible to others."[12] But too often Christian colleges have become too narrowly technical/professional or too narrowly disciplinary. They lack either the breadth of perspective or the ability to come down to earth necessary to be useful to pastors and parishioners.

Of course there are many exceptions. There are pastors who call upon faculty for help in counseling or social issues or preaching points. There are faculty who teach Church school classes and write books useful to the general Church population. But too often pastors and parishioners turn to popular secular sources instead. Sadly, the more academically prestigious the institution, the less likely it seems to be to take the lead in such matters. To perform this function in the Body of Christ, Christian colleges must take seriously the task of integrative scholarship.

Integrative Scholarship Is Worship

A Christian liberal arts college will provide an integrative education primarily because that is the best means for producing graduates who are able and willing to tackle complex real-world problems as their "reasonable service" to God.[13] But the word translated "service" in the book of Romans is rich in meaning. Of course it means concrete, practical action. But in a fuller sense, our worthy service is our worship. This brings us to a final reason why Christian liberal arts colleges should pursue integration.

For Christians, at least since the Reformation, worship includes their work. For Christian academics, their work is their scholarship. As we have seen, when undertaken properly, scholarship will be "service" because it includes direct and obvious practical benefits to students. Because it is integrative, it equips students to address real-world problems. But it should also be "service" in the fuller sense of worship. Just as the carpenter sees the fruit of his labor as worship to God and the artist offers her art as worship to God, the academic must do the same. Whether the craftsman works with wood, paint, metal, paper, or ideas, it should be worship. It should exalt Him. It should focus on Him. It should involve self-submission for those who worship. It should reinforce the idea that those who worship find their very identity in God.

Of course, no particular way of doing scholarship will guarantee that it is worshipful, just as no particular way of practicing medicine or carpentry or of conducting business can do so. But it does seem to me that integrative scholarship is particularly well suited to this purpose. Both narrow disciplinary scholarship and technical expertise can easily fall prey to false pride because they involve specialization. When specialization occurs, it makes the specialist "stand out." It can point to self. It can become an overly important substitute for the practitioner's proper self-identity in Christ. In his book, *The Culture of Professionalism,* Burton Bledstein says that "the culture of professionalism in America has been enormously satisfying to the human ego while it has taken an inestimable toll on the integrity of individuals."[14] Elaborating on this statement, Bruce Wilshire says,

> Typically we do not understand the power of the identity needs which fuel research efforts which are only apparently impersonal and detached. . . . [Professionalism] excites the self to pretensions of groundedness and stability, but at crucial points cuts the person's connectedness to the actual background of his or her behavior in the world and compromises stability and integrity. One's ego and one's professional sense of self are fragile, in need of constant defense.[15]

Wilshire's analysis may be too strong. Professionals—whether in a narrowly disciplinary academic sense or in a vocational/technical sense—have no monopoly on ego or pride. But the point is still well-taken and the problem of making such work true worship is apparent.

In contrast, when scholarship is integrative, the focus should be on the real problem to be addressed. It should not focus on the theory for its own sake or on the scholar for the ego's sake. Because the problem is not narrowly circumscribed, it will be easier, I believe, to submit the self. The burden of being the expert is reduced. And for these reasons it may be easier to make this kind of scholarship worship.

8

How Can a College
Pursue Integration?

In part III, I will turn to the practical matter of how colleges can implement
the distinctive genius of Christian liberal arts. That genius includes both the
intrinsic value of critical commitment I discussed in part I as well as the goal
of integration I have discussed in part II. But without anticipating the concrete suggestions I offer in part III, I conclude part II by spelling out what I
believe are two important principles—controversy and community—that
should guide any institution desiring to make integration a major goal of its
curriculum. These principles correspond closely with two of those described
in part I as means of producing critical commitment. This "overlap" will
make our discussion of practical matters much easier in part III.

COMMUNITY

The first principle for producing integration is community. It is necessary for
integration because integration presupposes that things not necessarily together are brought together: multiple disciplines, theory and practice, values
and learning. The very word "com-unity" reminds us that when integration
is sought, community will be critical. How else can the multiple perspectives
of various disciplines be brought together? Unless there is a group of people
who are deliberately committed to finding common interests, integration
cannot occur.

Many have affirmed the centrality of community to academic institutions.
Cardinal Newman described the university this way: "An assemblage of
learned [persons], zealous for their own sciences, and rivals of each other,

are brought, by familiar intercourse and for the sake of intellectual peace, to adjust together the claims and relations of their respective subjects of investigation. They learn to respect, to consult, to aid each other."[1]

Elton Trueblood puts it this way in *The Idea of a College:* "Teachers and taught work together, think together, play together, and pray together."[2]

Plainly, like "com-unity" the "uni-versity" is a place in which diversity is brought together. The lack of such coming together has prompted some to refer to modern universities as "multi-versities" instead. Good liberal arts colleges might turn out to be the only true "uni-versities" after all.

As we will see even more plainly when we turn to practical matters, community is an especially important principle for integration of disciplines. There was a day when a single person could bring together the necessary expertise in various disciplines to address complex problems. Today that is much more difficult. If authentic integration, in contrast to what we have called "pre-integration" requires understanding of the state of the art in multiple fields, then more than one person will likely be needed. Without community this integration cannot occur.

One beauty of community is its reciprocal relation to integrative studies. Community is a necessary cause and yet also an almost inevitable result of integrative scholarship. As Jerry Gaff puts it, "Interdisciplinary programs go beyond intellectual integration (as important as that is) to create a community of learning among students and faculty."[3] The cycle feeds on itself and is self-enhancing. Good communities of integrative scholarship only get better! Arthur Holmes describes the Christian college community as one based not on feelings but on common values, purposes, and tasks. If that common task is integration as I have described it, community will be enhanced and will grow in direct proportion.[4]

CONTROVERSY

A second principle for producing integration is controversy, which may seem contrary to community. But it is not hard to understand why controversy will be important if integration and attention to real-world problems is a priority. If there is not first a diversity to be brought together, there can be no integration and no community, only sameness. Students and faculty alike will find it very easy to lose sight of problems if the community is too homogeneous. Controversy as a deliberate strategy means to bring real-world problems into the environment and apply integrative approaches. The lack of controversy makes any college, and particularly Christian colleges, anemic. They are hothouses better suited to producing the dualistic dogmatists described in chapter 3.

Just as the problem discussed in chapter 3 for producing critical commitment with community and dissonance was the need for balance to avoid indoctrination, here the problem with community and controversy in producing integration is the need for balance to avoid fragmentation. Too little controversy means there is nothing to be integrated. There are no real-world problems to be addressed. Students are isolated from reality in Christian "summer camps." But too much controversy divides the community; it ceases to be a community at all. The shared purposes disappear. The shared task of integration cannot be accomplished. This effect will come just as surely because of too much controversy as because of too little community.

CONCLUSION TO PART II

The instrumental value of a liberal arts education is to produce graduates who are *able* to tackle real-world problems. This can be accomplished best if their education has been integrative of disciplines, of theory and practice, and of values and learning. If they have received the intrinsic value of a liberal arts education and are critically committed, they will be *willing* to do so. So with both the intrinsic and the instrumental values they will be able *and* willing. The obvious problems for producing both critical commitment and integration are practical. It is to such practical questions that I now want to turn.

Part III

The Practical Task of
Implementing Christian Liberal Arts

Part III

The Practical Task of Implementing Christian Liberal Arts

In the early 1980s, three small companies all caught a vision first imagined by researchers in Stanford's Xerox Park. The vision was to allow nontechnical people to use personal computers in an intuitive way. Although personal computers were beginning to emerge, the commands necessary to get them to do the simplest things were nightmarish. "Press ctrl-/ to insert the formatting code for . . ." "Type cd . . . to move up one directory and cd \ to go to the root." These DOS commands—an improvement over CPM—were bad enough; UNIX was much worse! The average person either could not or would not invest the time and energy required to learn to work a computer. The Xerox Park vision was to display a graphical representation of an ordinary desktop on the screen and allow users to manipulate small images representing ordinary papers or pictures or worksheets using a simple pointing device called a "mouse." Today this is commonplace because the vision for a graphical user interface (GUI) was spectacularly successful.

But only one of the three companies that caught this vision thrives, and almost everyone in America knows which one it is. Most experts say the smallest company had the very best product. It was compact, elegant, fast, and cheap. That company was and remains virtually unknown. Apple's embrace of this GUI vision was downright religious. The jury is still out on whether Apple will even survive. But Bill Gates is the richest man in the world, Microsoft leads the economy, and everyone seems to have Windows. It's all in the implementation.

A clear vision of Christian liberal arts is not enough. Vision must shape practice. It is said that "without a vision the people perish." But it is also said that "without works, faith is dead."

131

In parts I and II, I described the intrinsic and instrumental values of a Christian liberal arts education. The intrinsic value lies chiefly in the attitude of critical commitment engendered in students. The chief instrumental value lies in equipping graduates to tackle real-world problems. At the end of each part I laid out general guiding principles for accomplishing those ends. I suggested that instilling critical commitment requires at least three crucial elements: (1) an environment full of constructive dissonance, (2) living role models who promote the development of habits, and (3) genuine community. Teaching students to tackle real-world problems is facilitated by the presence of (1) controversy and (2) community.

Taken together, these five principles overlap and boil down to three: constructive controversy or dissonance, modeling to promote habits, and genuine community. In part III, these principles will inform all of the specific suggestions I would like to make about Christian liberal arts institutions. Furthermore, it seems to me that institutional distinctives may be roughly divided into those related to programs and those related to people. I believe people are more important, but let us defer that issue and begin instead with some discussion of programs.

At this point I must insert a major caveat. This book could end here. What follows are just suggestions. There is no claim to special insight or evidence of special success. When it comes to implementing the vision and applying the principles described in the preceding discussion, there can be no single path. Institutions will vary and so will circumstances. Most importantly, the faculty and administrators charged with this task will have creativity and perception far beyond my own. So I offer the following entirely in the spirit of illustration. It contains examples of how the two major values in Christian liberal arts that I have pointed out might shape a college, the intrinsic value of developing students to become critically committed, and the instrumental value of equipping students to tackle real problems. The examples merely illustrate one way to apply the three principles abstracted from these values. My few years in academic administration prevent me from claiming more.

9

How Can Programs Promote Christian Liberal Arts?

By "programs" I mean the curriculum. That includes both the formal curriculum (including the course requirements and the dominant modes of teaching) and the informal curriculum (noncredit granting aspects of the collegiate program and environment). Both make indispensable contributions to students' lives and are the major tools educational institutions use to accomplish their mission and implement their vision.

FORMAL CURRICULUM

Curriculum has been the subject of heated debate no doubt since the first faculty committee ever met. But it became the focus of special controversy in the latter part of the 1980s. William Bennett, who at the time was chairman of the National Endowment for the Humanities, issued a report in 1984, *To Reclaim a Legacy*, in which he decried the state of American university humanities curriculum.

> On too many campuses, the curriculum has become a self-service cafeteria through which students pass without being nourished. . . . The curriculum is no longer a statement about what knowledge mattered; instead it became the product of a political compromise among competing schools and departments overlaid by marketing considerations. . . . The curriculum has become a disaster area.[1]

I wish I could say that Bennett's criticisms do not apply at Christian liberal arts colleges. There is no doubt that by comparison with most state universities, such colleges retain a strong general education core. But I believe Bennett is right. Even at these colleges the design is haphazard, resulting largely from political considerations. One cannot sit through many curriculum reviews without becoming resigned to these facts. Consider the following examples.

First, there is the matter of departmental "turf," the "politics of the core."[2] Each department has to protect its own survival. Without a spot in the "distribution" requirement there is no guarantee of captive student audiences. And of course with fewer students there is less campus prestige or, worse still, fewer faculty positions.

Second, there are market demands. Christian liberal arts colleges are often enrollment driven. Financial survival depends on attracting students because endowments are often small. So when computer science is all the rage we create new majors, retrain our faculty, and consider adding computer literacy to the distribution requirement. Maybe computer programming could even count to fulfill the "language" requirement. Or when admissions announces that students demand communication studies, we add that to the general education requirement. If a travel program draws large numbers, we rationalize that Western civilization or Far Eastern civilization is really just as good as world civilization for fulfilling the requirement. These attempts to enhance financial survival are not necessarily wrong. Obviously, marketing is not all bad. In fact, it is only prudent to identify and articulate the overlaps between institutional mission and students' perceived needs. The danger arises when curriculum is entirely driven by student demand. Marketing becomes prostitution.

Third, there is the almost irresistible pressure of state teacher credentialing requirements. As if it were not hard enough to devise a coherent general education curriculum within the institution, the state often duplicates the effort with curricula of its own. Well intended to ensure the competence of elementary and high school teachers, these requirements impose a second "grid" on top of the institutional plan. The requirements often make good sense. But bullied or cajoled by departments of education and caught between "a rock and a hard place," many colleges find themselves modifying their general education requirements and departments find themselves modifying even the content of their courses to suit these expectations. Institutional vision for the curriculum, if it has been conceptualized at all, may be forced to play second fiddle.

Finally, but by no means the last of the real list, there is pressure to meet the content expectations of professional societies and standardized tests. This seems particularly true in the sciences, but probably also holds true elsewhere as, for example, in teaching logic to students preparing for the LSAT. Not only does it become necessary to teach a certain *amount* of information and skill for students to pass professional tests or certification, but also it must be taught on a particular *schedule* to ensure that students are ready by certain dates. These external disciplinary demands wreak havoc not only with the "elective time" of students in these majors with high unit requirements but with the principle of sequencing general education. Ironically, though rarely applied to the general education, this principle is sacrosanct within certain majors. Apparently this means that what is "good for the goose is not allowed for the gander."

Bennett's judgment about the state of curriculum was echoed by his successor at the National Endowment, Lynne Cheney. In a report released in 1989, *50 Hours: A Core Curriculum for College Students,* Cheney argued for a more "coherent" curriculum. The report pointed out that "colleges allow students to fulfill general education requirements with a long list of narrowly focused courses rather than with broad-based studies."[3] It is not primarily a problem of insufficient hours devoted to general education. For all four-year institutions the average was fifty-two hours. "There *is* time at most schools for a significant core of learning. As it is now, however, these hours . . . are all too often organized into loosely stated 'distribution requirements'—mandates that students take some courses in certain areas and some in others."[4]

These courses are often specialized and often not linked to one another in any coherent way. I believe this criticism holds true at Christian liberal arts colleges. Increasing pressure to publish on faculty at even these Christian liberal arts colleges may make the general education core more specialized. Often with little more than lip service to coherence, faculty dish up a smorgasbord of courses entitled "Introduction to X" where "X" stands for their own discipline. Even courses originally designed to be more integrative gradually become more specialized—in content if not in name—as it becomes more and more difficult to attract faculty to teach them in an integrative way.

I am not about to say that Christian liberal arts colleges should eliminate the traditional major.[5] Although the introduction of majors was a late arrival in American higher education, I believe it is now essential for students to obtain some depth of understanding and skill in one area.[6] The explosion of information in our age makes some specialization necessary. Even the idea that a curriculum ought to emphasize "transferable skills"—as important as it is in a day when graduates change careers on average three to six times in a lifetime—cannot substitute for disciplinary concentration.

But I do believe the formal general education curriculum should receive more attention than it does. For example, institutions might very well consider the suggestions made by Bennett and Cheney. Their reports, although published five years apart, were remarkably similar in advocating a strong foundation in history of world, Western, *and* American civilization. Foreign language and exposure to non-Western culture were also essential in both reports. But whether it derives from Bennett and Cheney or not, there should be more to the development of the formal curriculum than the politics I have described above. There should be vision that is tied to the distinctive mission of the institution.

For Christian liberal arts colleges, the curriculum might then be informed coherently by the two major goals we have suggested—development and integration—and therefore shaped by the principles of *constructive dissonance, modeling* to form *habits,* and *community.*

A Developmental Curriculum

If the goal is to produce graduates who are critically committed, then it seems crucial that the formal curriculum be developmental. The word "developmental" sometimes conjures up images of "student development" and that in turn is sometimes thought to contrast with "academic." Let me be plain in saying that I disagree with that dichotomy. But more importantly, by "developmental" I mean not just that the cocurricular is important. Rather, I mean that the formal curriculum itself should be informed by the very best we know about student cognitive, moral, and faith development. Faculty should do all we can to take students beyond dualism and beyond multiplicity to become persons of critical commitment.

The guiding principles are to promote constructive dissonance with modeling in community. But that means challenging students at the level of their current development and modeling alternatives at the next highest level. Is this *really* what our formal curriculum does? Do faculty *really* shake up and even challenge students' patterns of thought? Do colleges really offer alternatives modeled in the visible worldviews of its professors? As we saw in chapter 3, Lawrence Kohlberg says both are important. "As applied to educational intervention, the [interactionist] theory holds that facilitating the child's movement to the next step of development involves exposure to the next higher level of thought and conflict requiring the active application of the current level of thought to problematic situations."[7]

Nicholas Wolterstorff agrees and shows the connection to curriculum. "When the dissonance between one's environment and stage of reasoning becomes sufficiently severe, one moves on to a higher stage in order to attain equilibrium. . . . This goal of advancing the student in the form of his or her reasoning is accomplished by producing dissonance between the environment of [students] and that particular stage within which they find themselves."[8] The evidence is that students will not be attracted to lower stages and cannot even understand stages more than one level higher than their own.[9]

In chapter 3, I concluded that this requires (1) paying attention to the student's modes of thought, judgment, and faith, that is, to their level of development and (2) matching the stimulation (conflict, dissonance) to this information. In practical terms this might mean some or all of the following.

First, colleges need to have *better information about the students* they are admitting. Typically, the faculty are informed about grade point averages, SAT scores, demographic distribution, and even religious preferences. But from time to time faculty might participate in workshops describing the cognitive, moral, and faith development of their students. Periodic testing of incoming and graduating students might be helpful to establish these profiles.[10] While it is unlikely that basic developmental patterns will change much over time, the turnover in faculty and the tendency to forget such perspectives would justify repeated workshops.

Second, attention should be given to the *sequence in which general education courses are taught*. Some courses must come earlier rather than later because of method or content. This fact is obvious in teaching mathematics or the sciences. Of more interest is that in other areas some courses should come earlier rather than later because of cognitive, moral, or faith development. It may well be, for example, that the higher critical questions raised in Old Testament or New Testament will be less manageable than doctrine for beginning students, who are largely dualistic in their thinking. On the other hand, courses in Western civilization may not present such problems.

Of course it may depend on how the course is taught. Western civilization taught as the history of ideas may not be appropriate for incoming students at all. And depending, again, on how they are taught, Old Testament and New Testament might be more appropriate for the beginning student than doctrine. But in some cases the sequence may not be just a matter of how the course is taught. It may be unavoidably tied to the subject matter rather than the teaching. For example, a first course in philosophy might best be delayed until students have already begun to move out of dualism into multiplicity.

It is not my purpose here to determine which subjects should be arranged in which order. The point is only to say that allowing students to fulfill their general education requirements in any haphazard order neglects the obvious. Experienced teachers realize that assignments which require only memorization of facts are more appropriate for beginning students; those that require analysis and even original synthesis should be reserved for later stages of the course or for advanced classes.[11] Likewise, thoughtful departments do their best to sequence the program for their majors by building a foundation before proceeding to more advanced work. The point here is that this obvious principle should be applied to the formal general education curriculum as well. The question of whether the general education curriculum matches the developmental levels of students enrolled is largely unanswered because unasked.

Third, attention should be paid to the *range of developmental positions found in any given classroom*. One of the frustrations of college teaching comes from having students at widely divergent stages of cognitive, moral, and faith development in the same class. If you "pitch" to the most advanced, the less advanced are lost because they are overwhelmed. If you attend to the least advanced, the most advanced are lost because they are bored. Addressing the "middle" may lose both ends and hit just exactly no one. What I am describing is not a question of basic ability. The issue is development. Even the brightest will proceed through the same transitions. The problem is the range in one class. For example, students functioning at the level of dualism cannot even understand thinking that is more than one stage ahead of where they currently function. In the same class there may be another student functioning in multiplicity who cannot be challenged except by introducing problems with multiplicity and models of critical commitment. The teacher is set up to fail one or both. The answer, I believe, is to narrow this range as much as possible.

There are at least two possible objections. First, some say *they prefer a range* of students because more advanced students inform and enliven discussion. I am not convinced. Although it is certainly true that such discussion makes things more interesting for the instructor, it is not at all obvious that this is in the best interests of either the advanced or the beginning students. My point is not an argument against diversity. There is little doubt that diversity of opinion is healthy. But that kind of diversity is different from the diversity of developmental stage and orientation I am describing here.[12] Studies of the "freshman-year experience," for example, show that classes tailored to the beginning student increase retention, without which further development is obviously impossible. And at the other end of the spectrum, although the evidence is anecdotal, advanced students frequently report that classes in which developmental factors are more nearly homogeneous are among the most stimulating. And this may be true regardless of whether the class members are from the same disciplines.[13] I have found that advanced students in the sciences do better even in advanced philosophy courses than beginning philosophy students. To the objection that advanced students model higher stages of development to their less developed peers, I would only say that if the modeled stages are too advanced, the evidence suggests there can be no benefit anyway. And, of course, one hopes the teacher is providing that model and presumably in a more deliberately self-conscious way.[14]

Narrowing the range of development within general education classes can be addressed partly by sequencing the courses. Then informed faculty can tailor the content and expectations more closely to the student's development. But second, some may object that *it is impossible to group students* by levels of cognitive development merely by using their age because development occurs at different rates for each person. The point is important and well-taken. According to interactionist theories, the rate of development will depend both on the student's ability and previous environment. But in the first place, sequencing will certainly not hurt. Surely, it is more likely students will share comparable levels of development if they are all first-year students than if the class contains a wide distribution from first-year students to seniors. Second, we already creatively group students by ability through special "honors" sections and "advanced topics." Why not the same with regard to developmental progress? Different sections of general education courses would seem no less appropriate than different sections of chemistry or philosophy or English. Some studies have already been done and have confirmed that the introduction of different calculated incongruities (dissonance) was required to instigate developmental movement for differing groups.[15] Finally, although Kohlberg admits that development is "not age-specific" but rather "individual," he goes on to say that

> Nevertheless, gross age periods may be defined which are "open periods" for movement from one stage to another. The aim is not to accelerate development, but to avoid stage retardation and this means "presenting stimulation in these periods where the possibility for development is still open."[16]

Fourth, making the formal curriculum developmental should have *implications for teaching*. In addition to workshops for faculty in understanding their students there should be workshops for discussing the most appropriate techniques for promoting development at different levels.[17] It is one of the best-kept secrets of higher education that professors have typically received little or no training in teaching before they begin. And in too many cases they spend little time reflecting on teaching after they begin. Liberal arts colleges generally, and Christian liberal arts colleges in particular, should be the exceptions. They should take the lead in recent calls to reconsider the priorities of the American professoriate.[18]

Consider philosophy. Introductory courses generally bring me face-to-face with a group of students who are still functioning largely at a high school level of dualistic thinking. They become frustrated by discussions that to them "lead nowhere." They are interested in knowing only the "answer" and cannot understand why anyone would want to try to argue for what is "obviously ridiculous."

An example is the dilemma of how we could ever know that our senses give us an accurate representation of an external world. Obviously our senses often *do* deceive us. So how then can we ever be sure of their reliability? And of course, if our senses may deceive us about secondary matters like shape and color, they may, as Bishop Berkeley suggested, be fundamentally misleading about whether there is an external world at all. The "real" world may be, in fact, only a grand "virtual reality" in our mind or in God's.

In such cases provoking the kind of dissonance necessary to promote students' cognitive advancement means making them uncomfortable with their views. The technique of "playing the devil's advocate" is useful. I try to attack and undermine their stubborn belief in a real external physical world. I try to argue different sides on different days. I try *not* to answer my own objections on the same day. It takes time for intellectual "thorns" to work in. Because dualistic thinking usually entails strong passions, my advocacy for alternative ways of thinking must sometimes be equally forceful. I try to bring students into the process by warning them at the outset of the class: "Unless I get under your skin at least once this semester I may be failing in my responsibility to you." The trick, of course, is not to push any particular student too far. This is easier to avoid in a class with more homogeneous cognitive, moral, and faith development. Teachers are human and will inevitably fail; that is the cost of functioning on the cutting edge of student growth. Which brings us to another of our guiding principles: community.

The principle of constructive dissonance must never be isolated from the principle of community. Building a classroom environment in which there is a community of trust is crucial for the challenge of dissonance to be constructive. When students do not sense you are fundamentally "on their side," the induced dissonance may have the opposite effect of driving them backward in their development.[19] Community creates an atmosphere in which students can question. It creates an atmosphere in which the teacher is not only sensitive to individual students who have been pushed too far but is willing to confront them and be reconciled when necessary.

But development requires more than dissonance. At each step along the way, the "next stage" of development must be modeled attractively, even while the student's present stage is challenged. For the teacher, functioning simultaneously as the creator of both cognitive dissonance and personal community is the genius of good teaching. So the third principle, modeling, is essential too. By the time students have had several courses in philosophy they have become adept at criticism. They can play devil's advocate as well as I can. They have typically passed from dualism into multiplicity. One hopes their skepticism has not yet become cynicism. But now, because of their developmental progress, my approach to them changes. The last thing they need to see me model is devil's advocacy. What they need to see is that I have drawn some conclusions of my own in spite of the ambiguity surrounding such conclusions. I must now model critical commitment. The technique might be to lay out the alternatives and then marshal my arguments for what I believe to be the best case. Or the readings chosen might all represent the best criticisms of my own view, which I then defend against those readings. In short, professors should "profess" something. As with devil's advocacy, the students can be brought into the process by pointing out what they probably can see already, that I am arguing a particular view. But unless they see how to come to conclusions despite the human condition, I have only taken them halfway.

Again there are failings. This time both by my own inability or my failure to develop my own thinking adequately and by the temptation in those situations to pretend—to play a commitment "game." But honesty and vulnerability go a long way to compensate. Community engenders both because real community is not judgmental. When teachers are in community with students and with their own peers on the faculty, there is a much greater likelihood they can be honest and vulnerable. Without community, the positions faculty model may be only masquerades. Rather than model critical commitment, teachers will have modeled only sophistry.

Experienced teachers understand all this. I may be suggesting nothing new. But perhaps it bears articulation because it is not usually explicit. Workshops to investigate the techniques we use for promoting *constructive dissonance, community,* and *modeling* would all be useful.

I want to finish these comments on a developmental curriculum with a word in support of memorization and foreign language. In reaction to the "busy work" mentality of copy-book education, memorization has been largely shunned in higher education. It is seen as indoctrination, restriction of freedom—a relic of a parochial past. This is true despite the fact that faculty know the crucial role memory plays in our own ability to organize information and tackle new problems and the role it plays in students' own learning process. C. S. Lewis in *Abolition of Man* remarks how important those copy-book values become in shaping one's own worldview.[20] Although I would not advocate a return to the days of rote memorization and regurgitation for its own sake, perhaps we have thrown the baby out with the bath water. Aristotle's emphasis on habituation at the heart of character formation should not be forgotten. Modeling means constantly holding up for students incarnate examples of thinking and valuing at higher stages of development. Habituation, including memory work, can do the same. Used in the right way, such work holds up examples for students of principles and practices of more mature cognitive, moral, and faith development. If the liberal arts college is genuinely interested in educating the whole person, then good teaching should reconsider memory and habit.

Foreign language study, like memory work, may have fallen into some neglect. That is a little surprising given the vocational bent of most students, together with the obvious practical value of a language in an ever shrinking world. The trend of neglect may be changing, given the renewed emphasis on diversity and internationalization of the curriculum. However, I would like to suggest that foreign language study is also especially valuable for its developmental benefits and not just its instrumental ones. Our guiding principle in developmental education has been the use of dissonance in building abilities to see things in new ways. It seems to me that in addition to the practical cultural insights gained from study of a foreign language, that study generates a dissonance that forces a restructuring of thought processes.

Changing the way sentences are put together inevitably forces a reexamination of our own thinking. That must inevitably enlarge the student's ability to see in new ways. If discussion of Bishop Berkeley's radically mental world enlarges student perspectives, then recognition that some people have no words for "private property" or "individual," or that some languages are highly sensitive to gender or tone of voice, can dramatically enlarge a student's perspective as well. Often knowledge of another language sheds light on the roots of English words to the effect of broadening understanding.[21] Of course the case for broadened perspective can be made for virtually all subjects taught in the liberal arts, but because a new language cannot avoid a radical restructuring of thought with the inevitable dissonance and because it has been neglected, I believe it merits special attention in the curriculum.

I have suggested a number of ways in which I believe a curriculum can be made more developmental. It involves better knowledge of where students are already in their development, sequencing of coursework, narrowing the developmental range in classes, and thinking carefully about the implications for teaching. But the formal curriculum at the Christian liberal arts college must also be integrative.

An Integrative Curriculum

If our goal is to equip students to tackle real-world problems, then I believe integrative courses are essential. As with the word "developmental," "integrative" is also misunderstood. In chapter 6, I tried to clarify what I mean. Integration is *not* "preintegration," a mediocre dabbling conducted by faculty who are not cognizant of developments in their own field. It goes beyond that, as well as beyond the narrow guild-oriented disciplinary overspecialization often found in many research institutions. It means integration of multiple disciplines, of theory with practice, and of learning with faith. Real-world problems typically do *not* fall into the neat categories and frameworks of any particular discipline. Nor can they ever be really solved so long as the answers remain strictly theoretical. Finally, they rarely have solutions independent of the ethical and religious systems of those addressing them. Consequently I believe *problem-oriented integrative courses should be found at all stages of the formal curriculum.*

At the Beginning

Robert Bennett and Lynne Cheney have attacked the traditional "distribution" approach to general education and I agree. Bruce Wilshire has likened it to the "old fashioned Chinese menu, a little of this, a little of that." With such an approach, he says, the threat of raising up a race of "highly trained barbarians" is real.[22]

It is true that "we are creating the past faster than ever and the sum of what humankind has learned . . . is becoming lopsided in favor of the present."[23] But specialization is not the solution to providing the necessary foundation for students. Garrett Bauman describes the fallacy well. "Educators have responded . . . reasoning that perhaps if each graduate knows more about less, the sum total of what all men know will somehow keep pace. It won't work. People cannot 'access' each other. . . . A committee of myopic specialists . . . has never become the equivalent of one wise broad-minded brain."[24]

What seems to be missing is the interrelationship between the specialties. Men like Francis Bacon and Leonardo da Vinci not only understood a range of specialties but also understood the interrelation of those specialties. They did not stop short of specialties but went beyond them. We cannot inject our students with shots of this and that and then tell them to use their own skills to blend them into wisdom. We must model the very thing we are asking them to do. We must teach directly what we say will be our graduate's chief hallmarks.[25] General education courses that propose to produce graduates who can tackle real-world problems must integrate multiple disciplines under the umbrella of common themes or problems.

Imagine, for example, a general education course built around the problem of violence. It provides opportunity to expose beginning students to an actual controversial problem that demands insights from natural and social sciences as well as from the humanities. There is room for reading from classic as well as contemporary writing. The relevance is obvious to students; case after case can be drawn from history as well as contemporary social problems. Even though some may correctly point out that beginning students simply are not yet equipped to do this kind of integrative study, at the least it whets their appetite for education in a way introductory disciplinary courses often do not. And when used at the beginning of the general education curriculum, it poses the kinds of problems and hints at the alternative approaches possible, which will stir up the best kind of motivation to pursue a particular discipline. Those more specialized studies will not then be seen as ends in themselves but rather as sharper tools to be used later in tackling those real-world problems all the more effectively! Without this early recognition of the range of issues involved in real problems, students may never again have an interest in anything outside their major. If that specialized disciplinary training of a major is viewed as the only really practical part of their education, it will be small wonder that students want to get general education "out of the way."

In a sense we are talking here about adopting the same strategy for general education that many disciplines already use in requiring *practica*. Students involved in those kinds of courses typically tackle real problems in a real-world situation. Why not broaden that idea? Why not expand the operative framework from that of a single discipline to one encompassing several? And even the hands-on, off-campus component is appropriate, since integration includes that of theory with practice. The idea of hands-on, off-campus, beginning general education courses may seem radical, but it sets the stage for producing the graduates liberal arts colleges say they aim to produce.

By adopting such integrating structures, the general education curriculum can potentially build community. Students with widely diverse disciplinary goals can see from the beginning of their education the common problems everyone faces. Future physicists, poets, painters, philosophers, and psychologists can see the reason for their discipline in a common human condition. They can see the necessity for cooperation by acknowledging the contributions to be made by other disciplines. Otherwise, in only a few short months they may become so short-sighted they will not easily feel community with those from other disciplines ever again.

This community comes with less risk of reinforcing scholarship that is biased toward a particular class, race, culture, or gender. Too many general education courses are framed only by disciplinary theories. These are the "Introduction to X" courses and even the chronologically framed "civilization" courses. They often start with a "canon," or at least a paradigm, in which only certain aspects of human experience are highlighted and in which only certain kinds of solutions will be considered. Despite its excesses, the political correctness movement has rightfully criticized the bias and stereotyping such courses often promote. But why not start with a common problem and allow it to guide the inquiry instead of a canon or paradigm? Beginning general education courses might thereby not only produce community but also do so without the hardened categories that make some communities closed ones.

The popularity of freshmen seminars in recent years is an encouraging sign. Apparently these courses have been introduced because students want an earlier glimpse of how their education will be practical. Often they are topical so they may already tackle real problems. If not, it would seem a relatively simple matter to extend this popular idea by encouraging faculty to consider integrating the course in some or all of the three ways we have been discussing.

In the Middle

Integrative courses should not be limited to the beginning of the student's learning. Integration should characterize courses even within their major disciplines.

Case Studies within Regular Courses

Most disciplinary courses must presuppose the theoretical structures and problem agendas of the discipline. But if integration is indeed a goal, there must be occasions to step back and examine those presuppositions and con-nect them to the larger task of real-world problems of peace, justice, vio-lence, development, authority, ecology, and so on. Some of this might occur in brief sections of typical disciplinary courses. I do not believe such sections need to be superficial. For example, some courses might use case studies as effective tools to draw students into integrative study.[26] Cases drawn both from historical and current events have been effective across a range of dis-ciplines, particularly in the humanities and social sciences. But even the most theoretical natural science courses can benefit because often such courses are more deliberately intended to equip students for practical work or real problem solving than those in humanities anyway. So it is never too early to introduce those problems.

Seminars in the Major

In addition, most disciplines would benefit from required seminars in which majoring students would reflect more critically on the assumptions, limita-tions, and applications of their chosen specialty.[27] Natural and social science students would benefit from sections of courses or even whole courses in the philosophy of science. Analytic philosophers would benefit from sections on the contrasting methods of continental philosophy; creative writers from dis-cussions of critical theory. "Ideally, a major should give students under-standing of a subject in depth and also put that subject into perspective."[28] The perspective gained in early integrative general education courses must be nourished. This is possible even in the sciences in which the disciplinary paradigms and specialization are often judged to be the narrowest.

Practica for Real-World Accountability

I have already alluded to the value of including a practical dimension even to beginning general education courses. If integration includes the integra-tion of theory and practice, this is essential throughout the curriculum. Arthur Levine conducted a survey comparing students in the late 1960s with those in the late 1970s. In many ways students had not changed. But among the significant differences he noted was cynicism about social institutions and pessimism about the future.[29] Students seemed less interested than be-fore in discovering the real-world issues that needed attention. Even if this became less true in the 1990s, Levine's recommendations would still apply. He does not advocate abandoning liberal arts in favor of more practical train-ing but making modifications that immerse students in the real-world prob-lems of our day.[30]

Many disciplines already make good use of this curricular principle in the form of required *practica* and internships. Strong social and behavioral sci-ence programs have usually taken the lead. Economics and business studies also often include small business projects. Service-oriented religious studies programs sometimes require internships. But I believe a great deal more can be done creatively to incorporate practical experiences into the curriculum even of disciplines not usually thought to benefit from them. I do not mean only "off-site" experiences. And I do not mean only for the purpose of developing practical skills. Arguments for the benefits of practical curricular programs to those ends have been made much more effectively by others elsewhere. But I believe that "outside accountability" can enhance the goal of integration.

That accountability might come both to general education integrative courses and to disciplinary courses in the form of outsiders participating in course construction, in teaching, and even in evaluating students. It serves as a "reality check" in two senses. First, in the usual sense of verifying what will or will not "work" as solutions. But it is also a check in the less obvious sense of verifying what constitutes the real problems people face and the real questions they ask.

Obviously business students benefit from tackling a particular business in their community. The problems they address are real ones and the solutions receive the scrutiny of outsiders to the academic community. Chemistry and biology students grow from the pressure and reinforcement of collaborative projects with industry. Psychology, sociology, and anthropology students obviously benefit from contact with working counselors, welfare recipients, furloughed missionaries, and foreign service personnel. But theology courses can also be informed by recognizing the real struggles of parishioners and perspectives of working pastors and theologians. Writing projects in many disciplines benefit from input and evaluation by nonacademic writers and nonspecialists; poets by listening to those who have really felt pain, journalists from the red pencil of practicing journalists. Discussions of ethical issues will be enhanced by the presence of persons who grapple with these very issues on a regular basis in government, business, medicine, and so on. None of this is to suggest that faculty themselves are negligent or incompetent. But broader accountability enhances the integration of theory and practice.

Faculty–Student Cooperative Research

Student–faculty cooperative research is a final example of how the curriculum even within the disciplines can be integrative. In describing the distinctives of scholarship at liberal arts colleges, Kenneth Ruscio points out that faculty research at liberal arts colleges more often avoids excessive specialization because that would make it impossible to find collaborators among the limited group of colleagues and students found in smaller colleges. Such research is different from that at research universities. It more often crosses disciplinary or subdisciplinary boundaries.[31] Such research further integrates by putting students in touch with real problems in their discipline—whether in the sciences or in the humanities—whereby they can bring the theoretical framework they have acquired into play on a problem in the discipline. Such collaborative projects seem also to have the advantage of promoting student development by virtue of the modeling that inevitably occurs when faculty and students work together closely. This kind of research can be a model not only in the sciences but in other disciplines at Christian liberal arts colleges as well.

At the End

Perhaps most importantly, integration must be extended to the "end" of the undergraduate program and beyond. For too long, integration and general education have been synonymous with "introductory." That needs to change. What is needed is a new or renewed concept of advanced general studies. What a distinctive this might become for excellent liberal arts institutions! Why do we set the stage, teach the actors their lines, but then rarely dress rehearse for the performance of "Life after College?" We expect our graduates to "put it all together" but rarely teach them directly to do this.

To some extent a required major thesis can do this. It certainly asks students to draw together what they have learned *in the discipline* and apply it to a real problem *in the discipline.* I wholeheartedly support such requirements as a step in the right direction. But why not required "capstone courses" to the general education curriculum as well? These are advanced general studies courses that go beyond even the disciplinary thesis because they draw on the broader skills supposedly acquired throughout the curriculum and for which liberal arts institutions are supposedly noted. They draw on research; reading; analytic, synthetic, and writing skills; and, depending on the kinds of assignments made, on cooperative and value judgment skills as well. And they apply these skills to the real-world problems that go far beyond a single discipline.

Imagine a group of advanced students nearing the end of studies in their chosen major gathered together to address a problem such as "Government Approval of Controversial Drugs: Laetrile, AIDS ZX, and the French Abortion Pill." Students from psychology, sociology, political science, philosophy, chemistry, and biology could *all* make significant contributions. They would draw on their already well-developed disciplinary expertise as well as on the transferable skills of their general education. The topics might vary from class to class as the instructor's interest varied. Topics might even be selected to fit better the actual composition of the particular class. In general the topics might be more specific than those of beginning integrative general education courses but could be seen as manageable "bites" off those larger problems.

If such courses were viewed as the real culmination of the liberal arts education, students might better understand what is distinctive about what they have gained. They become matching "bookend" courses at the opposite end of their collegiate education from those interest-whetting opening integrative courses. By revealing the student's skills at tackling them, these courses help students understand more clearly just what they have learned in those four years. And by going beyond the disciplines, the courses help students see just how their liberal arts education differs from what they might have received elsewhere.

These capstone advanced general studies courses might even be reserved only for degree "candidates," students who had come to a stage in their education where they had completed a prescribed portion of both their disciplinary and general education requirements. A sense of pride of accomplishment might emerge which would go beyond that experienced by non–liberal arts graduates. Certainly, such a course would build community among its participants as they wrestled together to communicate with one another in addressing a common task. Without such opportunities we have stopped just short of delivering on the promise of liberal arts.

Interestingly, the integrative curriculum I have described is also developmental. Early general education raises questions. Disciplinary courses equip them with expertise. All courses provide broad transferable skills in reading, analyzing, thinking, and communicating. Advanced general studies courses bring students to the point where they begin to formulate real responses of their own.

I am not insisting that the only acceptable general education core must consist entirely of integrative problem-oriented courses. Some institutions have approximated this and with some success.[32] But others might prefer to supplement or substitute portions of their present distribution core with courses of the kind I have described.

Obstacles

But of course this brings us to the obvious problem that an integrative curriculum is very hard work. Hard to envision, hard to adopt, and hard to maintain. The barriers are enormous. "Almost all these efforts [at integrative general education] have run afoul of student career mania; parents' insistence that their sons and daughters be successful; national accreditation requirements for professional studies; professionalization of the liberal arts; inter-departmental haggling over team-teaching credit; emphasis on narrowly focused research; lack of academic rewards for interdisciplinary teaching; and especially the 'politics of the core.'"[33]

I have commented already on several of these as complications in shaping the formal curriculum: departmental turf politics, demands of professional accreditation, narrow research orientation, and even vocationalism. Let me remark about two others, which become barriers especially to integrative courses.

First, there is the problem of *motivating* faculty to teach integratively. Despite the fact that most faculty at Christian colleges would affirm the principle that their institution intends to educate more wholistically than the university, that often does not translate into any readily apparent differences in the content of their teaching. There may very well be greater personal attention to the students' individual needs, and even to their personal lives. There may be a willingness to let a small minority teach some truly integrative courses. But for the most part, disciplinary and integrative studies are seen as conflicting claims on the investment of their energy.

In part, I believe this is because our graduate training is generally narrow. And in part, it is because relatively greater rewards come from our efforts in disciplinary endeavors. This difference in rewards and reinforcement comes not only from the honor and reputation earned in professional societies but even from the promotion, tenure, and informal prestige structure of our own institutions. Who is promoted? Who is tenured? Who is held up as a model to the rest of the community by being asked to speak and by being quoted in talks by administrators? Is it those who have spearheaded distinctively integrative education or those who have become "stars" in their disciplines and published widely? As I have remarked above, when Christian colleges lose sight of their own potential distinctives, administrators and faculty committees look elsewhere—often inappropriately—for faculty evaluation criteria.

But perhaps an even greater reason why faculty are uninterested in integrative courses is the fact that *many of us have not really integrated our own thinking.* Even if we had been fortunate to attend a Christian liberal arts college which did this successfully—and I do not think there are many which do—the years of subsequent graduate training have most likely dissuaded us from giving such matters much further attention. So perhaps the deepest reason why we Christian college faculty do not teach integratively is that we do not know how. Our own thinking has not progressed to the stage we want our own students to achieve. We do not dress rehearse them because we cannot play our own roles. This would break what Jonathan Smith, former dean of the college at Chicago, called the "Iron Law": "Students shall not be expected to integrate anything that the faculty can't or won't."[34]

Good integrative teaching requires critical commitments on at least a few issues within our own fields. We must have already made some critical commitments. Furthermore, good integrative teaching requires considerable familiarity if not expertise in at least one other discipline. Without this we are dilettantes. As Arthur Holmes says, "The gaps between our disciplines too often prevent the benefits of interdepartmental interaction."[35] Finally, good integrative teaching requires the additional investment of thought in tying together the two disciplines, the theory with practice, and the topic with faith. With heavy teaching loads, increasing pressure to pursue the agenda of the discipline, and endless committee work, no faculty members in their right mind can invest the easily underestimated amount of time needed to equip themselves for this task. Time pressure and lack of personal life are already the two greatest sources of stress for college and university faculty.[36]

Second, then, is the obstacle of *equipping* faculty to teach an integrative curriculum. Integrative teaching of this kind requires a kind of preparation that most of us have never received and is largely unavailable in a formal institution. We are talking about retraining; but more than that, retraining of ourselves. There *are* no places to go for it because it is a distinctive that liberal arts and Christian liberal arts institutions have abandoned or neglected. I do not believe the situation is hopeless. I believe the answer is community, and in particular, I think teaching one another while we teach our students is the key. But how is this done?

Team teaching is an essential part. I can already hear my colleagues groaning. "We've tried that. It does not work. Besides, the students hate it, too." I do not believe it really has been tried as much as we think. Instead, what we have usually tried is "turn teaching." Having perhaps reluctantly agreed to work with colleagues in such a course, we plan a series of lectures, which allows us to draw as much as possible on the framework and content of what we already know. That's only human. Then we proceed to take our turn lecturing, modifying our content slightly to "hook" into the preceding and subsequent lectures. The result is that we give the students a miniaturized version of the distribution requirement within a single course. If it is hard for them to "integrate" an entire general education core when it is spread over four years and each course has an autonomy of its own, imagine how hard it is for them to "integrate" the pieces we give them in a single course. Small wonder they often find such courses fragmented and fractious.

But persistence is needed because faculty are unaccustomed to working with one another. In a recent survey by the American Council on Education (ACE) and UCLA, approximately 75 percent of faculty said they work essentially alone in their research. At some Christian colleges supposedly committed to integrative education, that figure ironically rises to 85 percent. Only about 30 to 40 percent of faculty have team-taught a course and, surprisingly, that figure sadly drops at some Christian colleges to 27 percent.[37] But if integration is sought, it will require working together. When asked in 1939 to explain the tremendous unity of aim and conviction at Johns Hopkins University fifty years earlier, Professor Rendel Harris said, "It was very simple; we all attended each other's lectures."[38] That means teaching each other, not learning alone.

Persistence is also needed because there is a natural progression to the development of integrative study. In the initial stage of sequential or turn teaching, students do most of the integrating themselves. But in a second stage, faculty learn to translate the ideas and terms of another discipline into their own, like learning a foreign language. Only in a final stage do faculty and students come to value each discipline, each perspective, in its own right and are equally able to illuminate the problem at hand.[39]

The obvious advantage of team teaching is that instead of retraining in another field and then integrating for oneself, we can rely on the expertise of colleagues, leaving only the task of integrating the topics in interaction with one another. In my mind this integration goes on in the team-taught classroom. Faculty learn to integrate before the students' eyes. Instead of "turn lecturing," why not "dialogical conversations"? Even when one faculty member frames the issues, why not have other team members not only physically present but actively engaged in *real* exchange and especially in *real* questioning. The idea would be to model for students just exactly how difficult it is to translate real issues across the jargon of different disciplines. The faculty would be teaching one another while teaching their students. The result for faculty themselves might often be little more than coming to understand the problem from the perspective of another field. But that's a start. If we can succeed in helping our students see that a major part of addressing real-world problems is learning to see them from many points of view, we will finally have begun to accomplish the integrative education we tout. Even to model the frustration and confusion of learning to see as another sees is often more than what is accomplished now in "canned" or "staged" presentations. This makes integrative thinking "visible," and students begin to identify with their instructors.

So in addition to the advantage for the aim of integration, team teaching also promotes the cognitive developmental goal of critical commitment. In studies of how students can be helped to move beyond multiplicity to critical commitment, William Perry found that "the most important support seemed to derive from a special realization of community . . . that in the very risks . . . of working out their Commitments, they were in the same boat . . . with their instructors."[40] Modeling and community found to be crucial in making the formal curriculum developmental emerge again here as benefits of the best kind of integrative curriculum as well.

Of course one might worry that the in-class dialogue between faculty team members will become so arcane that students would lose all benefit. Naturally, faculty will have to be sensitive to this. But on the other hand, I believe that "lay faculty" questions to a disciplinary team member may be exactly the questions students would like to ask but cannot yet articulate. In this way, team members, who are themselves learning, "take the point" for their students. And of course faculty teams must "teach one another" in other places besides the classroom. This can occur in regular team meetings that get beyond logistics to the subject matter of the course.

Overcoming this second obstacle of equipping one another to do integrative teaching will require more and perhaps even less than team teaching.

Economic realities may preclude team teaching because it is expensive. The college might consider collaborative "team-planned" courses. While not taught by a team, there would be a team from whom the instructor can learn. The benefit of faculty teaching faculty to compensate for our own narrow expertise is still there. The benefit to students of seeing integration modeled in their presence is not. Team planners should be compensated in some way lest the savings over team teaching be taken directly from faculty flesh. But one possibility would be to exchange team consultancies so that each planning team member would benefit equally in his or her own integrative courses from the investment of time and energy in conversation.

Overcoming the obstacle will require more than team teaching because conversation will need to occur also in regular open topical faculty gatherings or forums. It needs to occur in interdisciplinary summer institutes dedicated to the development of true integrative dialogue, perhaps with publishable results. Faculty professional development will take on a central role and perhaps an unusual form if real integration actually becomes an institutional distinctive. More on this below. Arthur Holmes summarizes the problem of equipping faculty and the solution of conversation: "Interdisciplinary courses are premature before the teachers involved know enough about each other's fields to construct and conduct a unified course. Time must first be found for interdisciplinary dialog among faculty."[41]

Obviously, integrative teaching requires genuine vulnerability. To expose one's own ignorance to students and —what's worse—to one's colleagues in institutes, forums, or the classroom, is extremely threatening. It can only occur in the context of a genuine community of scholars built on commitment without reservation to the value of this distinctive integrative education. As Jerry Gaff puts it,

> At their best, interdisciplinary programs go beyond intellectual integration . . . to create a community of learning among students and faculty. . . . although crafted to provide a better education for students, they are an important source of renewal for faculty. And although they are designed to be effective settings for teaching and learning, they also tend to stimulate interdisciplinary scholarship among faculty whose minds are stretched by their colleagues and students.[42]

The question is, Are we prepared to keep on learning ourselves?

INFORMAL CURRICULUM

There is obviously more to the curriculum than just what goes on in classes. Faculty may object to the idea that what goes on outside the classroom has a greater impact than what goes on inside. But particularly at residential

Christian liberal arts colleges, any program that purports to engender both the intrinsic and the instrumental values I have described cannot neglect attention to the informal curriculum. I would like to make suggestions for applying the principles of dissonance, modeling, and community in three areas of the informal curriculum.

Living-Learning Experiences

Both integration and development goals can be enhanced by programs that combine living and learning. I have in mind here any programs that put students in close proximity with fellow students and especially with faculty for extended periods of time with a common task.

But merely sharing common experiences is not enough. As Arthur Holmes has argued, experience is not enough for the purpose of education.[43] This is so, first, because from at least as far back as Plato, understanding that lasts cannot be entirely based on experience, which is changing and relative to the individual. Second, understanding is not just lasting, but general. Hume's problem of induction shows that experience cannot justify what is general and consequently that once again it is not enough for understanding. Finally, experience requires interpretation. In the battle between empiricists and rationalists, Kant reminded us that neither experience nor interpretation is complete without the other. Interpretation without experience is empty, but experience without interpretation is blind. For living-learning programs to be educational, they must be reflective. There must be time to reflect on what has been experienced and how the experiences illustrate principles, which in turn can be related to a conceptual framework.

Cross-Cultural Experiences

One common living-learning experience on Christian liberal arts campuses today is the cross-cultural experience. These programs include inner-city campuses, short-term missions, and study tours. These are life-changing experiences for the students involved, many of whom return to their home campus feeling like aliens. Their horizons have been expanded, their thinking challenged, and their attitudes changed. It seems to me that each of the principles of dissonance, modeling, and community can already be found at work in such programs, making them unusually powerful programs for accomplishing what Christian liberal arts colleges strive to achieve. By the same token, these principles can help make sure such programs do not stray from those purposes.

In the first place, it is obvious that cross-cultural experiences induce dissonance. As a tool for promoting personal development, they are probably unequaled. They force a reappraisal of the ways students think, the ways they relate to others, the things they value, and what they believe. To experience firsthand real people who think, relate, value, and believe differently is far more effective than imagining such alternatives in some classroom. This happens naturally in such programs not only from contact with those of the "foreign" culture but from other program participants when they are thrown into close living situations.

It is not so much that the alternative values, beliefs, and ways of thinking themselves will necessarily become attractive. That is usually neither the result nor the purpose of such programs. But the students must make room in their own thinking for the fact that real people hold and act on those alternatives. It is critical that those who develop such programs recognize the importance of this dissonance factor. Otherwise the programs can easily fall short of their potential for developmental goals. Unfortunately, study tours and inner-city experiences can insulate participants from the dramatic differences around them. Accommodations can be too much like those at home, the trappings of familiar culture and subculture can be "brought along," and contact with people of the other culture can be limited, making for sort of a "glorified television experience." Local expertise should be tapped, overly large groups should be avoided, and the "tourist mind-set" discouraged. There may, of course, be programs with more limited goals that happen to occur in cross-cultural environments. But as a tool for the liberal arts goal of development, such living-learning experiences are most effective when they are provocative and unsettling.[44]

Second, cross-cultural programs often include significant experiences of community. Rather than function alone, students may live, work, and perhaps travel together in another country. A group of students may be housed together with faculty in an inner-city environment. As we have seen, community is crucial to development. It can provide an environment of safety into which students can retreat when the dissonance is too troubling, a kind of safety net. But it also provides the context in which the reflection can be accomplished, without which the experience would not be education at all. This kind of reflection makes the program plainly integrative as well because the group may consist of persons from various disciplines, and social, economic, and religious backgrounds. The shared intimacy of living together will force encounters along a broad range of issues. Integrative conclusions will inevitably arise if community is promoted. The role of faculty is critical in ensuring the maintenance of community both for support and for stimulating reflection. The details of how this can be done best must be left to the creativity of those who lead. My point is only that the community found in such groups can be a powerful contributor to the goals of the Christian liberal arts college.

Finally, cross-cultural living-learning programs usually provide students with models for their own development that are more intimate and therefore more effective in shaping their character. Accompanying faculty and even families can be live examples of faith and learning. Faculty are more likely to be observed in a learning mode themselves, modeling the characteristics of openness, vulnerability, curiosity, or persistence, to name only a few. The same can be said for persons in the surrounding culture. To witness the patience of those less fortunate, the persistence of those handicapped, or the friendliness of those who have been oppressed can burn deep impressions into young minds. My hope would be that such programs are maintained and enhanced and, further, that faculty who participate in such programs will not be viewed as "second class" by colleagues who see such programs as "peripheral" or "soft" relative to the task of education. I believe they are unusually important if serious attention is given to the distinctive mission of the Christian liberal arts college.

Residence Life

Residence life is another obvious living-learning "program." For Christian liberal arts colleges, this is a crucial place for dissonance, community, and modeling to occur. Student development staffs devote enormous efforts to making this happen and, I believe, are generally more sensitive to some aspects of the developmental goals of a Christian liberal arts college than are the classroom faculty.

Sadly, there is evidence that student involvement in residential life is actually inversely correlated with their development of the characteristics usually associated with liberal arts learning.[45] No doubt there *is* dissonance, no doubt there *is* modeling, and no doubt there *is* community of some kind. But unless these factors are submitted to the overriding goal of promoting cognitive, moral, and faith development *as well as* social development, then they may actually be counterproductive to the aims of the educational institution. Christian liberal arts colleges especially must avoid the bifurcation of students' lives into academic and personal or, worse yet, into academic, social, emotional, spiritual, physical, and so on.

It is one of the great tragedies of these colleges that at many, there is a "divide" between those responsible for formal curriculum and those responsible for residence life. One staff is responsible for social development, another for faith development, another for cognitive development, another for physical development, and who knows, who cares for moral development? It has not always been so. In the days before the "professionalization" of student development, classroom faculty lived among the students. These faculty lived with students and ate with them, as well as taught them in the classroom. Today that is considered practically impossible, not to mention an unreasonable invasion of private life. Yet there are colleges, even large universities, where programs encourage faculty to live among students for periods of time ranging from a weekend to a year.[46] Some may be only token programs in which a "house master" rarely interacts with the student residents. But others can provide genuine opportunities for constructive interaction, for building community and understanding between students and faculty, and for students to watch more closely the models of faculty who, more than "talking heads," are real-live persons with families and opinions about matters outside their disciplines. The demands on faculty in such a program would be enormous. Compensatory release of work responsibilities might be necessary. Not all faculty would be well suited by temperament. More mature faculty might be better fitted. But if the goals of the Christian liberal arts college are taken seriously, such a program could be a powerful contributor to accomplishing that distinctive mission.

There are other kinds of living-learning experiences that could be mentioned. Science research stations come to mind. But my purpose has been only to show that these programs in the informal curriculum can make significant contributions to the distinctive developmental and integrative goals of Christian liberal arts colleges.

Mentoring Programs

Even when there are no opportunities for extended periods of living and learning together, students can benefit from longer-term, more regular contact with college faculty. Studies of the freshman year experience show that the most important factor influencing retention of students is the establishment of some connection to long-term members of institutional faculty and staff. I believe that principle holds for improving a student's personal development.

The effect of role models in promoting advance from one developmental stage to another has already been established. Why not capitalize on this? If we know that students grow when they see models of maturity, why not increase that exposure? It happens naturally in living-learning programs. Mentoring programs can make it happen even on campus. Students can identify faculty they already know, perhaps in the classroom, church, or gymnasium. The mentor and student make a commitment to remain in regular contact over a semester or year or even several years. Sometimes they meet just to talk about the week's activities. On other occasions they observe one another at work and discuss it together. Faculty benefit from student feedback sometimes as much as the reverse! They may socialize and worship together. They become friends with mutual commitment. Over time they come to know one another in a way rarely possible for instructors in the classroom or even for professional student development staff.

There is some awkwardness in naming the student in such relationships—"protégé" or, perhaps better, "apprentice."[47] The beauty of the word "apprentice" is that one recognizes that what the mentor does and has become already has value in itself. It is for that reason the apprentice wishes to learn. The college mentor manifests skills, perhaps in a disciplinary "guild," that are valuable apart from whether others learn them. But the mentor also embodies virtues that have value independently of whether they are passed on. The extension of the analogy is that while most apprentices follow their mentors in only one specialized area, the student at the Christian liberal arts college apprentices for moral, faith, and even social *as well as* cognitive development.

Time must be made for this purpose. It cannot become just another "straw" added to the faculty "camel's back." If time is released for research, for writing, and for governance, then how much more important to do the same for mentoring, which is at the heart of institutional purpose.

Students probably should not be compelled to participate. But in the right environment, all students, and especially advanced students, will want such relationships. At their best, the working relationships sometimes found between graduate students and their dissertation advisers might approximate what I am describing here. But why not adopt and adapt that structure for undergraduates?

If it is true that the most important virtues are caught and not taught, then surely without concentrated, consistent time with more mature mentors, students will be unable to grow as they might. It is the virtue of liberal arts institutions, and Christian ones in particular, that such programs are possible. They are already in place in some institutions. I believe they are an effective tool for implementing the principle of modeling, which I take to be essential to the goal of developing student maturity.

The Environment

Although the overall environment is not usually seen as a "programmatic" feature of the Christian liberal arts college, I believe it deserves more attention. There can be no doubt that the living-learning environment in which students find themselves at college has a tremendous impact on what they learn and how effectively they learn. In short, the environment is a significant part of the informal curriculum.

By "environment" I mean not only the location of the college campus but the architecture of buildings, the level of noise, the topics and tone of conversations, the orderliness of surroundings, the color of surrounding skins, the accents of friends' voices, and the topics and tone of all college activities; and the list goes on. I cannot possibly comment on most of these important factors. But I want to comment on two features over which most institutions have some control: college-wide activities and community diversity.

College-Wide Activities: Chapel/Convocation

College-wide activities include such programs as the orientation of new students, the celebrations of baccalaureate, commencement, year's end, admissions events, and of course chapel or convocation. Like the formal curriculum, such activities should also embody the spirit of aiming to produce graduates who are critically committed as well as able and willing to tackle real-world problems. This is what it means for such a college to be mission driven. But how often are such activities scrutinized with these eyes? Isn't it true that more often they are shaped and evaluated primarily by pragmatic considerations? Will the students have fun? Will balloons and boisterous behavior make the students feel at home? Will the students feel the mood is too somber? Can the speaker really communicate effectively? Is this the music students enjoy? Are the topics selected currently "hot?"

Of course those pragmatic factors cannot be forgotten lest such programs become irrelevant or, worse yet, self-defeating. A class session or chapel that does not engage students before moving them forward will leave them behind. An admission event that does not recognize how high school students think will fail and ultimately, perhaps, the entire college with it. A chapel program that lines up dusty, unattractive pedants week after week will accomplish little.

But we must never forget that colleges are *educational* institutions. As often as possible they must hold up what their faculty judge to be the very best. The same principles used in the classroom for promoting the college's intrinsic and instrumental goals should be considered for these college-wide activities as well.

Take, for example, the role of chapel/convocation. Chapel/convocation is often, or in some cases at least, a worship activity. But that need not preclude the educational function. It is the largest classroom on campus. In fact, I dare say that function will enhance the worship precisely because worship must always offer the very best we have. Of course there may be significant disagreement about what constitutes the "best" we have to offer. That is where it becomes crucial that the campus community be clear on its distinctives. In all of the preceding chapters, I have argued that the most basic—albeit most general—distinctive of institutions of liberal arts may be to produce graduates who have become critically committed and are willing and able to tackle real-world problems. If critical commitment and the willing ability to tackle real problems are among the highest aims to which the college aspires, then surely, like a carpenter's handiwork, manifesting them can become our worthy worship to God and so have a place in the chapel/convocation "curriculum."

If dissonance, modeling, and community promote development of critical commitment in the classroom and formal curriculum, then why not in chapel/convocation too? First, consider *dissonance*. Should the chapel/convocation program disturb the students? Should it not force them out of their usual ways of thinking and acting? This ought to be true in regard to not only the content of such activities but the style and methods of their presentation as well. If developmental principles hold true, it cannot appeal to something so far beyond them that it is unattractive but rather something that stretches them to the next step.

Second, consider *modeling.* Should not the chapel/convocation program be terribly concerned to put before students not just persons of excellence in communication but persons of excellence in content? Indeed not just persons of excellence in content but persons of excellence and depth of character. Even films on the lives of great souls can do this if followed by discussion. Lest this sound terribly idealistic or impossible, should we not rely heavily on the models we have already hired for students? Should we not rely heavily on our own faculty and staff for chapel/convocation? Otherwise we become guilty again of specialization. We employ professionals for cognitive development, professionals for social development, and professionals for spiritual development. Should we not let students apprentice in spiritual ways as well as cognitive ones? Should we not do all we can to let them see faculty as models of worshiping as well as models of thinking?

Finally, consider *community.* Should not the whole community feel ownership for this program? Will not the absence of this sense of community in a college-wide activity undermine its effectiveness in promoting development? Without community, dissonance is destructive. Community requires something in common and effort must be made to establish and affirm what that is. At some Christian colleges differences in styles of worship among faculty and students may be considerable, but the commitment to worship must not be lost. Ownership means involvement in creating, implementing, and most of all participating in these college-wide activities. Without the consistent presence of faculty and administration, the distinctive mission of the college has been compromised, an opportunity lost, a mixed message sent.

But community and controversy are also principles that promote willingness to tackle problems. These too ought to characterize chapel/convocations. First consider *controversy.* Should not chapel/convocation expose students to real needs in the world? Should it not advance them developmentally and provoke them to consider what they can do about such matters and how they might better equip themselves to such ends? Should not the information they receive there make it easier to *do* something and not just *become* something? Whether one believes worship and controversy can be combined in a single program is not the issue. They may need to be separated. The point is that chapel and convocation, as examples of college-wide informal curriculum, must reflect the institution's goals.

Second, consider *community* . . . again. The way in which community promotes integration in the formal curriculum works equally well here. As in team teaching, why not involve a range of persons from campus and beyond who bring various specialties, various forms of faith, and various methods of practice to bear on real issues. Their very coming together is a form of community. Should this not ensure that theoretical concerns, which often predominate in the classroom, are brought down to reality? Should this not ensure that a faith perspective is apparent on real issues?

Some may object, "But where is Christ in all this?" My point is that our distinctives as a *Christian* liberal arts institution should not be separated from the distinctives characteristic of liberal arts institutions in general. We do not want Christian goals and distinctives for chapel and liberal arts distinctives for the classroom. That's a disaster for both! Rather, our purposes as Christians must pervade our purposes as an educational institution in the liberal arts tradition.

That means that the *content* (object) of the critical commitment we desire for our students will be critical commitment to Jesus Christ and the virtues they acquire will go beyond just those of critical commitment in general. We hope they will become persons of more than just epistemological humility. They will show the fruit of the Spirit . . . love, joy, peace, patience, kindness, goodness, faithfulness, gentleness, and self-control. They will show purity of heart, meekness, peacemaking, hunger for growth, and all the other virtues of the Sermon on the Mount. As liberal arts institutions, we provide an environment conducive to character development and as Christian institutions we teach and model the character of Christ.

Likewise, the *selection* of real-world problems they tackle will focus on those problems that stand in the way of the advancement of Christ's kingdom. That kingdom preaches "sight to the blind, liberty to the captives" . . . "loving justice, showing mercy, walking humbly" . . . "peacemaking" and so on.[48] As liberal arts institutions, we equip graduates to grapple with the problems of society. As Christian institutions, we urge special attention to those that are of priority in the Kingdom.

Furthermore, each institution should consider its own heritage in identifying the content of critical commitment and the selection of real-world problems. Academic communities rooted in traditions of social justice can justifiably organize chapels to encourage the tackling of real-world problems of social justice. Those with traditions of evangelism can structure those programs around the problems of mission.

My point is that insofar as it is our desire and purpose to bring about these specific Christian and community ends in becoming and doing, the Christian college must not forget its more general liberal arts distinctives nor the means that have proven successful in bringing them about. Those liberal arts distinctives must guide the Christian and community distinctives just as the latter must pervade the former.

In summary, chapel/convocation, as but one example of college-wide activities in the informal curriculum, should apply the same mission-driven principles as the formal curriculum. Let me make one final caution. While the college must always offer and model the "best," this cannot be just the best of one culture or group. Without abandoning the objectivity of values at one level, we must recognize that in addition to variations in the *content* of one's critical commitments there are also differences in its *form*. And in addition to variations in the *selection* of real problems there are also differences in *means* for tackling them. That brings me to the second and final example of environmental factors.

Diversity

Diversity has become a buzzword. It has come to mean many things to many people. It is sometimes taken to refer to ethnic or racial diversity. It sometimes refers to religious diversity, or even just temperamental, political, or stylistic diversity. Sometimes it is thought to threaten standards. And in some cases it is a thinly disguised label for relativistic ethics and even godless existentialism. For others it is the path to excellence as well as to equity. I take diversity to be of many kinds, as I will elaborate below. But I believe that diversity—within the confines of institutional mission—promotes the goals of producing graduates who are critically committed as well as able and willing to tackle real problems.

I suspect this is an area of serious danger among Christian liberal arts colleges. Often founded by denominations, the colleges sometimes remain too narrowly homogeneous. Students often come largely from the same region of the country, largely the same socioeconomic class, the same racial group, the same political persuasions, the same denominational background, and even the same style of worship. In short, the students are often members of the same narrow subculture.

This homogeneity is not without its virtues. It reduces the secondary problems of adjustment for students already stressed by leaving home. It amplifies, as one African-American student pointed out, the actual benefit of what diversity does exist because subgroups simply cannot avoid interaction by hiding behind radical incompatibilities and retreating so easily into separate enclaves. It permits the examination of finer shades of differences in opinion, which in turn promotes discrimination in the best sense of the word. As Thomas Kuhn has pointed out, there is a proper place for narrowness of focus even in science. Exclusive focus on one paradigm extends and applies it more efficiently, systematizing the beliefs and values shared, checking for coherence. And of course *when combined with the proper attitudes of self-examination,* the same narrow focus reveals much more quickly the flaws in the prevailing paradigms.

However, if we grant the distinctive goals of promoting critical commitment and equipping graduates to tackle real-world problems and if we grant the effectiveness of dissonance, controversy, and modeling as means to attain those goals, then the value of diversity becomes clear.

Dissonance and Controversy

When there is diversity, dissonance and controversy is much more likely, and with it a greater likelihood of developing critical commitment. But what kind of diversity is needed?[49] Most importantly, there must be diversity of mind. There need to be differences of opinion about politics, film, theater, economics, music, styles of worship, medical ethics, social justice, epistemology, metaphysics, and even hermeneutics and theology. There should be clubs for Republicans and Democrats; outreach teams and Habitat for Humanity; summer mission fellowship and philosophy clubs; praise bands, rock bands, jazz bands, and string ensembles; Salvationists, Episcopalians, and even a Newman Club. Public faculty panels should be frequent and exciting. In short, the environment should welcome different points of view.

Diversity may or may not be accomplished by including persons of different racial or national origin. Usually, however, this does make a great difference. It usually forces everyone to reexamine more basic assumptions than they would otherwise. When students discuss workfare as a constructive alternative to welfare, those from poorer economic classes might uncover and challenge an assumption that welfare recipients are lazy. When justice and consistency and law are used as models for government, those who have known oppression can give tangible examples of how these have been misused inhumanely. When faculty discuss promoting the very best in art or culture, an international colleague can interject, "Whose 'best culture' are you referring to?" Gender diversity can do the same. Tremendous dissonance can arise when a faculty colleague suggests that the problem at hand should not be addressed by logical analysis but by attention to relationships. The perspective of both genders can be dramatically different. Carol Gilligan's criticism of Kohlberg's stages of moral development is just one well-known example. It seems obvious to me that the presence of such diversity of mind promotes a dissonance that can contribute to the development of critical commitment.

The presence of persons of color, a healthy balance of men and women, and variations of temperament, style, and so on also contribute to equipping students to tackle real-world problems. In the first place, the world is diverse whether their college institution is or not. Sooner or later, students will have to come to terms with this diversity if they hope to address real problems. They will be much farther ahead if their collegiate experience is diverse. Second, the kind of flexibility of approach they learn from working with persons of wide differences will better equip them for problem solving in all kinds of situations.

Modeling

Finally, I believe that the presence of diversity within the educational community is essential because it implements the principle of modeling. We have seen that modeling is crucial to development. If there are no models of women scholars, women students will be handicapped in their own development. If there are no models of black or Latino faculty, students of all colors will be handicapped, especially, of course, those who are black or Latino. If there are no models of faculty from formal liturgical or informal liturgical traditions, the students will be impoverished. We need to hire faculty of color. We need to admit and facilitate the inclusion of students of color. We need to cultivate international connections as a source of students and of visiting faculty. These things cost money. But the presence of a foreign faculty member even for a short time can have impact on lives far beyond what we can imagine.

Diversity in Community

I am not suggesting that this principle of diversity be taken to its extreme. Every Christian college must be faithful to its mission. Interestingly, the regional accreditation associations (e.g., WASC and MSA), to the chagrin of many from more politically correct institutions, have insisted in strong and unambiguous terms that each college must diversify, but only within the confines of own mission. Those that are charged to represent the demographics of a state must, of course, do so. Those that stand for distinctive religious beliefs need not hire atheists, homosexuals, or even persons of different religious traditions, for example. That allowance for distinctive mission extends even to admissions. So I am not suggesting that we would be truer to our principles as a Christian liberal arts college if we required our faculty and student body to match the diversity of the entire world, or even our country or state.

But I am suggesting that the informal curriculum will be more effective in accomplishing those principles to the extent that we make the environment diverse in every way we can. Can even the most conservative Protestant colleges be so bold as to consider short-term visiting faculty who are Catholic? Could Christian colleges consider short-term visiting faculty who are atheists? What about speakers who represent "the opposition"? Is even that too threatening? I hope not. What about films, art, music? All these can be used to create a diverse environment that is enriching educationally because it promotes dissonance, controversy, and modeling of alternatives.

But what is crucial is that in spite of diversity there must be community. Because diversity clearly embodies the principles of dissonance and controversy, it cannot be separated from the compensatory principle of community. By that I mean that if we have *only* a group of faculty, students, and staff who are different, then diversity becomes a force largely for division, not growth. In other words, diversity will be educationally effective only so long as it remains within the bounds of what defines the community. Disagreement with "outsiders" is brushed off and can entrench thinking and stunt growth.

The trade-off is plain. The broader the defining constraints of the community, the greater the opportunity for diversity and hence for the growth it produces. But by the same token, the broader the community, the less pervasive its effect in shaping development because of the greater likelihood members will dismiss the diversity as "them" rather than "us." On the other hand, the narrower, more sharply defined the community, the more effectively it affects its members' lives, but the less likely it is to find the breadth of diversity that stimulates growth. The critical tension both faculty and administrators must embrace is how to balance these two opposing forces to maximize student development.

Some have said that concepts like multicultural community and diverse community are self-contradictory. I disagree. But unless there is a clearly defined common unity, a clearly articulated, oft-repeated, regularly celebrated, concretely illustrable "tie that binds," diversity will not promote the intrinsic and instrumental values I believe should characterize the Christian liberal arts college. Faculty of different liturgical styles must worship together. Faculty of different gender perspectives must talk about them openly. Faculty of different temperament must affirm one another. Students of different ethnic backgrounds must spend time together as well as apart. Recognizing the compensatory principle of community is yet another illustration of how diversity, like all the other suggestions in this chapter, must be guided and supervised by mission. Diversity without community, like experience without reflection, *cannot* promote education.

This discussion of diversity as a principle to characterize the environment and therefore the informal curricular *program* of our campuses has actually been as much about *people* as programs. Let us now turn to that more directly.

10

How Can People
Promote Christian Liberal Arts?

In this chapter, I return to what I believe is the more important way in which institutional distinctives are put into practice: *people*. The people who constitute a Christian liberal arts college community will make it what it is—not only classroom faculty but also administrators, supporting staff of all kinds, and the students themselves. If I were more thorough and energetic, I would discuss the ways in which administration, staff, and students, as well as faculty, must embody and implement the distinctive characteristics of the Christian liberal arts college. Much could be said about how administrators and staff ought to be hired differently, oriented differently, reinforced differently, and assigned differently because the institution in which they work is a Christian liberal arts college, not a church, not a camp, not even a secular university. Furthermore, there is also much that could be said about how students should be admitted differently, oriented differently, reinforced differently, and advised differently because they attend such a college. But at the risk of parochialism, I will limit myself to the classroom faculty. I believe they are the heart of the institution. They are certainly the sine qua non, without which there is no educational institution. They should comprise a community of scholar-teachers. I would like to make some suggestions related to each of these three terms (scholars, teachers, and community) separately, even though I do not believe they can actually be separated.

SCHOLARS

The nature of the professoriate has become the subject of as much debate as that of curriculum. I agree with Ernest Boyer when he says that "liberal arts colleges provide an especially supportive climate for the scholarship of integration."[1] I have given my reasons above; integration is the key to enabling students to tackle real-world problems. Furthermore, I have explained there that I believe integration means integration of disciplines, of faith and learning, and of theory and practice. In short, I believe there is a distinctive kind of scholarship that ought to be found at Christian liberal arts colleges. It should go beyond both dabbling and esoteric scholarship; it should be integrative. But now I would like to explore what it takes to equip faculty at Christian liberal arts colleges to do this distinctive kind of scholarship. I want to group my suggestions about scholarship around the ideas of faculty hiring and faculty development.

Faculty Hiring

Hiring is absolutely crucial. As one university president told me, "Hire smart or manage tough." If we want faculty who will provide students with a liberal education, it seems obvious that they themselves must be liberally educated.[2] When they are not (and often they are not), a dean must be sure that they are willing to become liberally educated through both their scholarship and their teaching. If not, the distinctives of the liberal arts college are doomed from the outset. This is obvious, but I am afraid it is often ignored. If colleges are serious about recognizing and affirming their distinctives, they should be hiring faculty who match those distinctives. Community colleges should not hire like liberal arts colleges. And liberal arts colleges should not hire like universities. The problem is that they all seem to hire like Harvard! If integrative scholarship is the kind sought, then perhaps the following suggestions should be considered.

Student and Teaching Oriented

First, hire faculty whose vision of their scholarship is student and teaching oriented, not primarily research, publication, or performance oriented. The faculty member whose scholarship is primarily student and teaching oriented will be sensitive to the developmental needs of the student. Her scholarship will be predominantly a means to this end.

Some have said that putting the matter this way is simplistic. It mistakenly makes student and research orientations mutually exclusive. I agree wholeheartedly that they should not be made exclusive of one another. Those who hold such a dualistic view will typically choose one or the other. Some choose teaching and become the preintegrative dilettantes who should be avoided by academically serious Christian colleges. There must be a love for truth and for the ways faculty have learned to discover and create it within their disciplines. The others choose research and become esoteric disciplinarians like those found on most secular campuses. Page Smith offers a disheartening look at what comes of this excessive "publish-or-perish" mentality in his chapter by that name in *Killing the Spirit.*

But if scholarship and teaching are not exclusive, then their relative weight and, more importantly, the kind of scholarship practiced must reflect the distinctives of the college. It should be plain that I am talking about a question of priority, not exclusivity. Is the student secondary, a means to research and publication ends? Or is it the other way around? I believe that what is distinctive about the liberal arts college, and especially the Christian one, is that the scholarship will serve the student and the teaching. The faculty will be teachers of philosophy and not philosophers who teach, teachers of science and not scientists who teach, teachers of art and not artists who teach. The distinction is subtle and controversial but important. This must be made very clear to faculty candidates but often it is not. "They all hire like Harvard!"

Some attempt to excuse a dominant research orientation in candidates by saying that research makes better teachers. I don't buy the argument. Research does not automatically make for better teachers. As Page Smith puts it, "The notion that research enhances teaching, although thoroughly discredited by experience *and* research, is one that lingers on and is often trotted out by the ill-informed as a justification for the publish-or-perish policy."[3] He cites at least two studies that he says "directly contradict" this claim.

> Martin Finkelstein, in a study made in 1984, declared that he had been unable to find any grounds for the proposition that "good research is both a necessary and sufficient condition for good teaching." The facts were quite otherwise. He reached the conclusion that "research involvement detracts from good teaching. . . ." Hugh Brown and Lewis Mayhew in American Higher Education reached a similar conclusion. The fact is, they wrote, that, "whenever studies of teaching effectively are made as judged by students, no relationship is found between judged teaching effectiveness and research productivity."[4]

I believe that deans and department chairs must be unusually cautious that this subtle argument does not upset the distinctive priorities of the Christian liberal arts college.

It is also not enough to substitute student involvement in research for student-oriented research. Even the program of student involvement in research—much touted in the sciences—must be scrutinized. It can become a cover for using student labor to promote what are primarily research priorities not necessarily in the best interests of the students. They become narrow researchers cloned after their graduate school–trained instructors. The question we come back to is whether the research is primarily a means to the end of student development along the lines of critical commitment and the ability to tackle real-world problems. But this brings us naturally to the question of the nature of such scholarship.

Institution Orientation, Not Guild Orientation

Second, hire faculty who are institution oriented and not guild oriented. The first principle of putting priority on students addresses the goal of scholarship at liberal arts colleges. This principle of putting institution ahead of guild shapes the distinctive kind of scholarship that faculty candidates should be encouraged and even expected to pursue.

Just as the first principle of hiring promotes student development, this second principle promotes the other major distinctive goal of the Christian liberal arts college: to equip graduates to tackle real-world problems. Those problems typically integrate many disciplines, as well as faith and learning, with theory and practice. So the distinctive scholarship of faculty at such institutions should be integrative. Beginning with real-world problems, the scholarship brings together the best from many guilds, methods, conclusions, and perspectives. It does not fail to consider how distinctively Christian values inform the problem and either expand or restrict the solutions available that are consistent with revelation. Finally, it never overlooks the practical questions of how this scholarship can have a practical impact on the lives of real people. All of this makes the scholarship truly integrative.

I am not trying to say that every faculty candidate for every Christian college must limit his or her scholarly activities to projects exclusively of this sort. But I am saying that unless there is a substantial mass of faculty scholarship of this kind, the institution is in danger of failing to distinguish itself from other non-Christian and non–liberal arts colleges all around.

In addressing the question of the kind of scholarship that is consistent with making students the priority (my first principle above), Page Smith makes the following provocative comment:

> It is my contention that the best research and the only research that should be expected of university professors is wide and informed reading in their fields and in related fields. The best teachers are almost invariably the most widely informed, those with the greatest range of interests and the most cultivated minds. That is real research, and that, and that alone, enhances teaching.[5]

I have already described such integrative scholarship in an earlier chapter and I will make a few suggestions on how to promote it among faculty in the section below on faculty development.

Of course the catch in all this is to operationalize these two principles. How can those who make hiring decisions judge these things? It seems to me that what candidates do is more important than what they say. The track record of potential candidates should be examined closely. Have they published esoterically or integratively? Have they taught narrowly or integratively? What use have they made of sabbaticals? What variety have they built into their background? In the case of new graduates, what are their dreams?

What courses do they long to teach? What projects of scholarship would they like to undertake? It seems to me the answers to these kinds of questions, taken of course in the context of the environment from which they come, will make it easier to know whether this potential faculty member will contribute to the distinctive goals of the liberal arts college.

What saddens me about saying all this is that I am certain it will be misunderstood. It will be taken as a throwback to the days when liberal arts colleges, and especially Christian ones, tolerated a level of mediocrity that is unacceptable. I have labored throughout this book to resist the idea that there are only two choices—mediocre scholarship with teaching orientation and excellent scholarship with an esoteric focus. I have argued that what makes a Christian college distinctive is that it seeks to go beyond both. If my case for colleges to help their graduates become critically committed and to equip them to tackle real-world problems has not been made, then this call for hiring integrative scholars will fall on deaf ears.

Joint Appointments

Third, consider whether joint appointments may reduce the isolation of academic departments. Some have suggested that if disciplinary overspecialization is a major problem, we ought to solve it by eliminating departments altogether or by combining and renaming them under new rubrics. There may be some value in this but there is also great danger. The risk is that this "antidisciplinarianism" will undermine the foundation for doing the distinctive scholarship I am calling for. Without departments, disciplinary competence may be neglected. And without disciplinary competence, scholarship may lapse back into the dabbling I have referred to as "preintegration." There must be differences of framework and approach before anything can be integrated at all.

We ought to consider joint appointments instead. This will give a greater sensitivity to broader issues—the real-world problems—to the individuals hired. It will enlarge their perspective of what is worth studying. And it will set the stage for their own professional development as they learn from colleagues who may have different graduate training. It may reduce "turf consciousness" and give faculty a greater level of ownership for the distinctive mission of the institution. And if joint appointments cause administrative nightmares, then perhaps deans and chairs might at least make load assignments across departmental lines.

Open to Change

Finally, be sure to hire faculty who are open to change. A candidate who has progressed in his or her personal development to a stage beyond both dogmatism and skepticism is obviously preferable. If he or she does not already show evidence of student and institutional orientation, there needs to be evidence of an openness to accommodating the needs of the institution. Is he ready to join a "team"? Is the institution a means to her career ends or is she called to serve Christ through serving students in this place? What place does the institution play in his priorities? Are these even issues he recognizes as issues in the first place? Finally, this crucial attitude is important not only because of what it says about the faculty member's own development, and about her potential to adjust, but also because "openness" is an attitude that often signals the presence of another cluster of attitudes that are essential to building community. These include a willingness to listen, to withhold judgment, and to be flexible.

Faculty Development

Besides hiring the right faculty, it is crucial to encourage them to remain and to grow.

Promotion and Tenure Criteria

First, faculty promotion and tenure criteria concerning scholarship should reflect the distinctive institutional goals of integration and critical commitment. It seems to me that the present structures of faculty reward and recognition for scholarship often lean too heavily in one of two directions.

In some cases this is toward the criteria one would find on a secular university campus. Often publication is emphasized and sometimes the quality and nature of the publication is less important than it should be. I have described some of this tendency toward narrow and self-serving publication above. Articles have even been written about extending one's publication list with the least amount of effort as promotion and tenure reviews approach. There is lip service to teaching and sometimes real attention by promotion committees to the student evaluations so conveniently quantifiable as a measure of success. But the real agenda when it comes to scholarship, too often even in Christian colleges, is the number of published articles in refereed journals. One cannot help wondering, first, whether such evaluation has skipped over the issue of teaching without really making it a priority, without really taking a close look, and, second, whether the measure even of scholarship has been inappropriately construed. Where are the institutional distinctives in the judgment of the kind of scholarship?

In other cases, the criteria for promotion and tenure hardly mention scholarship at all. Or if they do, they make it so peripheral compared with teaching that one wonders if faculty are expected to remain intellectually active at all. Sometimes, in this situation, the argument is made that with heavy teaching and committee loads there is simply no time for scholarship. Although this is often true (more below), sometimes it reflects the misunderstanding that scholarship can only be done in narrow disciplinary ways and allows us to conclude that integration is merely treating students right and praying before class instead of modeling the active process of grappling with new problems ourselves. If promotion and tenure criteria do not include scholarship and expect faculty to cover new intellectual ground themselves but allows teaching to rehash old issues— however innovatively that may be done—a significant opportunity is lost to shape the institution in the direction of the distinctive goals of integration and development.

If Christian colleges make integration a goal, then why not require all faculty to show evidence they have stepped outside their training and background to expand their own perspectives? Why not require all faculty as a condition of tenure to write an integrative paper, to participate in some significant cross-cultural experience, preferably long-term and preferably related to the educational process?

If development is also a goal for students, why not ensure that faculty will experience the same kind of dissonance we might use to develop our students? For example, why not expect all faculty members to demonstrate their scholarship each year by presenting a colloquium to their own department or to the college as a whole? The stimulation to develop would be as important to them personally as the scholarly accountability would be to the institution.

If teaching is really the priority, then the definition of what counts as appropriate scholarship should include the writing of textbooks, the revision of syllabi, and the reviewing of books related to coursework. Stanford University has taken these kinds of steps, even limiting the number of scholarly pieces a professor can submit for promotion or tenure review. Presumably this is with the hope that the quality of what is published will be improved and that more time can be devoted to teaching.[6] Syracuse University has also taken steps with revised guidelines for promotion and tenure considerations.[7] "Paradoxically, as research universities emphasize teaching, campuses where professors mainly teach are pushing faculty members to do more scholarly work."[8]

It would be a shame for liberal arts colleges, and especially Christian ones, to lag behind on a matter so much nearer to their distinctive strengths than even Stanford. Fortunately, there are leaders. Evergreen State College and Roberts College both use teaching very heavily in personnel decisions.[9]

Francis Oakley, president of Williams College, has responded to what he judges to be overstated criticisms of American higher education. He argues that critics like Alan Bloom, Charles Sykes, Page Smith, and others often fail to present an adequately nuanced account of the present situation. Such critics do not put their criticisms in the appropriate context. They are "silent" about the vast amount of statistical data that witnesses to profound transformations in the variety of institutions, students, and faculty over the past thirty years or more. He is not convinced that faculty themselves are fleeing teaching for research or that overspecialization has become a problem. But Oakley admits that the data *do* support the problem that I am addressing here and the one I raised in part II. There is a mysterious gap between what faculty and even administrators say they want by way of priorities and what they believe actually exists. He says, "The research-oriented incentive and reward structure dominant in the academy appears at least to be poorly aligned with what most faculty are doing, want to do, and believe it to be their mission to do."

He agrees that it is hard to resist Ernest Boyer's conclusion that "the research mission, . . . appropriate for *some* institutions [has] created a shadow over the entire higher learning enterprise" and that "far too many colleges and universities are being driven not by self-defined objectives but by external imperatives of prestige."[10]

In other words, even if it is not true that faculty themselves are abandoning teaching for research, at least the criteria by which they are judged are pushing them that way.[11] So I believe it is absolutely crucial—a top priority—that these criteria reflect the distinctive institutional goals.

Professional Development Contracts

Second, faculty should be encouraged to enter into professional development contracts that reflect integrative and developmental goals. Such contracts can take into account the differences not only between faculty with different kinds of interests but also the important and often overlooked cycles within any particular scholar's own career. As Roger Baldwin says, "Higher education should acknowledge the changing character of these periods and help professors travel through successfully."[12] There will be some whose scholarship may include a significant amount of publication, others for whom curricular matters will dominate, and others still for whom institutional matters may be a major concern. And any of these may be the focus for a particular faculty member at different stages of his or her time at an institution. I believe it is important to acknowledge these differences and variations more openly and to reconcile them with the distinctive institutional mission as much as hiring.

When faculty recognize that what they are doing is explicitly recognized as making a direct contribution to the institutional mission, it is liberating. Faculty need no longer feel the strain and even the paralysis that can come from the self-contradictory task of focusing on all aspects of their job at once. Ernest Boyer calls them "creativity contracts" and calls on colleges and universities to use them to help faculty define their professional goals for three to five years at a time. He goes on to say that "down the road, we can see the day when staying with one dimension of scholarship—without a break—

would be considered the exception, not the rule."[13] There are a number of such plans already at work even in Christian liberal arts colleges, so it is not necessary to reinvent the wheel.[14]

The nature of the scholarship proposed should be consistent with the integrative and developmental goals of the institution. I do not mean that all scholarly work must be interdisciplinary or integrative of faith and learning or practical and applied. Some strictly disciplinary scholarship will be essential if faculty are to be equipped to go beyond dabbling as I have described in the last part. But I do believe there must be enough evidence of some scholarship of one of these kinds from every faculty member to distinguish them from scholars outside the Christian liberal arts tradition. And I do believe it is always appropriate to ask how it relates to the end of promoting the development of students.

Among the obvious examples of this kind of scholarship are projects that involve the creation of curricular materials. Such materials should constitute legitimate scholarship at Christian liberal arts colleges, particularly as they reflect the goal of students' cognitive, moral, and faith development toward critical commitment. There is a need for textbooks written by Christians as well as anthologies of readings for almost every discipline. Often the anthologies prepared by non-Christians omit readings that Christians might wish to use to provide the contrasts of worldviews essential for the faith and learning component of integration. Software development can also be a legitimate form of scholarship. I will say more about the link between teaching and scholarship in the major section on teaching below.

Scholarship should also include the work faculty do to keep themselves abreast of the developments in their discipline. I have already cited Page Smith's view that this is the "only research that should be expected of university professors."[15] Although Smith overstates the case, his remark underscores not only the legitimacy of this kind of scholarship but also its centrality. As I have tried to say before, Christian scholarship should go beyond; it should not be preintegrative or subdisciplinary but postintegrative or supradisciplinary. To do this, there *must* be a disciplinary foundation. Without it, there is risk of dilettantism. I believe one of the best ways for faculty to remain "up to speed" in their own field is to review current publications in their field.

Thus I believe a strong professional development contract at Christian liberal arts colleges will almost always include expectations for the publication by faculty of book reviews. It is a relatively simple way to ensure that faculty have and retain the basic tools necessary for moving on to tackle distinctively integrative issues in their classes and other research. Typically, once faculty find themselves commenting in print on the work others have done, it will be a relatively small step to move on to writing critical reviews, then critical studies, and of course articles of their own. So the book review not only can serve to ensure that faculty are abreast of their own field but can encourage further intellectual ferment and work. If the books and articles reviewed are chosen with care, the work will not only complement the teaching of the disciplinary courses but will move the faculty member in the direction of greater integration in all three senses I have described.

Faculty Loads

Third, faculty loads should be carefully examined to accommodate scholarly activity of all kinds and to ensure that faculty can realistically be expected to function as models for students. In a 1989 survey conducted jointly by the American Council on Education (ACE) and the University of California at Los Angeles (UCLA), faculty at private four-year colleges reported that the two greatest sources of personal stress—both of them far more significant than any other sources—were time pressures and lack of a personal life. Since my major theme in this volume has been to argue that Christian liberal arts colleges must go beyond what other institutions do, it would be criminal to fail to recognize the demands this places on faculty.

I believe faculty at Christian liberal arts colleges have carried a heavier load than colleagues at other kinds of institutions.[16] Faculty at large universities usually have fewer preparations, more teaching assistants, fewer expectations for wholistic education to compensate for demands for research and publication. Community college faculty do not have research and publication demands nor usually the expectation for involvement in students' lives, and this compensates for higher student numbers and greater numbers of preparations. But faculty at Christian liberal arts colleges are expected to do it all.

The teaching load has typically been high both in terms of the number of preparations and often in terms of the number of students.[17] And some might say the load is all the greater because excellence in teaching has been an advertised distinctive. In addition, such faculty have been expected to participate much more extensively in student advising and in the personal lives of their students. Expectations for administrative involvement has also been greater, perhaps, than at public institutions, with more than one committee assignment often the rule. It has often been assumed that the trade-off has been the lack of pressure to publish. But as we have seen, that is changing. How can they survive?

I believe administrators and faculty committees must study this problem carefully. There is an obvious need to be sure faculty are being productive. Without such productivity, small institutions, especially, may simply go out of business. But the following kinds of activities must be taken into account in setting faculty loads: advising time when student majors are numerous; laboratory preparation and time when assistants are not available; examination and assignment marking time when class size is large; differences among the work and time loads of various committee assignments; participation in college-wide activities such as speaking at orientation, chapel, community, and commencement events; and outside activities that are encouraged and that enhance the college's reputation and/or visibility.

And I think colleges must be cautious of addressing this problem by providing additional compensation for added tasks. Although it does have the advantage of resolving inequities in the distribution of faculty loads and is no doubt appropriate in limited contexts, as a panacea, added compensation can easily become counterproductive. The compensation of faculty at Christian colleges needs to be closely examined. Even though expectations for a self-sacrificial attitude may be both necessary and beneficial at such institutions, they should not mask manipulativeness or inequitable demands when compared with other persons or programs at the same institutions. Faculty compensation needs to be the very highest priority. There are two problems: compensation and load. The problem with addressing overload strictly with compensation is that it becomes a trap for faculty. Solving one problem exacerbates the other. With too many projects, too many tasks, faculty become too busy and harried to do any of them well. And even if the urgent tasks are completed, what about the important ones? What about the quality of preparation, time for reflection and reading, relaxed interaction with students, time with their children and family? Can faculty be models of persons mature in their own development and engaged in tackling real-world problems when their greatest source of stress is time pressure and lack of personal life? Unless we put tangible value on the amount of time faculty spend, the distinctive goals of the Christian liberal arts college will not be met.

A better approach, I believe, is to compensate overload with unload. I believe preparation reductions, course reductions, committee assignment reductions, minisabbaticals, sabbaticals, and leaves of absence all serve much more effectively to address problems of load than proliferation of stipends. These must be brought to bear on a case-by-case basis in consultation between faculty and those asked to hold both faculty and administration accountable to reasonable expectations of load. It would likely take the form of "load contracts" forming a part of the "professional development contracts" mentioned above.

Although such considerations of load will necessarily complicate life for deans and department chairs, that may be the cost of equipping faculty to perform the distinctive roles to which they are called at Christian liberal arts colleges. Taken together with professional development contracts, I believe it can be one of the most effective ways of affirming faculty who may otherwise feel unappreciated and incapacitated by unrealistic expectations.

Opportunities for Integrative Scholarship

Fourth, Christian liberal arts colleges should provide opportunities for integrative scholarship not found anywhere else. If Christian colleges are actually going to go beyond their sister institutions in academia, there must be evidence of this in tangibly distinct programs.

For example, I think it would be exciting for Christian colleges that are serious about being distinctive to operate what might be called integrative studies institutes. The idea is not new.[18] They could be planned for the summer or even during term. The institute would focus on a theme selected by faculty because it embodies all three dimensions of integration: multiple disciplines, faith and learning, and theory and practice. For example, there might be institutes on violence, on development and ecology, on equity and excellence in academe, on the meaning of multicultural community. The prospects are exciting to imagine. Each institute would involve a small group (perhaps only ten or twelve) of faculty from a range of disciplines, together perhaps—but not necessarily—with a distinguished Christian scholar from elsewhere. The participants might be selected on the basis of applications submitted to an appropriate faculty committee once the topic had been announced.

Faculty would be paid a stipend to compensate for the investment of time. If it were in the summer, this might, for example, free faculty from the need to teach in summer school for financial reasons. If it were during the term, a course load reduction would be appropriate. Funds would also be available to purchase books that the participants agree are essential shared texts. If during the summer, a significant period of time, from four to eight weeks, would be set aside.

If possible the participants, and even their families, might find a place isolated or immersed—depending on the issue—that would stimulate interaction. Days would be scheduled around joint discussions/seminars and time for reading and writing.

At the end, and as part of the expectation for a stipend or release time, faculty would write on the theme of the institute. It seems likely that many if not all of these results would be publishable either in independent media or by the college itself in an ongoing series of proceedings. I can imagine the benefit of such publications to Christians around the world. But of course the benefit to the students these faculty teach would be the greatest. As the faculty themselves learn what integration really means, they are much more able to practice it and model it for those students. The education the students receive will be much more likely to be the distinctive one I have envisioned.

I believe that such a program embodies a number of the principles I have suggested for implementing the distinctive goals of Christian liberal arts. Because the participants would be from various disciplines, there would inevitably be the dissonance and controversy that arises when persons with different perspectives and frameworks attempt to communicate. That dissonance would be as productive of growth for faculty as it would be for students. If the choice of outside scholar is considered carefully, that person can be a model of integration and critical commitment. If the length of the institute and even its location is right, a powerful sense of community can emerge. In discussing the need for Christian colleges to educate for community, Roberta Hestenes, former president of Eastern College, seems to agree: "research should be done more in teams. Teams of scholars working together on common themes and concerns have a better chance to model community, to discover things that need to be discovered, and to exhibit something of what Christian education ought to be about."[19]

In short, I believe that the idea of integrative institutes can provide for the expression of the unique distinctives of Christian liberal arts colleges. They can do something needed but unlikely in the larger universities. They can provide "think tanks" to help discover critical commitment and integration. They may help academia in general reclaim what Wordsworth called "the feeling intellect." This is a service such colleges can provide to the Church and to academia as whole.[20]

Another suggestion is that faculty in Christian liberal arts colleges should regularly participate and present in departmental and college-wide colloquia. I have in mind here a periodic occasion when members of a department would each be expected to present something to their colleagues. Suppose there are three members in a small philosophy department. Each member would be expected—it becomes part of the job description—to make an hour-long presentation to the other two members once a year. It would be designed primarily for colleagues in the discipline. It might focus on that faculty member's ongoing research in a particular topic. It might consist in a summary and critical analysis of several months of reading in the discipline. It might also, as Ernest Boyer suggests, consist in reporting on what the faculty member judges to be the "two or three most important new developments or significant new articles in their fields."[21] There should be ample time for genuine interaction, not just the token "are there any questions?" that sometimes follow faculty forums. Although students majoring in the discipline might be invited, the colloquium should not be aimed at them. Although colleagues in other departments would probably be invited, again, the focus should not primarily be on communicating to them.

The reader might object that this suggestion seems to fly directly in the face of the ideas developed above that scholarship should always be student oriented and bridges to colleagues should be built in team teaching. But on the contrary, I think that such colloquia actually accomplish both ideas better by *not* focusing on students and colleagues directly.

The fact is that for faculty who attend, colloquia such as I describe would promote cognitive dissonance as they work hard to integrate what they hear from another discipline into their own thinking. Like the program of team teaching, this kind of event promotes the integration that faculty themselves often lack but certainly need to help students do the same.

Without regular contexts for such stimulation, many faculty simply will not grow and will never go beyond their own graduate school training to acquire the distinctive skills they need to operate in the distinctive Christian liberal arts environment. And of course faculty will inevitably build community through encounters of this kind. Furthermore, it will more likely be the community of learning—the community of scholarship—that should distinguish an educational institution.

For students who attend, such colloquia would model true integration. They may not be able to follow the presentation completely and they may be surprised at the vigorous misunderstandings and struggles even other faculty have in translating the issues. But this will give them tangible examples of what real integration means. Often the hardest part is bridging the gaps from one perspective to another, and we do not give students enough examples of what this really is like. They will see the struggle "in the flesh" and realize that it is much if not most of what it means to be liberally educated. They will also see the attitudes of conviction with humility and critical commitment modeled by faculty they know and respect.

Regular college-wide colloquia are, of course, also desirable. Many institutions already have them. They might focus on broader topics and be integrated into themes set for the entire institution for a semester. But I believe these programs are no substitute for the need to have regular accountability within departments or divisions for ongoing growth in disciplinary foundations and integrative development.

Personal Attitudes and Commitments

Fifth, and finally, faculty should be reminded of the value of, and be encouraged to grow in, the development of their own personal attitudes and commitments. This is a pretty vague practical suggestion. I have described critical commitment as a major goal for students in Christian liberal arts colleges. But I have also made it clear that this is partly a matter of holding commitments and partly of how they are held—partly content and partly attitude. I have said that modeling is a crucial principle for accomplishing this. Finally, I have confessed that we who are faculty at such colleges may not have developed ourselves sufficiently to be the models we ought to be. Some of the suggestions above for scholarship will address this deficiency. But the problem is broad and this suggestion is probably little more than a wistful catchall.

I remember a lesson I learned in boot camp. I was the cocky graduate student among high school grads and college undergrads. I had quickly learned to play the "game." I regularly and disdainfully "beat the system." My shoes were polished and lined up with the edge of the bed. The bed was tightly tucked, and the floor was slippery with Lemon Pledge. My trouser zippers were zipped under the shirts on the hangers that were precisely spaced two inches apart. And the "gig sheets" were tucked in the front-buttoned pockets. When the major (yes, it was a major) did the inspection, he paused in front of me and, watching me out of the corner of his eye, tapped a shoe out of line. "Take two for misaligned shoes!" Still watching me stand at stiff attention, he smeared the spotless mirror and said, "Take two more for a dirty mirror." Two demerits ("gigs") meant forty-five minutes marching alone on the hot asphalt on Saturday morning while everyone else was in town. When I entered his office immediately after inspection and inquired about why he had been so grossly unfair, he said, "Mannoia, I can see you can do whatever you set your mind to do. But in the military, we care about more than performance; we care about attitude, and you have an attitude." I'm not sure what stunned me most, the fact that he was right or the fact that an apparently unsophisticated military man had reflected so thoroughly on human nature and education.

The kind of faculty we want at Christian liberal arts colleges need to "perform," but they also need to have an "attitude." We want to be faculty who do scholarship, who do teaching, who do hold integrative commitments with a critical perspective. But we want to be faculty who do so with attitudes that include epistemological humility. I have described this attitude more fully in chapter 3.

Skepticism and intellectual arrogance, problems of belief and attitude, may be endemic to academia. Thus in Christian colleges we all—colleagues, deans, administrators—want to do whatever we can to cultivate faculty who have actually drawn conclusions, professors who actually "profess" something but also embody the passion, the meekness, the tolerance, the open-mindedness, and the examining, humble attitude distinctive to Christian liberal arts.

The aim of cultivating faculty who profess something challenges the "myth of neutrality."[22] As Elton Trueblood puts it,

> Actually nobody is objective. Everybody has a perspective, a worldview. And one's worldview is taken on faith, it is not proven. . . . The claim that scholars can be impartial or neutral in anything of human importance is now an outmoded idea. . . . What is important, in intellectual honesty, is that basic assumptions or perspectives should be understood, admitted, and cogently defended. . . . Students have a right to know what the positions are which professors take on major issues.[23]

Without this, faculty themselves will not be liberally educated.[24] Amherst College recognized this clearly fifty years ago.

> In the first place, no teacher worthy of the name can avoid having convictions on vital issues, and no teacher can actually succeed in hiding these convictions from his students no matter how hard he may try to do so. Secondly, the student is much less likely to be victimized by the professor's beliefs if they are stated

openly and if the student is told, as he should be, that he is under obligation to accept them or reject them only on his own responsibility and at his own peril. . . . Thirdly, we believe that students should be made to realize that responsible men DO make up their minds, however tentatively, on questions of importance and that men are under moral obligation to do so.[25]

The pluralism of faculty disagreeing about real views they hold is what the community—and students in particular—need to see. When they see "that the most trusted adults and the most venerable disciplines of knowledge (even the natural sciences) must each compose reality in a pluralistic and relativized world," students begin to understand the importance of making commitments themselves.[26]

Arthur Holmes talks of cultivating faculty with the right attitude. He says students "need a teacher as a catalyst and guide, one who has struggled and is struggling with similar questions."[27] James Fowler and Sam Keen call it the need to show "vulnerability."[28] It is a set of related attitudes—passion, meekness, tolerance, open-mindedness, curiosity, humility, and more. These are attitudes that should permeate all aspects of the faculty members' life.

Christian colleges should encourage their faculty to form their own positions on difficult issues by identifying those who have done so and affirming them. If occasions for exchange such as I have suggested above are too few, the chances of this will be slim. Furthermore, means should be found for communicating to their colleagues the positions faculty have taken. Finally, colleges should provide an environment in which "trying on ideas" is encouraged. Senior faculty play an absolutely crucial role and should be urged by deans and administrators to set the stage by modeling vulnerability themselves. If senior faculty hesitate to speak either out of fear of appearing foolish or out of disdain for the level or topic of the discussion, an environment will quickly develop in which fewer faculty stake out positions at all. And when they do, there will be too much at stake to risk the proper kind of attitudes I have described. The end of becoming liberally educated themselves will be lost and the students will suffer. It is hard to define these goals of a faculty of beliefs and attitude. It is even harder to describe the steps that might be taken to promote them.

TEACHERS

I have recommended that the faculty of the Christian liberal arts college seek to be a community of scholar-teachers. Although I began by making some suggestions about how to cultivate faculty as scholars, the subjects cannot really be separated. Some of those ideas overlap with the means to cultivate faculty as teachers.

The movement described above to redefine scholarship has been as much a return toward teaching as it has been away from publication. As the American Association for Higher Education says, it is motivated both externally and internally to academe. Externally, students and parents are asking hard questions in the face of escalating costs. Internally, trustees and administrators repositioning their institutions and faculty who care deeply are looking again at teaching.[29] The Carnegie Foundation surveys I have cited show that 62 percent of all faculty believe teaching effectiveness should be the primary criterion for promotion. Seventy-six percent feel this way at the liberal arts institutions of special interest to us.[30] A Canadian study makes the same point. "Teaching is seriously undervalued. . . . Universities must pay far more attention to the role of teaching. . . . Scholarship is defined too narrowly in terms of publications and should include innovative teaching skills."[31] The problem, of course, is how to put into practice a priority everyone seems to agree on.

The recent teaching initiative has produced a wealth of literature and many institutions are actively involved. It is not my intention to survey that front or to reinvent the wheel. So let me first review places where I have already addressed the subject of teaching and then make two suggestions.

In chapter 9, on programs, I argued that a team-taught curriculum would enhance the distinctive goals of the Christian liberal arts college. In the present chapter, I have highlighted the crucial role hiring plays in finding the faculty who will become the right kind of scholars. In part, the goal was to find faculty who make scholarship serve students and serve teaching. There is no need to repeat the discussion of the relationship between research and teaching. We know that specialized research and guild orientation do not necessarily make for better teaching. I also discussed the role faculty development plays in shaping the people who will become the right kind of scholars. Part of this was to regulate promotion and tenure criteria so they give more than mere lip service to the priority on teaching that virtually all Christian liberal arts colleges profess. There, among other suggestions, I said that appropriate scholarship should include writing textbooks, revising syllabi, and reviewing books related to coursework.

Although I have already made some suggestions about teaching, there is much more to be said because it is so important. The purpose of the Christian college is to educate its students. Thus scholarship must serve teaching and teaching must be the higher priority. The best arguments about faculty scholarship and the faculty's "life of the mind" as valuable in itself or as worship cannot get around this priority. All aspects of the Christian college must center on teaching students—in class, on the field, in chapel, in the dining room, on the walkways.[32] Let me highlight only two suggestions for reinforcing this priority.

Master Teacher Programs

Much of the problem with undergraduate teaching comes from the fact that few faculty have had formal training in how to teach and some may not have had examples of really good teachers to follow. Laypeople are shocked that college faculty do not have any of the kind of training in teaching that the state mandates even for elementary school teachers. Many faculty dismiss this as irrelevant, assuming that by the time students arrive at college they have already learned to learn for themselves. If that were ever true in the first place, it may be less so today. There is a lot of talk about the underpreparation of high school graduates. This certainly puts increasing pressure on college faculty to teach well.

But what is perhaps equally unfortunate, the models most faculty have of teachers are those in graduate school who have made research and publication a priority.[33] Or perhaps they turn to undergraduate teachers often no better equipped to teach than the faculty members themselves. It's small wonder the faculty at liberal arts colleges—though perhaps highly committed to teaching—are often ill equipped to do so.

One solution may be a master teacher program. Once again the idea is not new, but it seems more common in elementary and high schools than in colleges. Perhaps this reflects the greater actual priority given to teaching in those institutions. Such a program at a Christian liberal arts college can serve two purposes.

It can identify and give recognition to those faculty who have already become excellent in this area, which will motivate others to follow suit. It will put "teeth" into the claim that teaching is valued if master teachers are given privilege and pay equal to that received by star researchers. I am not talking about the token "Teacher of the Year" awards given on most campuses. I am talking about the same kind of increases in base pay that often accompany promotions based on excellent research. Stanford has already taken such steps. Its recent $7 million program annually offers not only $5,000 cash bonuses for ten excellent teachers but permanent salary increases of $1,000 to twenty others.[34]

Richard Chait has suggested that on a national scale "The Pro-Teaching Movement Should Try Economic Pressures."[35] He proposes that master teachers be allowed to add the letters "M.T." after their name and that publishers of college guides list the number of such faculty in each institution. This, he says, might stimulate the market for good teaching. Whether such ideas make sense nationally, there is certainly no reason why individual institutions cannot do much more to recognize good teachers.

Second, such a program can provide the logical framework for training other faculty in teaching. Although it may not be the equivalent of formal training in teaching, in some ways it may be superior because it is done on the job. Short of increases in base pay or formal designations, smaller colleges might tangibly recognize their best teachers by annually selecting one or two to be designated master teachers. They can be offered course load reductions for the purpose of conducting a number of practical workshops for their colleagues on the improvement of teaching. Their familiarity with the institution and their colleagues can make this an effective in-service. What's more, it is cost-effective when compared with bringing in outside experts or sending faculty elsewhere for shorter-term training. It honors teaching and raises its visibility. Finally, such awards and workshops can promote community as faculty begin to see one another as resources for improving their own work. Master teachers already identified and recognized on campus can become the leaders of what Northwestern State University in Louisiana has called "Teaching Circles." Five to six faculty come together voluntarily to observe each other's teaching and review classroom events together.[36] MIT has recently begun a program of seminars on teaching for its faculty and teaching assistants.[37] The principle is to make faculty themselves responsible for their own good teaching.

Teacher Portfolios

The American Association for Higher Education published a monograph entitled *Teaching Portfolios* in direct response to the growing attention given to teaching as an essential part of scholarship. The monograph is based on the assertions of the Carnegie Foundation report, *Scholarship Reconsidered*, to which I have referred, as well as on the research of Lee Shulman, professor of education at Stanford. The purpose is to show that teaching can actually be a form of scholarship. It is not just a matter of taking subject-matter expertise and adding generic methods (how to plan a lecture, how to lead a discussion) to equal good teaching. Good teaching calls for the transformation of the concepts of a particular field into terms that can be understood by the particular students taught.[38] As Shulman puts it,

> we recognize . . . that a master chess player knows things that an ordinary chess player does not. But this knowledge is not a knowledge of principles; it is a knowledge of situations and ways of responding to them—the knowledge that comes of having been there before, and of which precedents might best apply in a new situation.[39]

It is the purpose of teaching portfolios to document a teacher's knowledge and performance. The documentation can include syllabi and artifacts of teaching over a period of the teacher's career. A portfolio is structured, selective, and above all reflective. As faculty members reflect on what changes they have made, the art of teaching itself becomes an expression of their scholarship. The initiative for presenting their teaching as scholarship goes into the hands of the faculty members themselves. This, then, can become the basis for more effective growth, especially when there is interaction with others about it. Furthermore, the portfolio can also become the basis for easier evaluation for promotion, for tenure, and for recognition of master teachers.

Such portfolios are cumbersome to create, maintain, and evaluate, although technology is making this simpler every year. But they can provide a key for Christian liberal arts colleges to operationalize their commitment to distinctive goals. If such colleges want to produce graduates who are critically committed, then there should be evidence in the teaching portfolios of its faculty that they have reflected deliberately on how to accomplish this. For those that have, there should be recognition and affirmation. What features of the faculty member's reading and writing assignments generate dissonance? What features model the higher stages of cognitive, moral, and faith development? If integration is a goal, how do the faculty member's class themes bridge disciplines, involve faith commitments, and apply clearly and plainly to practical, pressing, real problems? Does the teaching involve the use of habit formation to cultivate virtue? Does classroom discussion deliberately model an open and humble attitude toward the truth? All of these and more are questions that teaching portfolios might begin to answer as Christian liberal arts colleges move to sharpen the way in which strong teaching allows them to implement their distinctive educational goals.

COMMUNITY

Community seems to be the ubiquitous principle of Christian liberal arts education. In chapter 5, I showed that if we aim to produce graduates who have become persons of critical commitment, community must be an important (if not essential) part of the developmental process. In chapter 8, I argued that if we aim to produce graduates who can tackle real-world problems, community must be the foundation of all three elements of integration. In this part on practical suggestions, I have said that faculty are the heart of the institution and should comprise a community of scholar-teachers. I have suggested ways in which their role as scholars and their role as teachers can be informed by the distinctive purposes of Christian liberal arts. But scholarship and teaching cannot be separated. These are scholar-teachers *in community*. So let me conclude these suggestions about people with a few comments about community.

What Is Community?

Too often our notion of community includes tight control, consistency of behavior, homogeneity of makeup, and unity of opinion. But especially in an age of increasing diversity, this kind of community is often unattainable. Furthermore, to the extent that such community precludes healthy dissonance and controversy, it may actually be antithetical to the distinctive purposes we have ascribed to academic community. In short, what may be a warm, cozy community for some purposes may not be a very good liberal arts environment at all.

The academic community should not be characterized primarily by feelings but rather by an attitude. Of course affection and harmony among its members need not undermine academic community. But the essential ingredient, I believe, is the attitude of trust.

The descriptions of community offered by Sharon Parks and Sam Keen in the discussion of development seem to have this in common. They both describe communities of trust. Parks characterizes it as a place of interdependence and openness to "other." She likens the developmental process to the pilgrimage of God's covenant people.[40] And of course, the essence of Hebrew faith—unlike the Greek *pistis*—is trust.[41] Keen says the avoidance of tragic forward and backward development can be enhanced by faculty who liberate their students by becoming vulnerable to them. He says that students need to hear their teachers say, "I am extraordinarily perplexed over this problem too. Let me share with you the way it looks perplexing to me."[42] Plainly the issue for Keen is trust. Trust does not have to control; trust allows plurality, and it need not be limited to consistency and unity.[43]

Besides trust, community requires recognition of a common bond. Arthur Holmes says that the kind of community needed in Christian liberal arts colleges is one that promotes the recognition of shared purposes, heritage, and tasks.[44] This may or may not produce the feelings of mutual affection often taken to symbolize community. Faculty may or may not like one another. But there must be a recognition of shared educational task. This brings me to a practical question, How is this kind of community promoted?

How Is Community Promoted?

Both faculty and administrators have responsibility for community. It is at the heart of leadership to crystallize what are the shared purposes, heritage, and tasks of the particular Christian college. I say "crystallize" and not "create" because unless these shared values are present, however amorphously, in the minds and hearts of faculty, trustees, administrators, and even students, then the common bond will be artificial and will not bear the weight of diversity.

Administrators must take the lead. They must gather the leadership of the community and give time for reflection, arranging, for example, annual workshops, daylong sessions, retreats, and ongoing strategy-planning groups involving faculty along with administrators and trustees. To some these might seem "a waste of time." But over time, with patience, consensus emerges. It has been part of the purpose of this book to stimulate the kind of dialogue that will be essential to this process.

Then leadership must assume the crucial job of articulating the common bond over and over and over. It is sometimes said that the chief job of institutional leaders is to "manage values." They must tirelessly inject the overriding distinctive bonds of the community into every facet of its life. Like a good marriage, the bond of mutual commitment in trust cannot be taken for granted. It must be articulated openly and deliberately even when it might seem unnecessary.

In practice this means publicly honoring those who promote cognitive, moral, and faith development. Honoring those who model virtue and character. Recognizing those who have integrated many disciplines, those who function well both in their disciplines and in their church environment, those who are as comfortable in the world of government and industry as in academia. It may seem awkward to honor persons for their character: "We'd like to honor Professor Jones for her profound epistemological humility." But honor comes in many forms. If we call on Professor Jones for community functions and allude to Professor Jones as frequently as to those who may have shown more traditional evidences of academic success, the message will come across clearly.

For college leadership to articulate the common institutional purpose also often means having courage to avoid being all things to all people. This means being willing to identify and articulate what one's institution is *not*. It is tempting to prostitute these distinctives when marketing demands it. But if institutional purpose is really distinctive, it must unapologetically exclude some things. It might mean saying, "We are unapologetically not a graduate school" or "we are not well equipped to prepare Christian education workers without additional training" or "we cannot accommodate completion of a state teaching credential in the basic four-year program."

Maintaining this sense of trust and shared task means ensuring that faculty and staff are able to spend time together. That means attention to work loads. It means serious attention to the role of college-wide events as I have described above. It means concern for the physical layout of the campus and of offices so as to facilitate cooperative tasks. Industry long ago recognized the value of open offices and cooperative tasking, yet academia often still consists of rows of closed faculty office doors.

This task will fall not only to administrative leadership—above all the president and vice presidents—but also to faculty leadership, especially senior faculty. They must articulate what it is that makes this college distinctive. Younger faculty will learn by this model. The senior faculty must beware of majoring on minors, of propounding their own personal vision or style. Senior faculty must be empowered to assume this role. Many of the best may modestly conclude they have no such role to play precisely because they have acquired those virtues (e.g., humility) that ought to be modeled. So it falls to others to help them take up their role in this way.

Finally, of course, community is the responsibility not only of leadership but of every individual. All members of the community are responsible for their own attitudes. Why are many Christian college campuses characterized by lack of trust? Why do faculty not trust administrators whom they view as "self-serving unsophisticated sellouts to business and politics?" Why do administrators barely conceal their disdain for "elitist, arrogant, impractical" faculty? Trust is not just intellectual recognition of the common bond. Words of vision, articulated over and over will only become clichés and engender cynicism unless they are combined with real evidence of interdependence, openness to other perspectives, and vulnerability. All members of the community, whether leaders or not, should ask themselves whether they embody healthy dependence, openness, and vulnerability in their relations with others. Are they trustworthy? Do they keep promises, answer letters, and meet deadlines? Do they say different things in different contexts? Do they give credit where it is due? Do they "play politics"? Do they willingly confront disagreement?

To those who object that these attitudes cannot arise unless someone else first makes an environment in which this is possible, or someone else first makes him- or herself worthy of trust, I can only reply that this will not work any more in a community than it does in a marriage. If I wait for my spouse to ask forgiveness before I become vulnerable or if I wait for my spouse to change before I acknowledge my part, I may protect myself from harm but I will not build trust.

The healthy community, like the healthy marriage, requires reconciliation of individualistic attention to rights with social attention to responsibilities. In their extremes the latter can become oppressive while the former translates every dispute into the language of entitlements. Many of the issues in our society today can be framed in these same terms of rights versus responsibilities: abortion, racism, feminism, and so on. New interest in communitarianism in American society may provide a helpful resource for answers.[45] What a tragedy it would be, if, once again, secular society took the lead in promoting community. Could it be that in addition to neglecting their teaching distinctive just as secular campuses are embracing it, Christian colleges may also be embracing an entitlement perspective on community just as many in the secular culture are struggling to abandon it?

CONCLUSION TO PART III

Getting specific is risky. Even those who agree with the principles I outlined in earlier chapters may take issue on particulars. There will be readers who will judge some ideas in part III to be idealistic or impossible to implement.

Others will see some suggestions as naive or uninformed. Still others will see certain ones to be too radical or risky. I do not pretend to have the same confidence or conviction about these suggestions that I do about the instrumental and intrinsic values and even principles of dissonance and community enunciated earlier. I hope that those who agree with the vision I have described will not abandon that vision merely because the path I offer seems unworkable. The suggestions here are intended mostly to stimulate thinking.

My feeling is that the task of figuring out exactly how to produce *critically committed graduates tackling real-world problems* is an ongoing responsibility of the faculty in every institution committed to Christian liberal arts. If my suggestions are objectionable and better alternatives are found for producing such graduates, then so much the better. At least we can then have a sharper vision of what makes the Christian liberal arts college distinctive and how that distinctive mission might be accomplished. In the final analysis, the purpose of part III is to encourage institutions to make their practices more consistent with the distinctive mission of producing graduates who are becoming critically committed and are integrating multiple disciplines, faith with learning, and theory with practice to tackle real-world problems.

11

Final Remarks

WHY CHRISTIAN LIBERAL ARTS CAN GO BEYOND TRADITIONS

At the end of chapter 2, I explained why I believe that Christian liberal arts institutions can combine the aims of two major traditions in education: intrinsic and instrumental values, becoming and doing. In a nutshell, I argued that Christian faith means becoming like Christ and that includes serving the world. Since both demands are essential to following Christ, they encourage both traditions in education. But they also show how Christian liberal arts education can go beyond these same major traditions.

Because Christ Himself is the Truth, the academic pursuit of knowledge is to become like Him. But this means more than merely achieving a particular state of mind. For the Christian, the aim of knowledge is more; it is the development of the character of Christ Himself, including especially His attitude of humility.

Because Christ's conception of service extends beyond one's own community of shared interests, the notion that education is intended to equip one for service must also be extended. It must address real-world problems by means that will require the integration of many disciplines, values with learning, and theory with application.

HOW CHRISTIAN LIBERAL ARTS CAN GO BEYOND TRADITIONS

In parts I–II, I described in detail what the intrinsic and instrumental values of a distinctively Christian liberal arts education might look like. In part I, I tried to illustrate from developmental psychology *how* liberal arts can produce graduates who have become persons of critical commitment. This character illustrates the attitude that I take to be the distinctive intrinsic value of Christian higher education. It strives to take graduates beyond both the dogmatism and the skepticism that often result from alternative educational programs. In part II, I tried to show how, by following an integrative approach, liberal arts can equip graduates for doing the work of tackling real-world problems instead of only those contrived by narrow disciplines. This is the chief instrumental value for Christian higher education. It strives to take graduates beyond both the dabbling of dilettantes and the esoterica of narrow specialists.

Community and Diversity: Both Needed

As I described how both of these distinctives could be implemented, two important guiding principles emerged: the need for diversity as well as for an undergirding community. Their role in promoting both character development and integration should by now be plain.

Diversity includes the presence of dissonant influences necessary to stimulate the moral and cognitive development of students. It also means the deliberate inclusion of controversial alternatives so that there is actually something to integrate.

On the other hand, community is equally crucial. It provides the necessary context without which dissonance, modeling, and habit formation cannot effectively promote development. And community also provides the environment in which those diverse controversial alternatives might actually be brought together for integration.

For example, the integration needed for tackling real-world problems suffers equally from a lack of community as it does from a lack of diversity in opinion. Without a concerted effort to bring real-world problems to students and to take students to those real-world problems, students will never be aware of how the integration of multiple disciplines, of values and learning, and of theory and practice are essential to serving the world. In other words, without the controversy that arises from exposure to diversity of opinion and culture, integration has no raw material. On the other hand, unless there is a community of faculty with a commitment to such issues, there will be no forum for bringing the diversity together, no community of integration. Both diversity and community are clearly needed for integration.

By the same token, the development of critical commitment can collapse into indoctrination when there is too much homogeneity of community but collapses into relativism when there is too much diversity of opinion without community. In his recent book, *Universities and the Future of America*, Derek Bok put it this way:

At this point, universities confront a serious dilemma. They can try to impart a preferred moral code by every reasonable means at their disposal: classroom instruction, exhortation by academic leaders, rules of conduct backed by discipline, and the like. If they do, they risk imposing their views on students in a manner that conflicts with principles of intellectual freedom basic to the modern university [and a fortiori to the liberal arts]. To avoid this danger, they may elect simply to teach students to think more carefully about moral dilemmas without attempting to dictate answers. This is the method followed in most contemporary courses in applied ethics. Useful as it is, however, it runs the risk of making students clever casuists, adept at arguing any side of a difficult moral or social problem but lacking strong convictions of their own that they try to put into practice. In short, efforts to create a serious program of moral education seem to be caught between the evils of indoctrination, on the one hand, and the hazards of ethical relativism, on the other."[1]

Bok is describing precisely what I have called the need to go beyond both moral and cognitive dualism with its characteristic dogmatism as well as beyond moral and cognitive multiplicity with its characteristic skepticism. Both community and diversity are needed.

Community and Diversity: A Tension

But as I have already said, these two factors—diversity and community—may seem at odds with one another, even irreconcilable. This apparent tension has certainly not escaped the notice of those who struggle with the issue of diversity in American higher education today. As I have already noted, some believe the whole idea of a multicultural community may be a contradiction in terms. One would hope not.

In the first place, this is more and more what America is becoming: a multicultural community. There can be no question about the multicultural side of this label; the demographic change in our country is probably inexorable. The real question is whether America can remain in any significant sense a community at all. From Tocqueville to Bellah, many have warned against the loss of community. Unless "multicultural community" can make sense, the prospects for American society are not bright.

But second, and more to our purpose, unless the concept of diversity in community makes sense and can actually be created, there is little hope for the vision of Christian liberal arts education I have described here. Bok goes on to say that

Escaping this dilemma is the key to success in helping students to develop stronger ethical standards and a greater concern for the welfare of others. How this can be managed and whether it can be done at all are questions that still await an answer.[2]

I submit that the dilemma Bok poses here is precisely the problem of reconciling diversity and community. With only a homogeneous community there is danger that the task of moral and cognitive development will degenerate into indoctrination. But with only diversity of opinions, there is equal danger it will degenerate into relativism. As with the goal of integration, the goal of development also requires a reconciliation of community and diversity.

Furthermore, I also submit that even the goal Bok proposes, "to help students develop stronger ethical standards and a greater concern for the welfare of others," echoes the twofold distinctive of Christian liberal arts education I have envisioned in this book: to develop the intrinsic value of critical commitment and to exercise the instrumental value of serving the world by addressing problems in an integrative way. I believe Christian liberal arts education can answer Bok's question: How can it be managed and can it be done at all? His dilemma is one Christian liberal arts can address.

RESOURCES THAT ENABLE CHRISTIAN LIBERAL ARTS TO PURSUE THIS DISTINCTIVE MISSION

I believe Christian liberal arts institutions have resources that equip them to uniquely undertake the distinctive mission I have described. They can be places where students are taught to become and to do, to develop critical commitment, and to tackle real-world problems. These resources would allow such institutions to stand out distinctively by pursuing goals no other colleges can adequately undertake. These goals can be the genius of such institutions.

Small Size

Many Christian liberal arts colleges are relatively small institutions. Size is certainly not a sufficient condition for pursuit of the goals I have described, and it may not even be necessary. But it seems to me that the small size improves the chances that genuine community will arise even when there is diversity.

Community surely rests on communication, and the potential for communication across wider differences of disciplines is greater in small institutions than in large ones. Faculty meetings and campus-wide forums will probably draw together a wider range and larger percentage of the whole community. It seems more likely that there can be the shared heritage, the shared vision, and the sense of common educational task that Arthur Holmes says must characterize Christian liberal arts colleges.

But communication is only the first step toward the kind of attitudes (not just feelings) that I believe can hold community in diversity. In chapter 10, I said I believed the essential attitude was trust. Both Sharon Parks and Sam Keen describe communities of trust as places in which there is interdependence and openness to others. Parks even builds on the Hebrew understanding of faith as trust. Keen talks about the willingness to be vulnerable to colleagues and students alike. This vulnerability can extend, with time and persistence, to the sense of shared "risk" in the journeys traveled of faith and learning. It seems to me that small size can improve the likelihood of interdependency and openness to one another. When people resolve to treat one another as human beings and not representatives of positions or departments or groups, trust emerges, which reconciles community and diversity.

Faculty Calling

It probably goes without saying that most faculty at Christian institutions do not take their jobs primarily as a way to become wealthy. Nor is it likely that they do it to achieve an exalted reputation. Some may actually turn away from other opportunities much more conducive to those ends. For others, the market may not offer an abundance of alternatives, yet their decision to join a Christian institution is made with full awareness of the economic and career implications. In short, many, if not most, faculty at Christian institutions see their work as a calling of God.

By this I mean, first, that that their chief motivation is internal. To some extent this is true for all professionals, and academics are no exception. The drive to study, to learn, to write, to teach comes from personal desire as much as from external factors such as a paycheck. Professionals' sense of identity is tied up with the work they do.[3] The quality of their work is a reflection on their own person.

But for Christian faculty, the calling is more than just internal motivation. It is a sense that the purposes of their work have a kind of ultimate value because they arise out of the person's Christian view of the world and of life. No matter how mundane the task may seem, it contributes to what is really important in life. Whether it is the discipline of remaining current in their own field, the attention given to how students will receive classroom content, the concern for students as persons with needs beyond the curriculum, or the responsibility to model virtue in their relations with colleagues, everything Christian faculty members do will take on special, even eternal, importance. The quality of their work, then, is more than a reflection of their own person; it becomes an act of worship, even a sacrifice to God.

My point is that because many faculty at Christian institutions see their work as a calling, there is usually a higher standard for virtually all the tasks they undertake. This should show itself in the excellence of their disciplinary studies. But it should stand out in their attention to those aspects of the educational task that I have described as distinctive to Christian liberal arts. Faculty who see their own purposes in terms of becoming like Christ and following His example to serve the world should more readily attend to promoting character and integration in their own students. They should more eagerly urge students to develop in their character an increasing knowledge of cognitive and moral truth. They should more eagerly urge students to bring together all they know and can do in order to address the actual problems facing the world today. If this does not happen, then perhaps Christian college faculty are no different from their non-Christian colleagues at secular institutions.

The Model of the Body of Christ

To the problem of diversity in community, Christian institutions can bring the model of the Body of Christ. The Body of Christ worldwide seeks to be just what is required—a community of diversity. Followers of Christ do not succeed as often as they would like, and the world will no doubt dwell on obvious instances of failure. Yet the fact that Christians all believe this model is possible and struggle to see it manifest is a resource that Christian colleges bring to the vision I have described.

As St. Paul describes the Body, it, like a human body, contains diverse members. Each Christian brings his or her own gifts and individuality. Each has an important function often not valued in proportion to outward appearances.[4] Yet this diversity is knit together into a unity that is more than organizational. It is organic; it is a living Body. This community is accomplished only by virtue of the "headship" of Christ Himself. He has arranged the parts. Only by virtue of this supernatural coordination can reconciliation of diversity and community be accomplished. Christian colleges can bring this resource to the task of higher education.

I have sometimes compared the working of Christian community with the engaging of gears that do not naturally fit one another. Somehow the Holy Spirit functions as a supernatural lubricant that enables those gears to mesh in spite of their differences. Francis Schaeffer has called this the "final apologetic." Referring to Christ's "high priestly prayer," Schaeffer points out that ultimately the most persuasive way the world will know that Jesus was God, as He claimed, is when Christians live in community by loving one another.[5] If reconciling community and diversity is as unnatural as it seems, then when it occurs in the Body of Christ it must testify to the supernatural quality of that which holds it together, namely, Christ Himself.

In the same way, I believe the Holy Spirit can provide Christian liberal arts colleges with the means to bring together diversity and community. In so doing, these institutions can provide the essential ingredients to accomplish the distinctive task I have described and testify to Christ's work among them.

CONCLUSION

Are there Christian colleges prepared to come of age, to recognize their distinctive genius, to do what others likely cannot do? Are there Christian colleges prepared to be different from both Bible colleges and secular universities, as valuable as these others may be? Are there Christian colleges prepared to go beyond both dualism and multiplicity, beyond both dabbling and overspecialization? Are there Christian colleges prepared to embrace both the intrinsic and the instrumental values of higher education? Are there Christian colleges prepared to focus on educating graduates with the character of critical commitment and the calling to integrate by tackling real-world problems? Are there Christian colleges prepared to be genuine communities of trust, communities of diversity? Are there Christian colleges willing to address Derek Bok's dilemma—to struggle with the tension of avoiding both indoctrination and relativism? At the present time, I am not convinced there are many (if any) institutions prepared to do this. But there are some with the potential for it. I pray the Holy Spirit will equip and empower them to the task.

Notes

CHAPTER 1. INTRODUCTION

1. Ernest Boyer, *Scholarship Reconsidered: Priorities of the Professoriate* (Princeton, N.J.: Carnegie Foundation for the Advancement of Teaching, 1990), p. 55.

2. E. Lynton and S. Elman, *New Priorities for the University* (San Francisco: Jossey-Bass, 1987), p. 13.

3. Karen Grassmuck, "Rankings of Colleges by Magazines Grow in Popularity, Putting Campuses on Spot," *Chronicle of Higher Education* [hereafter referred to simply as *Chronicle*], October 16, 1991, p. 1.

4. Thomas W. Langfitt, "The Cost of Higher Education," *Change* [magazine of the American Association of Higher Education], November-December, 1990, p. 13. Langfitt reported that the cost of health care was up 4 percent over inflation, whereas higher education costs were up 5 percent above inflation.

5. Ibid. Confidence in the health care industry dropped from 73 percent in the 1960s to 33 percent in 1986.

6. Jean Evangelauf, "1991 Tuition Increases Expected to Outpace Inflation," *Chronicle,* March 6, 1991, p. A28.

7. Michele N-K Collison, "Applications Down at Private Campuses," *Chronicle,* March 6, 1991, A28.

8. Donald Kennedy, "Stanford in Its Second Century," address to Stanford Academic Council, April 5, 1990, quoted by Ernest Boyer in *Scholarship Reconsidered*, p. 1. See also Boyer's concern with teaching throughout this report in which he describes a new concept of scholarship. See also Larry Gordon, "Stanford to Focus on Undergraduates," *Los Angeles Times,* March 3, 1991, p. A3.

9. Scott Heller, "Stronger Push for Research on Liberal-Arts Campuses Brings Fears That Their Culture Is Threatened," *Chronicle,* July 5, 1990, p. A11. Cf. *Bulletin of the*

American Association of Higher Education 44, no. 4 (1991), which reports on a survey of over 18,000 faculty and administrators at forty-seven research institutions and indicates that while a clear majority favor a shift back to teaching, they also believe most of their colleagues do not agree. The "closet teacher" has to come out.

10. Examples: *Illiberal Education, Closing of the American Mind, ProfScam, Killing the Spirit, The Moral Collapse of the University.*

11. Cited in R. J. Schenkat et al., *It Stands to Reason: The Rationale and Implementation of a Development Based, Liberal Arts Oriented, Teacher Education Program* (Winona, Minn.: College of St. Teresa, 1985), p. 5.

12. Ibid.

13. Ted Marchese, "TQM Reaches the Academy," and Daniel T. Seymour, "TQM on Campus: What Pioneers Are Finding Out," *Bulletin of the American Association for Higher Education* 44, no. 3 (1991): 3–13.

14. Philippians 1:21; 2:5

15. Philippians 2:7; cf. www.greenville.edu/publications/mannoiatexts.

16. Earl J. McGrath, *The Graduate School and the Decline of Liberal Education* (New York: Bureau of Publications, Teachers College, Columbia University, 1959), pp. 8–9, cited in Bruce A. Kimball, *Orators and Philosophers: A History of the Idea of Liberal Education* (New York: Teachers College Press, 1986), p. 210.

17. David Breneman, "Are We Losing Our Liberal Arts Colleges?" *Bulletin of the American Association of Higher Education* 43, no. 2 (1990): 3–6.

18. Kenneth P. Ruscio, "The Selective Liberal Arts College," *Journal of Higher Education* 58, no. 2 (1987): 205–222.

19. Parker Marden, academic dean, Beloit College, quoted by Scott Heller in "Stronger Push," p. A11.

CHAPTER 2. WHAT DOES "CHRISTIAN LIBERAL ARTS" MEAN?

1. In Britain, the term "public" refers to schools of the people (private schools), and the term "government" or "state" is used to refer to what Americans call public institutions. Even the word "school" is used differently in Britain to refer only to elementary schools.

2. Samuel Capen, "The Dilemma of the College of Arts and Sciences," *Educational Review* 61 (1921): 277–278.

3. Ernest Boyer, *Scholarship Reconsidered: Priorities of the Professoriate* (Carnegie Foundation for the Advancement of Teaching, 1990), p. 129, appendix C. Drawn from *A Classification of Institutions of Higher Education,* Carnegie Foundation for the Advancement of Teaching (Princeton: Princeton University Press, 1989), pp. 191–192. The alteration of "liberal arts" to become "bachelor's" and "comprehensive" to become "master's" was effected in 1993 and reflects the ambiguity about use of the term "liberal arts."

4. David Breneman, "Are We Losing Our Liberal Arts Colleges?" *Bulletin of the American Association for Higher Education* 43, no. 2 (1990): 3, confirming reports by William Bowen, president of the Mellon Foundation.

5. The bachelor of arts (B.A.) category was changed in 1994 from liberal arts I and II and the percentage of arts and sciences degrees required for the category was dropped from 50 percent to 40 percent.

6. Randolph Schenkat et al., *It Stands to Reason: The Rationale and Implementation of a Development Based, Liberal Arts Oriented Teacher Education Program* (Winona, Minn.: College of St. Teresa, 1985), pp. 32–33.

7. David G. Winter et al., *A New Case for the Liberal Arts* (San Francisco: Jossey-Bass), pp. 9–11.

8. *National Forum* [a journal of Phi Kappa Phi], Spring 1989, p. 11.

9. Winter et al., *New Case,* pp. 12–13. Thinking critically included *differentiation* and *discrimination* of particulars and abstractions, *formation* of abstract concepts, *integration* of abstract concepts, *judgment, evaluation* of evidence and *revision* of hypotheses, *articulation* and *communication* of abstract concepts, *comprehension* of the logics governing relations among abstract concepts.

10. Bruce A. Kimball, *Orators and Philosophers: A History of the Idea of Liberal Education* (New York: Teachers College Press, 1986), p. 4. Kimball notes Jacques Barzun, "Humanities, Pieties, Practicalities, Universities," *Seminar Reports, Program of General Education in the Humanities,* November 14, 1973, p. 1.

11. This taxonomy of liberal arts definitions comes from Kimball, *Orators and Philosophers,* pp. 4ff. On pages 6–11 he describes and notes some of the historical approaches taken from an operational, a basket, and an a priori point of view.

12. Ibid., pp. ix–x.

13. Ibid., p. 13.

14. The use of the word "men" reflects Cicero's own thinking and should not be construed to mean that liberal education is not for women today.

15. Aristotle, *Politics* 8.2.

16. Plato, *Gorgias* 502–522.

17. Isocrates, *Against the Sophists* 2–11, 19–20.

18. Those who try to trace the meaning of the words "artes liberales" to Greece cannot seem to make a strong case for one tradition over another. Kimball, *Orators and Philosophers,* pp. 15–16. "Liberalis" seems closest to *eleutherios* or "fit for a free man." Yet this word has been found to be associated with all three of the Athenian approaches to education—Platonic, Isocratic, and Sophistic—hence one cannot tie "liberal arts" to any one of these particular schools. Comparable ambiguities arise with *skole,* from which we get "school," and *enkuklios paideia,* from which we get "general education" and even "curriculum."

19. Kimball, *Orators and Philosophers,* p. 19, citing Marrou (1956), p. 194. Henri I. Marrou, *A History of Education in Antiquity,* trans. George Lamb (New York: Shield and Word, 1956).

20. Kimball, *Orators and Philosophers,* p. 19.

21. *Higher Education Today: Facts in Brief,* ed. Cecilia Ottinger (Washington, D.C.: American Council on Education, 1989).

22. Leo Marx, "A Case for Interdisciplinary Thinking," *National Forum,* Vol. LXIX, No. 2 (Spring 1989), p. 8. This author says that many see liberal knowledge to be subjective, unpredictable, contingent, imprecise, not susceptible to exact verification or

disproof, soft, and feminine (p. 9). Newman agrees, saying that critics often associate liberal knowledge with the failure to cultivate the "solid and masculine parts" of the student's understanding (p. 123).

23. John Locke, noted in John Newman, *The Idea of a University* (New York: Holt, Rinehart, Winston, 1960), p. 120.

24. No doubt this answer has come from the influence of Arthur Holmes's book, *The Idea of a Christian College* (Grand Rapids, Mich.: Eerdmanns, 1975). Holmes (p. 33) poses the questions as "What can I do with it?" and "What can it do to me?"

25. Noted in Holmes, *Idea,* p. 38.

26. Noted in McGill, p. 25.

27. Newman, *Idea,* p. 81.

28. Ibid., p. 81.

29. Ibid., p. 77.

30. Ibid., p. 85.

31. Ibid.

32. Ibid., p. 78.

33. Ibid., p. 115.

34. Christians often find Newman's Aristotelianism unobjectionable, even quite suitable. And the defense he makes of liberal education follows quite reasonably. I will have more to say about this below.

35. Newman, *Idea,* p. 82, citing Aristotle, *Rhetoric* 1.5.

36. Holmes, *Idea,* p. 35.

37. David Elton Trueblood, *The Idea of a College* (New York: Harper, 1959), p. 11.

38. Newman, *Idea,* p. 76.

39. Noted by William Bennett in *To Reclaim a Legacy: A Report on the Humanities in Higher Education* (Washington, D.C.: National Endowment for the Humanities, 1984), p. 24.

40. Dinesh D'Souza, *Illiberal Education* (New York: Free Press, 1991), p. 229.

41. Ibid.

42. John Silber, *Straight Shooting* (New York: Harper, 1989), noted in *Change,* November-December 1990, p. 50.

43. Unless, of course, one adopts a nonnormative meta–ethical view, as many today are doing. But then to continue to *call* this a value at all falsely trades on the usual understanding of value as "normative" to give the impression that there is something here by means of which one can take decisions and direct one's life.

44. D'Souza, *Illiberal Education,* p. 179.

45. Robert Sandin, *The Rehabilitation of Virtue: Foundations of Moral Education* (New York: Greenwood/Praeger, 1992), pp. 159f.

46. Georg Henrik von Wright, *The Varieties of Goodness* (London: Routledge & Kegan Paul, 1963) p. 145. Noted in Sandin, *Rehabilitation,* p. 164.

47. Sandin, *Rehabilitation,* p. 165.

48. Ibid., p. 164.

49. Newman says the fruit of a liberal education is a habit of mind. Besides freedom it includes equitableness, calmness, moderation, and wisdom (p. 76). It is intended to produce the ability to think, to reason, to compare, to discriminate, to analyze, and to form judgments (p. 125). The ability to form judgments is a kind of

"master principle" such that regardless of the subject matter, it enables the educated person to "seize the strong point in it" (p. 125).

50. *In Defense of Archias,* noted in McGill, p. 25.

51. Josef Pieper, *Leisure: The Basis of Culture* (New York: New American Heritage Library, 1963).

52. Ibid., p. 21. Cf. the first paragraph of Aristotle's *Metaphysics!*

53. Leo Marx, *National Forum,* Vol. LXIX, No. 2 (Spring 1989), p. 17.

54. Noted in Boyer, *Scholarship Reconsidered,* p. 67.

55. *Liberal Learning and the Arts and Sciences Major,* Vol. 1, *The Challenges of Connecting Learning,* American Association of Colleges, 1991, p. 3.

56. *Involvement in Learning,* report of the Study Group on the Conditions of Excellence in American Higher Education. Reprinted in *Chronicle of Higher Education,* October 24, 1984, p. 49.

57. See Patricia McCormack, "Corporate Chiefs Take a Liberal View of Current Graduates," *Santa Barbara News Press,* February 26, 1984. Cf. Edwin Delattre, "Real Career Education Comes from the Liberal Arts," *Chronicle of Higher Education,* January 5, 1983.

58. George O. Kemp Jr., "Three Factors of Success," in *Relating Work and Education,* ed. Dychman W. Vermilye (San Francisco: Jossey–Bass, 1977), p. 103, noted in Arthur Chickering, "Liberal Education and Success at Work," *Bulletin* 5, no. 1 (1982), Center for the Study of Higher Education, Memphis State University, Memphis, Tennessee. Chickering's list of skills included four cognitive skills (information processing skills like learning, recall, and forgetting; conceptualizing skills like analysis and synthesis; ability to understand many sides of a controversial issue; ability to learn from experience). It also included two interpersonal skills (communication skills like fluency in speaking and writing as well as nonverbal skills; accurate empathy).

59. Winter et al., *New Case.*

60. Variations in admissions at one institution over several years, attrition from freshman to senior year, and interaction of maturation effects.

61. Winter et al., *New Case,* pp. 26ff.

62. Winter et. al., pp. 63, 66, and 67.

63. There is a closer positive correlation between improvements in critical thinking skills and participation in varsity (not intramural) athletics than there is between those improvements and academic involvement (including relatively great personal contact with faculty); there is a fairly strong negative correlation between improvement in critical thinking skills and participation in dormitory life.

64. Marx, *National Forum,* p. 9.

65. *Daedalus,* Winter 1988, noted in Marx, *National Forum,* p. 9.

66. Marx, *National Forum,* citing Herbert and Stuart Dreyfuss in *Daedalus,* Winter 1988.

67. Kimball, *Orators and Philosophers,* p. 238.

68. Ibid., p. 219.

69. Ibid., p. 230.

70. Derek Bok, *Universities and the Future of America* (Durham, N.C.: Duke University Press, 1990), p. 10.

71. Kimball, *Orators and Philosophers,* p. 26, referring to the *Gorgias* (462b–465e) and the *Phaedrus* (259e–261a), respectively.

72. Kimball, *Orators and Philosophers,* p. 19. The reference in Aristotle is *Rhetoric* 1354a.

73. Kimball, *Orators and Philosophers,* p. 36.

74. Newman, *Idea,* p. 78.

75. Cicero, *Offic. init.,* noted in Newman, *Idea,* p. 79.

76. Newman, *Idea,* p. 80.

77. Ibid., p. 77.

78. Ibid., p. 116.

79. Ibid., p. 86.

80. Ibid., pp. 114ff.

81. Ibid., p. 123.

82. Ibid.

83. Ibid., p. 93. Aristotle would distinguish moral virtue and intellectual virtue. Sandin, *Rehabilitation,* p. 166, citing *Nicomachean Ethics* 2.1.1103a15–18.

84. Newman, *Idea,* p. 125.

85. Ibid.

86. Ibid., p. 126.

87. Ibid., p. 121.

88. Ibid., p. 134.

89. Ibid., p. 79, citing Cicero. Cicero's words were that the search after truth comes "as soon as we escape the pressure of necessary cares."

90. See Kimball, *Orators and Philosophers,* pp. 26, 31, for discussion of the debate in terms of dialectic and rhetoric.

91. In the preface (page xiii), Joseph Featherstone talks about bringing the two schools of thought about liberal education together, but only in the sense of holding them in ongoing real, open tension. "A decent liberal education now contains—ought to contain—conflicting elements from both the philosophers and the orators. Not mixed up in a chowder the way most colleges are these days but in open tension. . . . Socrates was right about the truth; the orators were right about community. . . . And that fight must go on if our students are to be educated. They must learn to hold elements of the two ideals in some real tension, not a flabby compromise."

92. Newman, *Idea,* p. 134.

93. The idea of developmental becoming (chap. 2) goes beyond the oratorical tradition of uncritical belief in tradition and the sophistical tradition of skepticism to a kind of critical commitment that balances both. The idea of tackling real-world problems (chap. 3) goes beyond the philosophical tradition of narrow specialized research to a kind of integration that serves others.

94. Kimball, *Orators and Philosophers,* p. 239.

95. Ibid., p. 240.

96. John 8:32.

97. James 1:22; Romans 7:15.

98. Philippians 2:8.

PART I. CHRISTIAN LIBERAL ARTS
MEANS BECOMING AND NOT JUST DOING

1. "Report of Commission on Liberal Education," *American Association of Colleges Bulletin* 38 (1952): 110, cited in Bruce A. Kimball, *Orators and Philosophers: A History of the Idea of Liberal Education* (New York: Teachers College Press, 1986), p. 210.

2. Cited by D. K. Winter in comments to Westmont College faculty, March 11, 1987. Cited also by Sharon Parks in *The Critical Years* (New York: Harper & Row, 1986), p. 50, citing Robert Rankin, "Beginning," in *The Recovery of Spirit in Higher Education: Christian and Jewish Ministries in Campus Life* (New York: Seabury, 1980), p. 10.

3. Dr. S. Mackenzie, Grove City College, 1975.

4. See Robert Sandin, *The Rehabilitation of Virtue: Foundation of Moral Education* (New York: Praeger, 1992), chap. 10, esp. pp. 164ff.

5. This seems to be the primary argument of writers like Bok, for whom the value of moral education seems to lie in its usefulness for enhancing the "future of America."

CHAPTER 3. WHAT IS CRITICAL COMMITMENT?

1. Sadly, the faculty are, of course, chiefly to blame. Dinesh D'Souza in *Illiberal Education* (New York: Free Press, 1991) describes well the cynicism of faculty in narrow disciplines who believe nothing but perpetuate their own work nevertheless, becoming, for example, "closet capitalists" or "the richest Marxists in the country" (p. 181). Socrates long ago recognized this kind of "education" for what it was, sophistry. In the *Euthydemus,* he said that "mastery of this sort of stuff would by no means lead to increased knowledge of how things are, but only to the ability to play games with people, tripping them up and flooring them with different senses of words, just like those who derive pleasure and amusement from pulling stools from under people when they are about to sit down, and from seeing someone floundering on his back." Michel Foucault put it more pithily when remarking on Jacques Derrida, a hero of deconstructionists in the political correctness movement: "He's the kind of philosopher who gives bullshit a bad name" (cited in D'Souza, *Illiberal Education,* p. 190).

2. Robert Sandin (*The Rehabilitation of Virtue: Foundation of Moral Education* [New York: Praeger, 1992]) makes much the same point when he says, "The present crisis in values is deepened by the disarray of moral education, which has too often been polarized between the extremes of being restrictively doctrinaire [what I will call dogmatic] and being explicitly subjectivistic [what I will call skeptical]" (p. 17).

3. Credit for this line of thinking goes to D. K. Winter, president of Westmont College, in a chapel address at Westmont College, October 2, 1991.

4. Allan Bloom calls it "openness" in his book *The Closing of the American Mind* (New York: Simon & Schuster, 1987). (Cf. Sandin, *Rehabilitation,* pp. 24f.)

5. D'Souza, *Illiberal Education,* p. 215.

6. Abigail Thernstrom, political scientist from Harvard and Boston Universities, cited in D'Souza, *Illiberal Education,* p. 227.

7. If, as I have noted in chapter 1 (under subheading "Liberation To"), the movement *actually* tolerated everything, it would be self-defeating because it could then never permit an argument that made its own view preferable to any other (e.g., to the view that intolerance was better than tolerance).

8. Sharon Parks, *Those Critical Years* (New York: Harper & Row, 1986), p. 45, provides what may be a clue to this odd paradox. In describing the earliest stage of cognitive development, she points out that it is not the content of one's views which identify that one is at the earliest, "dualistic/authoritarian," stage but the intolerance of it. Dualists are intolerant of ambiguity. Because the language of "relativism and tolerance" is so commonplace and accepted by societal "authorities," we find ourselves hearing paradoxical expressions like "it is totally wrong for anyone to think that truth is not merely relative" or "you *must* be tolerant." Though the content sounds developed, the attitude suggests an immature developmental stage. Could it be that the PC movement emerged because of the failure of the American educational system to provide a liberal education? Could it be that the problem reflected in the political correctness movement is the lack of a liberal education in the *faculty* of our colleges and universities?

9. D'Souza, *Illiberal Education,* pp. 183–190.

10. Cited in Sandin, *Rehabilitation,* p. 23. Nietzsche would describe this as the naked will to power.

11. D'Souza, *Illiberal Education,* p. 192.

12. D'Souza says the dogmatic skeptic is "critically arbitrary" (*Illiberal Education,* p. 179).

13. Arthur Holmes, *The Idea of a Christian College* (Grand Rapids, Mich.: Eerdmans, 1975), p. 84.

14. Ibid.

15. Some of the best-known studies are those of Jean Piaget, Lawrence Kohlberg, and William Perry. Piaget concerned himself with cognitive and moral development, especially of young children (*The Moral Judgment of the Child* (New York: Free Press, 1965). Kohlberg extends Piaget's work more specifically into questions about how developmental theory should shape education ("Cognitive-Developmental Approach to Moral Education," *Humanist,* November–December 1972; "Cognitive-Developmental Theory and Practice of Collective Moral Education," in *Group Care: The Education Path of Youth Aliyah,* ed. M. Wolins and M. Gottesman (New York: Gordon & Breach, 1971); "Education for Justice: A Modern Statement of the Platonic View," in *Moral Education,* ed. T. Sizer (Cambridge: Harvard University Press, 1970); and especially "Development as the Aim of Education" [with R. Mayer], *Harvard Educational Review* 42, no. 4: (1972). William Perry pays special attention to higher education in his well-known 1968 book, *Forms of Intellectual and Ethical Development in the College Years* (New York: Holt, Rinehart, & Winston, 1968). Carol Gilligan, *In a Different Voice: Psychological Theory and Women's Development* (Cambridge: Harvard University Press, 1982), takes issue with Kohlberg's male bias and proposes an "ethic of care" to complement his ethic of justice. James Fowler, *Stages of Faith: The Psychology of Human Development and the Quest for Meaning* (San Francisco: Harper & Row, 1981), addresses faith development. Sharon Parks, *The Critical Years*

(San Francisco: Harper & Row, 1986), pulls together the thinking of many of the above in a discussion of faith that builds on Fowler.

16. Parks, *Critical Years,* p. 32.

17. Piaget, *Moral Judgment.*

18. Ronald Duska and Mariellen Whelan, *Moral Development: A Guide to Piaget and Kohlberg* (New York: Paulist, 197), p. 8.

19. Parks, *Critical Years,* pp. 33–34.

20. Ibid., p. 35.

21. Duska and Whelan, *Moral Development,* p. 47.

22. Kohlberg used eighty–four males in his twenty–year longitudinal study. Lawrence Kohlberg, "The Development of Modes of Thinking and Choices in Years 10 to 16" (Ph.D. diss., University of Chicago, 1958). Kohlberg, *The Philosophy of Moral Development* (San Francisco: Harper & Row, 1981).

23. Gilligan, *Different Voice,* chap. 1.

24. This example is cited in Parks, *Critical Years,* p. 39, and refers to Carol Gilligan, "Remapping the Moral Domain: New Images of Self in Relationship" (paper presented at the Reconstructing Individualism conference, Stanford Humanities Center, February 18–20, 1984). The example was given to Gilligan by Anne Glickman, mother of the boy.

25. Sandin, *Rehabilitation,* p. 81. Kohlberg freely admits this weakness.

26. Described in Parks, *Critical Years,* p. 41.

27. James Fowler, *Stages of Faith.*

28. Perry's scheme is based largely on two studies. One was done from 1954 to 1959 with thirty–one students at Harvard, producing ninety–eight interviews and seventeen complete four–year longitudinal records. The second was done from 1960 to 1963 with 109 students, producing 366 interviews and 67 complete four–year longitudinal records. William Perry, *Forms of Intellectual and Ethical Development in the College Years* (New York: Holt, Rinehart, & Winston, 1968), pp. 7–8.

29. Perry prefers the word "position" to the word "stage" because (1) it better suits the idea that these are "points of outlook" or "positions from which a person views their world," (2) it makes no assumption about duration, and (3) it allows for greater variation in the range of structures reported by students at any given time. See Perry, *Forms,* p. 48.

30. Cited by Parks, *Critical Years,* p. 41.

31. Perry himself uses these groupings on page 57 but refers to the second group by the name "Multiplicity" rather than "Relativism" because there is ambiguity in position 4 about whether multiplicity has led to relativism in all cases.

32. Perry, *Forms,* p. 56.

33. Ibid., pp. 190ff.

34. Ibid., p. 130.

35. There is considerably more discussion of this principle and its dangers below under the subheading "Response to the Right."

36. Kohlberg, "Development," pp. 451–452, 455.

37. Ibid., pp. 452–453, 456.

38. For the romantic, "extreme deprivation will retard or fixate development, but. . . enrichment will not necessarily accelerate it" (ibid., p. 459).

39. Ibid., pp. 454–455, 456–457.

40. Ibid., p. 455. Cf. pp. 475, 491.

41. Ibid., p. 471, citing John Dewey, *Experience and Education* (New York: Collier, 1963), p. 75. Originally published in 1938.

42. See chapter 1 on political correctness.

43. Kohlberg, "Development," p. 472.

44. The connection between the philosophical justification for valuing principles and the psychological theory of development is important and should not be confused. Kohlberg calls his view a "developmental–philosophic approach" (p. 484) to make the distinction and connection clear. Empirical research shows that principled thought and judgment is characteristic of the later stages of cognitive and moral development. And empirical research may also show that these later stages of development are more adequate with respect to the rational ethical principles Kohlberg affirms. However, these empirical facts do not make rational principles in general or particular rational principles right (naturalistic fallacy). That requires ethical warrant that can come from a variety of sources that may differ from one another while still all avoiding the naturalist fallacy. For example, they may be right because God says so or because their value is intuited. This question is addressed from the Christian's perspective in the next section of this chapter. Kohlberg puts the relationship this way: "Thus, the strategy attempts to avoid the naturalistic fallacy of directly deriving judgments of value from judgments about the facts of development, although it assumes the two may be systematically related. It takes as an hypothesis for empirical confirmation or refutation that development is a movement toward greater epistemological or ethical adequacy as defined by philosophic principles of adequacy" ("Development," p. 484).

45. Kohlberg, "Development," p. 484: "Moral development cannot be justified as adaptive by standards of survival [romantic view] or of conformity to cultural standards [cultural transmission view]."

46. Ibid., p. 473.

47. Ibid.

48. Ibid., p. 475.

49. This may seem to raise the specter of the naturalistic fallacy again—"Just because this cognitive and moral sequence is a fact doesn't make it right." But interactionists are not using the fact that it is natural to justify the development, but only as a way to avoid the charge of indoctrination. The justification of the interactionist's principles (e.g., liberty) will come from a variety of sources, including, for Christians at least, the authority of God and Scripture.

50. Kohlberg, "Development," p. 476.

51. These common features are discussed in Duska and Whelan, *Moral Development,* pp. 47–50, who apply them to Kohlberg (cf. Kohlberg, "Development," p. 458). But I believe Kohlberg and Perry agree on these general features of the developmental process. They themselves represent extensions, not significant departures, from Piaget, so I see no reason to believe that the characteristics do not apply to him as well. Since others such as Fowler, Gilligan, and Parks seem not to have parted company with Kohlberg and Perry, at least on these issues, the result, I believe, is considerable consensus across the constructive–developmental school. One notable disagreement has to do with whether development is "reversible." Kohlberg seems quite sure the developmental process is *not* reversible. In contrasting his progressive

developmental approach to education with that of the behaviorist, Kohlberg says reversible development is not development at all (Kohlberg, "Development," 1981, pp. 462, 486). On the other hand, Perry talks at length about obstacles to development, including "retreat" or "regression" (Perry, *Forms,* pp. 182ff.).

52. Perry, *Forms,* p. 80.

53. Ibid., p. 111.

54. T. S. Kuhn, *Structure of Scientific Revolutions,* (Chicago: University of Chicago Press, 1962).

55. On page 131 Perry suggests that because the religious Absolute is incompatible with relativism, any attempt to integrate them would be fatal, hence, "as an alternative to the usual loss of belief, the only possibility lies in the unstable dissociated condition of Relativism Competing."

56. Perry bemoans the lack of information here himself (*Forms,* p. 110).

57. Cited in Perry, *Forms,* pp. 111, 114.

58. Ibid., p. 33.

59. Parks, *Critical Years,* p. 48.

60. Fowler does not provide an intermediate stage of faith corresponding to Perry's positions 4, 5, and 6, but that is not surprising given the skeptical characteristics of those positions. See Parks, *Critical Years,* appendixes A and B for excellent charts comparing the various developmental schema.

61. Parks, *Critical Years,* p. 70.

62. Ibid., p. 50.

63. Cited by D. K. Winter in March 11, 1987, in comments to Westmont College faculty. Cited also by Parks, *Critical Years,* p. 50, citing Robert Rankin, "Beginning," in *The Recovery of Spirit in Higher Education: Christian and Jewish Ministries in Campus Life* (New York: Seabury, 1980), p. 10.

64. Perry, *Forms,* pp. 145–148. See also the excellent interview of an actual student with these balances annotated in the margins (pp. 167–176).

65. In Kohlberg's terms this is, of course, the development beyond conventionalism with its attention to others as the basis of values.

66. Gilligan, *Different Voice,* p. 155, cites here the work of George E. Vaillant, *Adaption to Life* (Boston: Little, Brown, 1977) and Daniel J. Levinson, *The Seasons of a Man's Life* (New York: Knopf, 1978).

67. Gilligan, *Different Voice,* p. 155.

68. Ibid., pp. 155–165 passim.

69. Perry, *Forms,* p. 160.

70. Ibid., p. 136.

71. G. W. Allport, "Psychological Models for Guidance," in *Guidance: An Examination,* ed. R. L. Mosher et al. (New York: Harcourt Brace & World, 1965), pp. 13–23. Cited in Parks, *Critical Years,* p. 69.

72. T. S. Kuhn, "The Function of Dogmatism in Scientific Research," in *Readings in the Philosophy of Science,* ed. B. Brody (Englewood Cliffs, N.J.: Prentice Hall, 1970), pp. 356–373.

73. Robert N. Wennberg.

74. Rev. Peter Griffiths, Northside Community Church, 1988.

75. Holmes, *Idea,* p. 85.

76. V. J. Mannoia, University of Zimbabwe, Christian Union talk.

77. Fowler's description of what Parks calls "convictional commitment" is in J. Fowler and S. Keen, *Life Maps: Conversations on the Journey of Faith,* ed. J. Berryman (Waco, Tex.: Word, 1978), pp. 17–21. Parks also alludes to Ricoeur and to pages 82–83, 81, so the source here is unclear.

78. Samir Masouh, conversation at Seattle Pacific University, June 1990.

79. Cited in Parks, *Critical Years,* p. 51. No reference to Ricoeur is given.

80. Newman, *Idea,* p. 87.

81. Trueblood, *Idea,* p. 19.

82. If this is really Kohlberg's argument, it is specious. Although it is true that from the fact cultural relativism ethical relativism does *not* follow, it is true for the same reason that from observations of cultural "objectivism" ethical objectivism does *not* follow. Cf. Sandin, *Rehabilitation,* p. 74.

83. Cf. Sandin, *Rehabilitation,* pp. 38ff.

84. "Kohlberg is an ethical formalist in the sense that he views the content of morality as derivable from an analysis of the formal character of moral judgment" (Sandin, *Rehabiliation,* p. 76).

85. Ibid., pp. 80f.

86. Ibid., p. 79. He says Kohlberg leaves out a "theory of good" and a "theory of virtue," addressing only a "theory of rights, duties, and obligations" (p. 79). The irony here is that Sandin himself seems formalistic. He sounds very much like a moral methodist when he stresses that "the basic aim of moral education is not to inculcate virtues but to nurture the capacity for autonomous moral thinking and decision making" (p. 8). Cf. "moral education is concerned not with the prescription of conduct or of policy, but with the general principles of morality and with the *methods of moral judgment*" (p. 8). In fact, this stress on rational, free, dialectic method is Sandin's solution in moral education to reconciling ethical objectivism with the pluralism of contemporary moralities (p. 7).

87. *Nicomachean Ethics* 2.6.1106b36.

88. See Sandin, *Rehabilitation,* p. 164. He is describing "academic virtue."

89. For him the chief virtue is self–control.

90. Perry, *Forms,* p. 112, describing the habit of relativism.

91. Newman, *Idea,* p. 76.

92. Ibid., p. 86; emphasis added.

93. Paraphrasing Aristotle, *Nicomachean Ethics* 2.4.1105a28–1105b12. Cited in Sandin, *Rehabilitation,* p. 167.

CHAPTER 4. WHY IS CRITICAL COMMITMENT CHRISTIAN?

1. Ibid.

2. William G. Perry, *Forms of Intellectual and Ethical Development in the College Years* (New York: Holt, Rhinehart, Winston, 1970), p. 39.

3. Ibid., p. 37.

4. Ibid.

5. Perry, *Forms,* p. 38; emphasis added.

6. Arthur Holmes, *The Idea of a Christian College* (Grand Rapids, Mich.: Eerdmanns, 1975), p. 87.

7. Ibid., pp. 89f.

8. Perry, *Forms,* p. 33.

9. Parks, *Critical Years,* p. 52.

10. Perry, *Forms,* p. 144.

11. Ibid., p. 175.

12. Ibid., p. 131.

13. As Arthur Holmes says, "Faith and intellect like love cannot be forced and must not be, if each is to play its part" Holmes, *Idea,* p. 78.

14. Perry, *Forms,* p. 176.

15. Paul Tillich, *The Courage to Be* (New Haven, Conn.: Yale University Press, 1952); Perry acknowledges his own existential bent on page 203.

16. Parks, *Critical Years,* p. 49.

17. David Elton Trueblood, *The Idea of a College* (New York: Harper, 1959), p. 23.

18. Holmes, *Idea,* p. 26.

19. Earl Balfour in Belle Valerie Gaunt and George Trevelyan, *A Tent in Which to Pass a Summer's Night: An Anthology for a New Age* (London: Coventure, 1977), p. 6; cited in Parks, *Critical Years,* p. 71.

20. Perry, *Forms,* p. 203.

21. Ibid., p. 202.

22. Robert T. Sandin, *Rehabilitation of Virtue: Foundations of Moral Education* (New York: Praeger, 1992), p. 63.

23. Ibid., p. 63.

24. Parks, *Critical Years,* p. 50.

25. Ibid., p. 44.

26. To whatever extent that Kierkegaard must be interpreted as antirational (irrational), I find analogies with his fideistic "uncritical commitment" not helpful. What I do want to affirm, however, is that critical commitment goes beyond reason, as virtue theory goes beyond formalistic ethics. It is certainly more like Kierkegaard than Sartre, more like James than Clifford, and more like Peirce than even James.

27. Sandin, *Rehabilitation,* pp. 63–64. Cf. Sandin's reference to "generating meaning" (p. 63) and the contrast of "creating" knowledge and "discovering" it (p. 69). His entire chapter 4, "Anti–Intellectualism of the Schools," is directed quite plainly at "the new ethical and epistemological subjectivism." Although ethical subjectivism seems more clearly inconsistent with orthodoxy, Sandin lumps it together with radically subjectivist epistemology, which to me oversimplifies matters.

28. These properly basic beliefs may include those that are self–evident, incorrigible, and others.

29. Sandin, *Rehabilitation,* p. 62.

30. Ibid., pp. 62–63.

31. See, for example, Stephen Toulmin and gestalt psychology.

32. See, for example, Thomas Kuhn, Larry Laudan, and Imre Lakatos.

33. George Marsden describes the unwillingness of many secular institutions to recognize their assumptions, calling it "methodological secularization" in his article, "The Soul of The American University," in *First Things* (New York: Institute on Religion and Public Life, January 1991), pp. 44–47.

34. Roberta Hestenes, *Christian College Coalition Bulletin,* January 1991, Special Section, page 2.

35. Additional comments immediately preceding those quoted: "In the past, the educational establishment has allowed the public to believe that subject matter is presented by teachers in a neutral, objective manner. The major threat to academic freedom . . . came from those with religious commitments, such as conservative Christians. Now it is increasingly clear that most professors have at least implicit political or religious positions, and these positions are expressed in the classroom, whether it is a Christian college or state university. . . . This is exciting." David K. Winter, "Political Correctness, and American Higher Education Today," Westmont College, chapel address, October 2, 1991.

CHAPTER 5. HOW IS CRITICAL COMMITMENT PRODUCED?

1. In part III, I will turn to the practical matter of how colleges can implement the distinctive genius of Christian liberal arts. That genius includes both the intrinsic value of critical commitment we are discussing here as well as the goal of integration to be discussed in part II. But without anticipating the concrete suggestions in part III, I want to conclude part I by spelling out what I believe are four important principles that should guide any institution desiring to make critical commitment a major goal of its curriculum. They are dissonance, habits, modeling, and community. I must remind the reader of my interactionist assumption about development. Although these principles *may* be consistent with, or even helpful to, maturationist and cultural transmission theories of development, they are not shaped with those alternatives in mind.

2. Arthur Holmes, *The Idea of a Christian College* (Grand Rapids, Mich.: Eerdmanns, 1975), p. 91.

3. Lawrence Kohlberg and Rochelle Mayer, "Development as the Aim of Education," *Harvard Educational Review,* Vol. 42, No. 4, Nov. 1972, p. 459.

4. Ronald Duska and Mariellen Whelan, *Moral Development: A Guide to Piaget and Kohlberg* (New York: Paulist, 1975), p. 104.

5. James Fowler and Sam Keen, *Life Maps: Conversations on the Journey of Faith* (Waco, Tex.: Word, 1978), p. 138.

6. Nicholas Wolterstorff, *Educating for Responsible Action* (Grand Rapids, Mich.: Eerdmanns, 1980), p. 27.

7. Duska and Whelan, *Moral Development,* p. 103.

8. And even then *only* when combined with modeling of the higher stage, as I describe in the section below on community. In other words, dissonance is a necessary but *not* sufficient condition for development.

9. Parks, *Critical Years,* p. 47.

10. Perry, *Forms,* p. 90.

11. Perry, *Forms,* p. 210, citing D. E. Hunt, "A Conceptual Systems Change Model and Its Application to Education," in *Experience, Structure, and Adaptability,* ed. O. J. Harvey (New York: Springer, 1966), pp. 277–302.

12. Winter, David G., David C. McClelland, and Abigail J. Stewart, *A New Case for the Liberal Arts* (San Francisco: Jossey-Bass, 1981), p. 138.

13. Winter, McClelland, and Stewart, *New Case,* p. 139, citing P. Woodruff, *The Men Who Ruled India* (London: Jonathan Cape, 1953). This principle of deliberately in-

troduced dissonance remains true, though perhaps to a lesser degree, of select private schools in England and especially in former British colonies (e.g., Zimbabwe and South Africa).

14. Fowler and Keen, *Life Maps*, p. 123.

15. Keen says that there are conditions under which "once-born" journeys can replace the revolutionary "multiborn" journeys so often characterized by failure.

16. Holmes, *Idea,* p. 91.

17. James H. Bryan and Nancy H. Walbek, "Preaching and Practicing Generosity: Children's Actions and Reactions," *Child Development* 41, no. 2 (1970): 346.

18. Wolterstorff, *Educating for Responsible Action*, makes this distinction among knowledge, ability, and tendency (e.g., p. 51).

19. Aristotle, *Nicomachean Ethics* 10.9.

20. Ibid., 2.3: "Virtues are concerned with actions and passions."

21. Perry, *Forms,* p. 112.

22. John Henry Newman, *The Idea of a University Defined and Illustrated: In Nine Discourses Delivered to the Catholics of Dublin,* ed. M. J. Svaglic (New York: Holt, Rinehart, Winston, 1960), pp. 76–115.

23. Plato, *Meno* 573, 577.

24. One might be tempted to say Plato's distinction is not the same as Aristotle's. One might say that what Plato calls knowledge differs from what Aristotle calls intellectual virtue in that the former is merely cognitive while the latter adds a tendency to act. But for Plato, knowing the good is to do it, and thus the two seem the same.

25. Aristotle, *Nicomachean Ethics* 2.1. Aristotle agreed with Plato that to a certain extent both are the result of nature, independent of education. But when it comes to the part that *can* be played by education, Aristotle makes plain the relative superiority of habituation over teaching in 10.9: "Now some think that we are made good by nature, others by habituation, others by teaching. Nature's part evidently does not depend on us, but as a result of some divine causes is present in those who are truly fortunate; while argument and teaching, we may suspect, are not powerful with all men, but the soul of the student must first have been cultivated by means of habits. . . . It is hard, if not impossible, to remove by argument the traits that have long since been incorporated in the character; and perhaps we must be content if, when all the influences by which we are thought to become good are present, we get some tincture of virtue."

26. Aristotle, *Nicomachean Ethics* 2.1.

27. Winter, McClelland, and Stewart, *New Case,* p. 140.

28. Wolterstorff, *Educating for Responsible Action,* p. 29.

29. Bruce Wilshire, *The Moral Collapse of the University* (Albany: SUNY Press, 1990), p. 91.

30. Perry, *Forms,* p. 212.

31. Ibid., p. 101.

32. Ibid., p. 213. Interviews revealed this at work. "Somehow I wanted to emulate [such people] because they seemed in some way noble people, and what they were doing seemed somehow noble and lofty—a very moral and superior type of thing. I think I fastened on this" (p. 158).

33. Kohlberg, "Development," p. 459.

34. R. J. Schenkat et al., *It Stands to Reason: The Rationale and Implementation of a Development Based, Liberal Arts Oriented, Teacher Education Program* (Winona, Minn.: College of St. Teresa, 1985), p. 5.

35. William Bennett, *To Reclaim A Legacy: A Report on the Humanities in Higher Education* (Washington, D.C.: National Endowment for the Humanities, 1984), p. 8.

36. James H. Bryan and Nancy H. Walbek, "Preaching and Practicing Generosity: Children's Actions and Reactions," *Child Development* 41, no. 2 (1970): 329, opening abstract.

37. A. Bandura, D. Ross, and S. Ross, "Vicarious Reinforcement and Imitative Learning," *Journal of Abnormal Social Psychology* 67 (1963): 601–607; and A. Bandura and F. L. Menlove, "Factors Determining Vicarious Extinction of Avoidance Behavior through Symbolic Modeling," *Journal of Personality and Social Psychology* 8 (1968): 99–108. These dealt with courage and aggression, not generosity.

38. Bryan and Walbek, "Preaching and Practicing Generosity," *Child Development* 41, no. 2 (1970): 334, table 2, "neutral" columns (13 vs. 7).

39. Wolterstorff, *Educating for Responsible Action,* p. 53. Stein's article is found in *Child Development* 38 (1967): 157–169.

40. David Rosenham and Anne Burrowes, "Preaching and Practicing: Effects of Channel Discrepancy on Norm Internalization," *Child Development* 39, no. 1 (1968): 297, fig. 1. Interestingly, Rosenham and Burrowes also showed that although there were fewer violations associated with the consistently strict model than the self–indulgent one (W. Mischel and R. M. Liebert, "Effects of Discrepancies between Observed and Imposed Reward Criteria on Their Acquisition and Transmission," *Journal of Personality and Social Psychology,* 1966, 3, pp. 45–53, said *none*), there were even fewer such violations with a model who was consistently lenient with both herself and the child. And there were still fewer violations where the model held herself to a higher standard than the child ("child indulgent"). The "down side" of these latter two cases of few violations is that it entailed a dramatically lower internalization of the highest standard: fewer "criminals" but also fewer "stars." Cf. Elizabeth Midlarsky, James H. Bryan, and Philip Brickman, "Aversive Approval: Interactive Effects of Modeling and Reinforcement on Altruistic Behavior," *Child Development* 44, no. 2 (1973): 321–328; and James H. Bryan, Joel Redfield, and Sandra Mader, "Words and Deeds about Altruism and the Subsequent Reinforcement Power of the Model," *Child Development* 42, no. 5 (1971): 1501–1508.

41. Wolterstorff, *Educating for Responsible Action,* p. 57.

42. James Bryan and M. Test, "Models and Helping," *Journal of Personality and Social Psychology* 6 (1967): 400–407; and M. A. Test and J. H. Bryan, "Dependency, Reciprocity, and Models," *Journal of Social Psychology* 78 (1969): 205–212.

43. Paul Harmon and Kay Evans, "When to Use Cognitive Modeling," *Training and Development Journal* 38, no. 3 (1984): 67–68. Quoted from the abstract in *Psychology Abstracts.*

44. George M. Marsden, "The Soul of the American University," *First Things,* January 1991, p. 45.

45. Some who have followed Wolterstorff's work on internalizing tendencies (*Educating for Responsible Action*) notice the absence of reference to "discipline," the second of Wolterstorff's two major strategies for education (chap. 5). I omit it here because it seems to me that it is less appropriate for developmental transitions usually occurring in college–age students. There may be empirical data to justify this claim, but I have not found it.

46. Some will point out that the catch is to know which students are appropriately developed and which are still too immature to be exposed to such diversity. This is

absolutely correct. In the first place this objection argues for a low faculty–student ratio so exposure can be more tailored to the individual student. Second, while this is a slippery slope, I would argue that Christian institutions may tend to err more on the side of avoiding diversity than on the side of exposing students to too much.

47. Perry, *Forms*, p. 65.

48. Ibid., p. 96.

49. Ibid., pp. 162f.

50. Ibid., p. 200.

51. Duska and Whelan, *Moral Development*, p. 107. In practical applications of this notion, Duska and Whelan make many practical suggestions for the role community plays in promoting moral development (pp. 113ff).

52. Fowler and Keen, *Life Maps*, p. 147. He says that the journey of the multi-born is much more disruptive to self and to others than he would like. It brings tragedy. He goes on to admit that while it has not been his own experience, there are better ways.

53. Ibid., p. 159.

54. Parks, *Critical Years*, p. 61.

55. Ibid., p. 63. This criticism is also raised against Kohlberg because he restricted his studies to male Harvard students. Carol Gilligan's *In a Different Voice* stresses the need to consider alternative characterizations of mature cognition, faith, and moral development. This alternative, like Parks's and ours, takes very seriously the place of community.

56. Parks, *Critical Years*, p. 70.

57. Ibid., p. 145.

58. Ibid., p. 141.

59. Ibid., p. 140.

60. Parks, *Critical Years*, p. 137.

61. Kohlberg, "Development," pp. 475f.

62. Ibid., p. 475.

63. Sandin, *Rehabilitation*, p. 38.

PART II. CHRISTIAN LIBERAL ARTS
MEANS TACKLING REAL-WORLD PROBLEMS

1. Geoffrey Hartman, *Saving the Text: Literature/Derrida/Philosophy* (Baltimore: Johns Hopkins University Press, 1984), pp. 60–61.

CHAPTER 6. WHAT IS INTEGRATION?

1. Arthur DeJong, *Reclaiming a Mission* (Grand Rapids, Mich.: Eerdmans, 1990); Ernest Boyer, *Scholarship Reconsidered: Priorities of the Professoriate* (Princeton, N.J.: Carnegie Foundation for the Advancement of Teaching, 1990); George Marsden, *The Soul of the American University: From Protestant Establishment to Established Nonbelief* (New York: Oxford, 1994); David B. Tyack, ed., *Turning Points in American Educational History* (New York: Wiley, 1967).

2. Theodore M. Benditt, "The Research Demands of Teaching in Modern Higher Education," in *Morality, Responsibility, and the University,* ed. Steven Cahn (Philadelphia: Temple University, 1990), p. 2.

3. Boyer, *Scholarship Reconsidered,* passim.

4. Bruce Wilshire, *The Moral Collapse of the University* (Albany: SUNY Press, 1990), p. 64.

5. Ibid.; cf. p. 73.

6. Boyer, *Scholarship Reconsidered,* p. 37.

7. George Douglas, *Education without Impact: How Our Universities Fail the Young* (New York: Carol Publishing/Birch Lane Press, 1992). Cited in *Chronicle of Higher Education,* March 10, 1993, p. B6.

8. Charles Eliot, *Educational Reform: Essays and Addresses* (New York: Century, 1898), p. 27, cited in Walter Metzger, "The Academic Profession in the United States," in *The Academic Profession: National, Disciplinary, and Institutional Settings,* ed. Burton Clark (Berkeley: University of California Press, 1987), p. 135; and in Boyer, *Scholarship Reconsidered,* p. 4.

9. E. Shils, "The Order of Learning in the United States," in *The Organization of Knowledge in Modern America,* eds. A. Oleson and J. Voss (Baltimore: Johns Hopkins University Press, 1979), p. 28, cited in Boyer, *Scholarship Reconsidered,* p. 9.

10. Boyer, *Scholarship Reconsidered,* p. 9.

11. Douglas, *Education without Impact,* p. B6.

12. Allan Bloom, *Closing of the American Mind* (New York: Simon & Schuster, 1987); Wilshire, *Moral Collapse;* Dinesh D'Souza, *Illiberal Education* (New York: Macmillan, 1991); Douglas, *Education without Impact.*

13. Francis Oakley in his book *Community of Learning* (Oxford, 1992) identifies and tries to rebut the following three threads: (1) the dominance of research over teaching, (2) the overspecialization of knowledge, and (3) the denigration of Western traditions (pp. 111–112ff.).

14. *Involvement in Learning: Realizing the Potential of American Higher Education,* reprinted in *Chronicle of Higher Education,* October 24, 1984, p. 36.

15. Ibid., p. 43. Cf. Ezra Bowen, "Bringing Colleges Under Fire," *Time,* October 29, 1984, p. 78.

16. *Involvement in Learning,* p. 43.

17. Ibid., p. 44.

18. Ibid., p. 49.

19. William Bennett, *To Reclaim A Legacy: A Report on the Humanities in Higher Education* (Washington, D.C.: National Endowment for the Humanities, 1984); cited in *Chronicle,* November 28, 1984, p. 16.

20. Boyer, *Scholarship Reconsidered,* p. 13.

21. He says that critics decry "academic specialization, the balkanization of disciplines, the fragmentation of knowledge, [and] the inability (or unwillingness) to honor and nurture the generalizing spirit." According to Oakley, they conclude that overspecialization is a problem because it entails a loss of particular content (*Community of Learning,* p. 122).

22. Ibid., p. 124.

23. Oakley, *Community of Learning,* p. 124, citing William Bennett, *To Reclaim a Legacy,* pp. 7, 22.

24. A. N. Whitehead, *"*Aims of Education and Other Essays," in *Alfred North White-head: An Anthology,* ed. F. S. C. Northrup and Mason W. Gross (New York: Macmillan, 1955), p. 135.

25. C. Jencks and D. Riesman, *The Academic Revolution* (New York: Doubleday Anchor, 1969), cited in K. Ruscio, "The Distinctive Scholarship of the Selective Liberal Arts College," *Journal of Higher Education* 58, no. 2 (March-April 1987), p. 206.

26. *Involvement in Learning,* p. 46.

27. *To Reclaim a Legacy,* p. 16.

28. Boyer, *Scholarship Reconsidered,* p. 11, citing Dolores Burke, *A New Academic Marketplace* (Westport, Conn.: Greenwood Press, 1988), p. 22, citing T. Caplow and R. McGee, *The Academic Marketplace* (New York: Basic Books, 1958).

29. Ibid., p. 11.

30. Courtney Leatherman, "Definition of Faculty Scholarship Must Be Expanded to Include Teaching, Carnegie Foundation Says," *Chronicle,* December 5, 1990, p. 16.

31. John Goldman, "Universities Rated 'F' for Inability to Help Solve Society's Problems," *Los Angeles Times,* August 7, 1990, p. A5.

32. Boyer, *Scholarship Reconsidered,* p. 12, table 1.1.

33. Ibid., table A–32.

34. Carolyn Mooney, "Critics Within and Without Academe Assail Professors at Research Universities," *Chronicle,* October 28, 1992, p. A17.

35. Thomas Langfitt, "The Cost of Higher Education," *Change,* November–December 1990, vol. 2, no. 6, p. 14.

36. David Savage, "Seniors Assail Undergraduate Education at UCLA Campus," *Los Angeles Times,* May 23, 1985, p. 3.

37. Peter J. Gray et al., "Myths and Realities," *AAHE Bulletin,* December 1991, p. 4.

38. Scott Heller, "Stronger Push for Research on Liberal Arts Campuses Brings Fears That Their Culture Is Threatened," *Chronicle,* July 5, 1990, p. A14.

39. Ibid.

40. David Savage, "Seniors Assail Undergraduate Education at UCLA Campus," *Los Angeles Times,* May 23, 1985, p. 3.

41. Robin Wilson quoting Jennifer Ellard in "Undergraduates at Large Universities Found to Be Increasingly Dissatisfied," *Chronicle,* January 9, 1991.

42. Scott Heller, "Stronger Push for Research on Liberal Arts Campuses Brings Fears That Their Culture Is Threatened," *Chronicle,* July 5, 1990, p. A14.

43. Ibid.

44. Wilshire, *Moral Collapse,* p. 74.

45. Martin Trow and Oliver Fulton, "Research Activity in American Higher Education," in *Teachers and Students: Aspects of American Higher Education,* ed. Martin Trow (New York: McGraw-Hill, 1975), pp. 57–58.

46. Trow and Fulton, *Teachers and Students,* pp. 42–45, cited in Oakley, *Community of Learning,* p. 116.

47. Peter Gray, Robert Froh, Robert Diamond, "Myths and Realities," *AAHE Bulletin* 44, no. 4 (1991): 4–5. First data from a national study funded by the Lily Endowment on the balance between research and teaching at research universities through the National Study of Research Universities, Center for Instructional Development, Syracuse University, 111 Waverly Avenue, Suite 220, Syracuse, N.Y. 13244-2320; tel. 315-443-4571.

48. Gray, Froh, and Diamond offer some interesting data relevant to this issue. They report that although faculty, department heads, deans, and the office of academic affairs each believe they themselves hold teaching and research to be of equal importance, "faculty perceive that the higher one's position in the university administration, the greater one's bias toward research" (p. 4). Sadly, the greatest gap in perception is between faculty perception of deans' emphasis and the deans' own perception of that emphasis. It appears that deans may be preaching one thing and practicing another when it comes to personnel actions.

49. If the liberal arts colleges are taken out, the ratios approach or exceed 2 to 1, moving toward research. R. Miller, H. Chen, J. Hart, and C. Killian, "New Approaches to Faculty Evaluation—A Survey, Initial Report" (submitted to Carnegie Foundation, September 4, 1990). Cited by Boyer, *Scholarship Reconsidered,* p. 31. Oakley goes on to say that, in any case, research does not come at the expense of teaching or even administrative involvement. Citing Trow's analysis of the 1969 data, he says that faculty who publish most frequently were neither less likely to see undergraduates outside of office hours and informally nor less likely to be involved in administrative matters. He concludes that "one should not simply assume that some sort of zero–sum game is necessarily involved. . . . The common view that a heavy commitment to research is necessarily bought at the cost of reduced attention to teaching and other institutional service is clearly not warranted" (Oakley, *Community of Learning,* p. 117).

Oakley speculates that some faculty may simply be more energetic than others. Apparently he means that some can do it all while others cannot. I wonder if that is a kind way of saying that faculty who only teach are lazy. But aside from the fact that one might ask whether "time outside of office hours" or "informal time with students" is a measure of teaching, and his own admission that such data say little about the *quality* of the teaching or administrative work, his speculative conclusion seems contrary to the direct question asked of 1989 faculty respondents. When asked whether they felt "pressure to publish reduces the quality of teaching" at their institution, a sizable group of the faculty at institutions where research is most emphasized clearly believe it *does* detract from teaching: 53 percent at research institutions, 54 percent at doctorate-granting institutions, and 41 percent at comprehensive institutions. If the trend is really toward research criteria for promotion, then it does not seem unreasonable to expect that more and more faculty *will* come to see the trade-off as a zero–sum game played with their own time and energy.

50. Gray, Froh, and Diamond, "Myths and Realities," pp. 4–5.

51. Wilshire, *Moral Collapse,* p. 66, citing Michael Moffatt, *The Coming of Age in New Jersey* (New Brunswick, N.J.: Rutgers University Press, 1989) dealing with dormitory life at Rutgers.

52. Quoted by John Goldman, "Universities Rated 'F' for Inability to Help Solve Society's Problems," *Los Angeles Times,* August 7, 1990, p. A5.

53. Page Smith, *Killing the Spirit* (New York: Viking, 1990), p. 179.

54. Ibid., pp. 178, 197. In an even more scathing critique of research done by the American professoriate, Charles Sykes concludes that "much of what passes for knowledge creation makes only the most piddling contribution to the pool of human wisdom. Much of it is merely humbug." Charles Sykes, *ProfScam: Professors and the Demise of Higher Education* (New York: St. Martin's, 1990), p. 103.

55. Pablo Parrish, "Seven Ways to Lengthen a Publication List Without Doing Anything Very Original," *Chronicle,* May 18, 1983.

56. First items printed in Anne Matthews, "Deciphering Victorian Underwear and Other Seminars: Or How to Be Profane and Scholarly—All While Looking for a Job—at the Modern Language Association's Annual Convention," *New York Times Magazine,* February 10, 1991. Second-to-last item from *Sociological Abstracts,* where you will also find "Agrarian Processes within Plantation Economies in Guyana and Coastal Ecuador," "Macro–Micro Linkages and Structural Transformation: The Move from Full–time to Part–time Farming in a North Florida Agricultural Community." To the last might be added, "A Comparative Study of Cuticular Folds in the Anthers of Lycopersicon–SPP and Solanum–Pennellii by Scanning Electron Microscopy" and from *Philosophers' Index,* "Smolensky's Interpretation of Connectionism: The Implications for Symbolic Theory" and "Heidegger and Epideictic Discourse: The Rhetorical Performance of Meditative Thinking." My own undergraduate thesis was "Detection of the Hanle Effect Using Intense Cadmium–Ion Vapor Laser Systems." And my own Ph.D. dissertation was "Whitehead's Ontological Principle: A Defense and Interpretation."

57. Scott Heller, "Stronger Push for Research on Liberal Arts Campuses Brings Fears That Their Culture Is Threatened," *Chronicle,* July 5, 1990, p. A14.

58. Hugh Brown and Lewis Mayhew, *American Higher Education* (New York: New York Center for Applied Research, 1965). See, for example, pp. 68ff.: "Whenever studies of teaching effectiveness are made as judged by students, no relationship is found between judged teaching effectiveness and research productivity." Brown and Mayhew cite F. C. Rosecrance, *The American College and Its Teachers* (New York: Macmillan, 1962) and insist that Rosecrance's defense of the connection between teaching and research is "clearly ideological."

59. Smith, *Killing the Spirit,* pp. 178, 197.

60. I support the model of research institutes associated with universities (e.g., the Jet Propulsion Lab with Caltech and the Lincoln Labs with MIT). But it is helpful only so long as the priorities for staff on each side are kept clear and distinct. Although dominant in natural sciences, this model might be used effectively in social sciences and even the humanities.

61. Richard Chait, "The Pro–Teaching Movement Should Try Economic Pressures," *Chronicle,* July 11, 1990, p. A36.

62. Larry Gordon, "Stanford to Focus on Undergraduates," *Los Angeles Times,* March 3, 1991. The $7 million plan includes cash bonuses to outstanding teachers, creation of sophomore "cluster" seminars, and easing the publish-or-perish mentality by limiting the numbers of articles a professor can submit for promotion reviews and allowing textbook writing, previously sometimes ridiculed, to be given equal attention with research.

63. Ernest Boyer (an alumnus of the college I now serve as president) has also called for a redefinition of "scholarship" in *Scholarship Reconsidered.* His redefinition is intended for all in higher education whereas mine is concerned primarily with those in Christian liberal arts. However, there is still considerable overlap. What I call integrative scholarship below plainly includes his "scholarship of integration" (my "integration of disciplines") and "scholarship of application" (my "integration of theory and practice"). His "scholarship of discovery" I take as a foundation or at most a means to the end of integrative scholarship. His "scholarship of teaching" I take as

the end of integrative scholarship. And, finally, I do not believe he has clearly affirmed what I call the "integration of values/faith and learning." But that is not surprising given the wider audience he addresses.

64. "Unnecessary" is probably a foolish overstatement because there are many Christian liberal arts institutions today at which self–sacrificial faculty continue to wear many "hats." And they sometimes still teach heavy course loads out of their areas of specialty and even competence.

65. Boyer also repudiates this dilettantism (*Scholarship Reconsidered,* p. 19).

66. The topic of defining integration in the Christian context seems to be one of growing interest. See, for example, Ken Badley, "Integral Learning and Faith/Learning Integration: Competing Christian Conceptions," *Journal of Research on Christian Education* 3, no. 1 (1994): 13–33; or "Two 'Cop–Outs' in Faith Learning Integration: Incarnational Integration and Worldviewish Integration," *Spectrum* 28, no. 2 (1996): 105–118. See also efforts by the Council for Christian Colleges and Universities and the Consortium of Christian Colleges to promote faculty discussion around this long-standing theme.

67. Richard Cummings, "Interdisciplinary Challenge," *National Forum* [Phi Kappa Phi journal], Spring 1989, pp. 2–3.

68. Jerry Gaff, "The Resurgence of Interdisciplinary Studies," *National Forum,* Spring 1989, pp. 4–5.

69. Some might say that this aspect of integrative studies is what should be called multidisciplinarity, not interdisciplinarity. I prefer to use "interdisciplinarity" more generically and use general studies and bridge studies to distinguish the ways in which interdisciplinary studies both combine the questions of multiple disciplines *and* address questions belonging to no single discipline.

70. Marx, Leo, "A Case for Interdisciplinary Thinking," *National Forum,* Spring 1989, p. 11.

71. Cummings, "Interdisciplinary Challenge," *National Forum,* Spring 1989, p. 2.

72. John Goldman, "Universities Rated 'F' for Inability to Help Solve Society's Problems," *Los Angeles Times,* August 7, 1990, p. A5.

73. Derek Bok, *Universities and the Future of America* (Durham, N.C.: Duke University Press, 1990), p. 105. He goes on to illustrate this by showing that people like Rachel Carson, Ralph Nader, Michael Harrington, and Betty Friedan raised consciousness of important social issues from *outside* academia.

74. Nicholas Wolterstorff, *Educating for Responsible Action* (Grand Rapids, Mich.: Eerdmans, 1980).

75. Garrett Bauman, "Interdisciplinary Studies for the 21st Century," *National Forum,* Spring 1989, p. 40.

76. Bok, *Universities,* p. 69.

77. Ibid., p. 70, citing the *Harvard Report* (1945), p. 72.

78. Louis E. Raths, Merrill Harmin, and Sidney B. Simon, *Values and Teaching* (Columbus, Ohio: Merrill Books, 1966), cited in Wolterstorff, *Educating,* p. 121.

79. Wolterstorff, *Educating,* p. 122.

80. Or relative at most to the individual's community.

81. For further criticism of "values clarification" in education, see Sandin, *Rehabilitation,* pp. 56–61.

82. For more discussion on the avoidance of indoctrination in moral education, see the section on community in the preceding chapter; Parks and Kohlberg on democratic community (passim), and Sandin on the role of dialectic in educational community.

83. Kenneth Ruscio, "The Distinctive Scholarship of the Selective Liberal Arts College," *Journal of Higher Education* 58, no. 2 (1987): 207.

84. Ibid., pp. 213, 220.

85. Ibid., p. 214.

86. Ibid., p. 216.

87. Ibid., p. 219.

88. Ibid., p. 217.

89. Ibid., p. 218.

90. Ibid., p. 216.

91. Ibid., p. 219.

92. Ibid.

CHAPTER 7. WHY PURSUE INTEGRATION?

1. William G. Perry, *Forms of Intellectual and Ethical Development in the College Years* (New York: Holt, Rhinehart, Winston, 1970), p. 166.

2. Perry, *Forms,* p. 167.

3. Ronald Marstin, *Beyond Our Tribal Gods: The Maturing of Faith* (Maryknoll, N.Y.: Orbis, 1979), p. 34.

4. Micah 6:8.

5. Matthew 25:45.

6. Luke 4:18; first acknowledgment of mission.

7. Philippians 2:4–8.

8. Jerry G. Gaff, "The Resurgence of Interdisciplinary Studies," *National Forum* [Phi Kappa Phi journal], Spring 1989, p. 4.

9. Gaff, "Resurgence," p. 4.

10. Ibid.

11. It is interesting that Troy Martin at Berkeley studied the effects of racial diversity there and found that although students of various racial groups do not want to mix socially, they want more joint work projects in classes because they believe it builds community and the ability to work together.

12. Ernest Boyer quotes Derek Bok, who says the situation is no better for secular institutions providing leadership: "Armed with the security of tenure and the time to study the world with care, professors would appear to have a unique opportunity to act as society's scouts to signal impending problems long before they are visible to others. Yet rarely have members of the academy succeeded in discovering the emerging issues and bringing them vividly to the attention of the public." Derek Bok, *Universities and the Future of America* (Durham, N.C.: Duke University Press, 1990), p. 105.

13. Romans 12:1.

14. Bruce Wilshire, *The Moral Collapse of the University* (Albany: SUNY Press, 1990), p. 66; Burton Bledstein, *The Culture of Professionalism: The Middle Class and the Development of Higher Education in America* (New York: Norton, 1976), p. xi.

15. Wilshire, *Moral Collapse,* pp. 68f.

CHAPTER 8. HOW CAN A COLLEGE PURSUE INTEGRATION?

1. John Henry Newman, *The Idea of a University Defined and Illustrated: In Nine Discourses Delivered to the Catholics of Dublin,* ed. M. J. Svaglic (New York: Holt, Rinehart, Winston, 1960), p. 76.

2. Elton Trueblood; reprinted in *Faculty Dialogue,* Spring 1991, p. 18.

3. Jerry G. Gaff, "The Resurgence of Interdisciplinary Studies," *National Forum* [Phi Kappa Phi journal], Spring 1989, p. 5.

4. Arthur Holmes, *The Idea of a Christian College* (Grand Rapids, Mich.: Eerdmanns, 1975), p. 96.

CHAPTER 9. HOW CAN PROGRAMS PROMOTE CHRISTIAN LIBERAL ARTS?

1. Cited in the *Chronicle of Higher Education,* November 28, 1984, p. 16.

2. Leland Miles, "Renaissance and Academe," *National Forum* [Phi Kappa Phi journal], Spring 1989, p. 17.

3. Scott Heller, "Model Curriculum for Colleges Proposed by Humanities Chief," *Chronicle,* October 11, 1989, p. 1.

4. Lynne Cheney, "50 Hours," cited in *Chronicle,* October 11, 1989, p. A16.

5. Departments perhaps but not majors. More on this below.

6. See Page Smith, *Killing the Spirit: Higher Education in America* (New York: Viking, 1990), passim.

7. Lawrence Kohlberg and Rochelle Mayer, "Development as the Aim of Education," *Harvard Educational Review,* Vol. 42, No. 4, Nov. 1972, p. 459.

8. Nicholas Wolterstorff, *Educating for Responsible Action* (Grand Rapids, Mich.: Eerdmanns, 1980), p. 27.

9. Ronald Duska and Mariellen Whelan, *Moral Development: A Guide to Piaget and Kohlberg* (New York: Paulist, 1975), p. 103.

10. The CIRP Project at UCLA and the Council for Christian Colleges and Universities Project funded by FIPSE are good examples that should be considered very carefully, especially the longitudinal studies in the latter.

11. Some school reformers will argue that Bloom's taxonomy should be applied at all levels or grades. I agree that when a new subject is introduced, new factual information must be introduced. The point I am making has to do with how far beyond that stage—how far along Bloom's scale—we can and should expect students at different stages of development to proceed. Haphazard sequencing will ask students to do more with the material than they are able to do and frustrate them as well as the teacher.

12. I can, however, imagine skill courses such as writing or public speaking, or largely content courses, say, for example, that deal with current events, where the requisite cognitive or moral development is not high. In this case it seems any disadvantage arising from having students with a wide range of such developmental stages is overridden by the benefits of having students with a wide range of experience and diversity.

13. For example, *Report on England Semester,* Westmont College, 1990.

14. I do not mean to suggest that there is only one way to learn. Multiple intelligence theory is making that clear. Each faculty member should attempt to teach in a variety of ways in order to accommodate as much as possible this variation in students' learning styles. This does not, however, make them any less responsible for modeling higher levels of cognitive, moral, and faith development for students of all learning styles in their classes.

15. Perry, *Forms,* p. 210, citing L. G. Wispe ("Evaluating Section Teaching Methods in the Introductory Course," *Journal of Educational Research,* 1951, Vol. 45, pp. 161–186), and D. E. Hunt ("A Conceptual Systems Change Model and Its Application to Education," in O. J. Harvey, ed., *Experience, Strategy, and Adaptability* [New York: Springer, 1966], pp. 277–302).

16. Kohlberg, "Development," p. 490.

17. My main point here is to reflect on how one's teaching should vary depending on which cognitive, moral, or faith transition the teacher wishes to facilitate. This is similar to, but not identical with, a related issue that also merits attention in faculty training. Theories about "learning styles" and "multiple intelligences" argue that faculty should adopt a "range" of pedagogical styles in order to facilitate learning by students of differing "intelligences" or "styles." Often faculty know as little about these variations as they do about the developmental theory I am emphasizing here.

18 Boyer, *Scholarship Reconsidered,* including survey data finding that 85 percent of faculty are primarily interested in teaching.

19. There is some controversy about whether cognitive regression is possible. At the very least, dissonance without community will stunt growth.

20. C. S. Lewis, *The Abolition of Man* (London: Oxford University Press, 1943).

21. For example, in teaching the problem of freedom and determinism, the discussion is enhanced when students reading the "cans and ifs" exchange between G. E. Moore and J. L. Austin recognize the difference between the indicative mood and the subjunctive mood. Unless they've had truly excellent preparation in English grammar, they are unlikely to know the difference without having studied a foreign language.

22. Bruce Wilshire, *The Moral Collapse of the University* (Albany: SUNY Press, 1990), p. 79. He also cites Clifford Geertz, who says, "The question of where the 'general' went in 'general education' and how we might contrive to get it back so as to avoid raising up a race of highly trained barbarians . . . is one that haunts anyone who thinks seriously about the intellectual life these days" (*Local Knowledge* [New York: Basic Books, 1983], p. 160).

23. Garrett Bauman, "Interdisciplinary Studies for the Twenty-First Century," *National Forum,* Spring 1989, p. 39.

24. Ibid.

25. Ibid.

26. There are textbooks based on the "case study" approach for virtually every discipline.

27. Cf. Ernest Boyer's approach cited by Jerry Gaff in "The Resurgence of Interdisciplinary Studies," *National Forum*, Spring 1989, p. 5. "Boyer suggests that students should acquire a perspective of their disciplinary subject in an 'enriched major' that requires them to examine three questions: a) What is the history and tradition of the field? b) What are the social and economic implications to be pursued? c) What are the ethical and moral issues within the specialty that need to be confronted?"

28. Ibid., p. 4.

29. Arthur Levine, *When Dreams and Heroes Died: A Portrait of Today's College Student* (San Francisco: Jossey-Bass, 1980).

30. Ibid., pp. 131–132. Cf. the discussion of Levine in Robert Sandin, *The Rehabilitation of Virtue: Foundation of Moral Education* (New York: Praeger, 1992), pp. 21-23.

31. Kenneth Ruscio, "The Distinctive Scholarship of the Selective Liberal Arts College," *Journal of Higher Education* 58, no. 2 (1987): 205ff.

32. Grove City College (although there are no capstone courses); University of Utah Honors Program (described in Phi Kappa Phi *National Forum*, Spring 1989, p. 26.

33. Leland Miles, "Renaissance and Academe," *National Forum*, Spring 1989), p. 17.

34. Cited by Jerry Gaff, "Resurgence," p. 5.

35. Arthur Holmes, *The Idea of a Christian College* (Grand Rapids, Mich.: Eerdmanns, 1975), p. 57.

36. Cooperative Institutional Research Program, conducted jointly by the American Council on Education and UCLA, 1989 results.

37. Ibid.

38. Cited in Elton Trueblood, "The College in America," *Faculty Dialogue,* Spring 1991, p. 17.

39. Jerry Gaff, "Resurgence," p. 5.

40. Perry, *Forms,* p. 213; cited in Randolph J. Schenkat et al., *It Stands to Reason: The Rationale and Implementation of a Development Based, Liberal Arts Oriented, Teacher Education Program* (Winona, Minn.: College of St. Teresa, 1985), p. 5.

41. Holmes, *Idea,* p. 57.

42. Jerry Gaff, "Resurgence," p. 5.

43. Holmes, *Idea,* p. 66.

44. Initial results of the study on student outcomes conducted by the Council for Christian Colleges and Universities and supported by FIPSE suggest that the best way to accelerate identity development is by as little as two weeks immersion in another culture.

45. See David G. Winter, David C. McClelland, and Abigail J. Stewart, *A New Case for the Liberal Arts* (San Francisco: Jossey-Bass, 1981).

46. University of Southern California; Dallas Willard, chair of philosophy, participated.

47. Robert Wennberg, November 25, 1992, conversation citing Randy VanDerMey.

48. Luke 4:18 (Isaiah 61:1); Micah 6; the Sermon on the Mount in Matthew 5.

49. Dinesh D'Souza, *Illiberal Education* (New York: Free Press, 1991), p. 230.

CHAPTER 10. HOW CAN PEOPLE
PROMOTE CHRISTIAN LIBERAL ARTS?

1. Ernest Boyer, *Scholarship Reconsidered: Priorities of the Professoriate* (Princeton, N.J.: Carnegie Foundation for the Advancement of Teaching, 1990), p. 59.

2. Compare ibid., p. 65. "Simply stated, tomorrow's scholars must be liberally educated."

3. Page Smith, *Killing the Spirit: Higher Education in America*. New York: Viking, 1990. p. 178.

4. Ibid., pp. 178–179.

5. Ibid., p. 179. Ernest Boyer makes essentially the same comment in *Scholarship Reconsidered*, p. 28, where he discusses scholarship as "staying in touch with one's field."

6. Larry Gordon, "Stanford to Focus on Undergraduates," *Los Angeles Times*, March 3, 1991, p. A3.

7. National Study of Research Universities, Center for Instructional Development, Syracuse University, 111 Waverly Avenue, Suite 220, Syracuse, N.Y. 13244–2320; tel. 315–443–4571.

8. Carolyn Mooney, "Critics within and without Academe Assail Professors at Research Universities," *Chronicle Of Higher Education*, October 28, 1992, p. A18.

9. R. Edgerton, P. Hutchings, and K. Quinlan, *The Teaching Portfolio: Capturing the Scholarship of Teaching*, (Washington, D.C.: American Association of Higher Education, 1991), p. 3.

10. Francis Oakley, *Community of Learning: The American College and the Liberal Arts Tradition* (Oxford: Oxford University Press, 1992), p. 119, citing Ernest Boyer, *Scholarship Reconsidered* (Princeton, N.J.: Carnegie Foundation for Advancement of Teaching, 1990), pp. 12, 55, and appendix A, table A–23.

11. I find it hard to explain why faculty would report on Carnegie Foundation surveys that the pressure and criteria had shifted while still insisting that *they* had not changed in their own judgment about the relative importance of teaching and research. What's going on here? Who *is* changing the criteria if not the faculty themselves? Are they being hoodwinked by a powerful elite among them? By administrators with skewed perceptions about scholarship or with fantasies about the public relations value for their institutions of faculty with long lists of published work?

12. "Faculty Career Stages and Implications for Professional Development," in *Enhancing Faculty Careers: Strategies for Development and Renewal*, ed. Jack Schuster, Daniel Wheeler et al. (San Francisco: Jossey–Bass, 1990), p. 24.

13. Boyer, *Scholarship Reconsidered*.

14. One example is the "Gordon Plan" at Gordon College in Wenham, Massachusetts. This program has received national attention. See recent mention of the plan in R. Edgerton, P. Hutchings, and K. Quinlan, *The Teaching Portfolio: Capturing the Scholarship of Teaching*, (Washington, D.C.: American Association of Higher Education, 1991).

15. Smith, *Killing the Spirit,* p. 179.

16. There is some evidence to the contrary. A national faculty workload study shows the hours of class preparation for faculty at small liberal arts colleges to be lower than for faculty at research institutions.

17. Community colleges may well have even higher student and preparation loads. But here the expectation for both publication and involvement in students' lives is clearly diminished.

18. The Houghton Institute of Integrative Studies and Calvin College's summer institutes are examples. The Council for Christian Colleges and Universities has also sponsored a series with some of these features, although they have tended to be less thematic and more disciplinary even while attracting faculty from various disciplines. Naturally, they also did not bring together faculty from just one institution, so the benefit to a particular community was not as great. See also Boyer, *Scholarship Reconsidered,* p. 57.

19. Roberta Hestenes, "God's Mission for Higher Education," *Bulletin of the Christian College Coalition,* Special Section, January 1991, p. 1.

20. See Bruce Wilshire's description of this unique function in *The Moral Collapse of the University* (Albany: SUNY Press, 1990). Robert Cross picks up on it in his review of Wilshire's book in *Change,* November–December 1990, p. 52.

21. Boyer, *Scholarship Reconsidered,* p. 28.

22. L. Kohlberg and R. Mayer, "Development as the Aim of Education," *Harvard Educational Review* 42, no. 4 (1972): 464.

23. Elton Trueblood, "The Concept of a Christian College," reprinted in *Faculty Dialogue* 14 (Spring 1991): 26–28.

24. W. Bennett, *To Reclaim a Legacy: A Report on the Humanities in Higher Education* (Washington, D.C.: National Endowment for the Humanities, 1984), p. 25.

25. "Amherst Tomorrow: A Report of the Alumni Committee on Postwar Amherst College," *Amherst Alumni Council News* 18, no. 3, pp. 95–96, cited by E. Trueblood in "The Concept of a Christian College," reprinted in *Faculty Dialogue* 14 (Spring 1991): 29.

26. The quotation is from Sharon Parks, *The Critical Years* (New York: Harper & Row, 1986), p. 47. I do not mean to suggest that in the end truth is pluralistic and relativized. But it is crucial, first, for students to consider that possibility and then, second, to distinguish that view from the view that while Truth may not be plural and relative, the human condition does call us to believe with attitudes of humility. Trueblood calls it the "value-centric predicament" ("Concept," p. 27).

27. Arthur Holmes, *The Idea of a Christian College* (Grand Rapids, Mich.: Eerdmanns, 1975), p. 48.

28. James Fowler and Sam Keen, *Life Maps: Conversations on the Journey of Faith* (Waco, Tex.: Word, 1978), p. 158.

29. *Teaching Portfolio,* p. 1.

30. Carnegie Foundation National Survey 1989, cited in Boyer, *Scholarship Reconsidered,* table 5, p. 32.

31. Stuart Smith, chairman of the Science Council of Canada, quoted in Jennifer Lewington, "Report on Canadian Higher Education Calls for More Emphasis on Teaching," *Chronicle,* October 23, 1991, p. A42.

32. See Holmes, *Idea,* pp. 101ff.

33. Cf. Thomas Langfitt, "The Cost of Higher Education," *Change,* November-December 1990, p. 15.

34. Stanford has also changed its promotion and tenure guidelines. Only a limited number of publications can be submitted for reviews, and the development of cur-

ricular materials including software is recognized. Syracuse University has taken others steps. Its Focus on Teaching project includes significant revisions in the promotion and tenure guidelines.

35. Richard Chait, "The Pro-Teaching Movement Should Try Economic Pressures," *Chronicle,* July 11, 1990, p. A36.

36. Described in Boyer, *Scholarship Reconsidered,* p. 38.

37. Their president, Charles Vest, says that "the tough issue of how to weigh teaching in tenure decisions is also receiving attention" (letter to alumni dated November 1992).

38. *Teaching Portfolio,* p. 2.

39. Ibid.

40. Parks, *Critical Years,* p. 70.

41. Martin Buber, *Two Types of Faith* (New York: Harper, 1961), passim.

42. Fowler and Keen, *Life Maps,* p. 158.

43. Ibid., p. 113.

44. Holmes, *Idea,* p. 96.

45. Amitai Etzioni, *The Moral Dimension* (New York: Free Press, 1988); Philip Selznick, *The Moral Commonwealth* (Berkeley: University of California Press, 1992); Mary Ann Glendon, *Rights Talk* (New York: Free Press, 1991); William Galston, *Liberal Purposes: Goods, Virtues, and Diversity in the Liberal State* (New York: Cambridge University Press, 1991). Cf. works by Robert A. Nisbet and William Galston, "Clinton and the Promise of Communitarianism," *Chronicle,* December 2, 1992, p. A52. Communitarians emphasize rights *and* responsibilities. Their recommendations seem weakest when applied on a large scale. But that criticism should not apply to the Christian liberal arts college.

CHAPTER 11. FINAL REMARKS

1. Derek Bok, *Universities and the Future of America* (Durham, N.C.: Duke University Press, 1990), pp. 77–78.

2. Ibid.

3. Sometimes this can become all-consuming and lead to workaholism. Full-time Christian workers are no exception to this danger and, in fact, may be particularly susceptible. See Engstrom and Juroe, *The Work Trap* (Old Tappan, N.J.: Fleming Revell, 1979).

4. See 1 Corinthians 12.

5. John 17. See Francis Schaeffer, *The Mark of the Christian* (Downers Grove, Ill.: InterVarsity Press, 1970).

Bibliography

Adler, Mortimer. *Reforming Education*. New York: Macmillan, 1988.

Barzun, Jacques. *The American University*. Chicago: University of Chicago, 1993.

Bennett, William John. *To Reclaim A Legacy : A Report on the Humanities in Higher Education*. Washington, D.C.: National Endowment for the Humanities, 1984.

Blanshard, Brand. *The Uses of Liberal Education and Other Talks with Students*. LaSalle, Ill.: Open Court, 1973.

Bloom, Alan. *The Closing of the American Mind*. New York: Simon & Schuster, 1987.

Bok, Derek. *Universities and the Future of America*. Durham, N.C.: Duke University Press, 1990.

Boyer, Ernest. *Scholarship Reconsidered: Priorities of the Professoriate*. Princeton, N.J.: Carnegie Foundation for the Advancement of Teaching, 1990.

———. *College: The Undergraduate Experience in America*. New York: Harper & Row/Carnegie Foundation for the Advancement of Teaching, 1987.

Brubacher, J. *On the Philosophy of Higher Education*. San Francisco: Jossey-Bass, 1977.

Contemporary Thoughts on Christian Higher Education: Pacific Lutheran University. Tacoma, Wash.: Pacific Lutheran University, 1961.

D'Souza, Dinesh. *Illiberal Education*. New York: Free Press, 1991.

De Jong, Arthur J. *Reclaiming a Mission: New Direction for the Church-Related College*. Grand Rapids: Eerdmans, 1990.

Duska, Ronald, and Mariellen Whelan. *Moral Development: A Guide to Piaget and Kohlberg*. New York: Paulist, 1975.

Facts in Brief. Washington, D.C.: American Council on Education, 1989.

Fowler, James. *Stages of Faith*. New York: Harper, 1981.

Fowler, James, and Sam Keen. *Life Maps: Conversations on the Journey of Faith*. Waco, Tex.: Word, 1978.

Freire, Paulo. *Pedagogy of the Oppressed*. New York: Continuum, 1970.

Gilligan, Carol. *In a Different Voice: Psychological Theory and Women's Development.* Cambridge: Harvard University Press, 1982.

Higher Education Today: Facts in Brief. Edited by Cecilia Ottinger. Washington, D.C.: American Council on Education, 1989.

Holmes, Arthur. *The Idea of a Christian College.* Grand Rapids, Mich.: Eerdmanns, 1975.

Howell, J., and D. Eidson. *The Idea of an Ideal Liberal Arts College.* Lanham, Md.: University Press of America, 1985.

Kimball, Roger. *Tenured Radicals: How Politics Has Corrupted Higher Education.* New York: Harper & Row, 1990.

Kimball, Bruce A. *Orators and Philosophers: A History of the Idea of Liberal Education.* New York: Teachers College Press, 1986.

Kohlberg, Lawrence. *The Philosophy of Moral Development.* San Francisco: Harper & Row, 1981.

Lerner, Max. *The Mind and Faith of Justice Holmes.* Boston: Little, Brown, 1945.

Levine, Arthur. *When Dreams and Heroes Died: A Portrait of Today's College Student.* San Francisco: Jossey-Bass, 1980.

Lynton, E., and S. Elman. *New Priorities for the University.* San Francisco: Jossey-Bass, 1987.

Martin, Warren Bryan. *College of Character.* San Francisco: Jossey-Bass, 1982.

Mayers, M., L. Richards, and R. Webber. *Reshaping Evangelical Higher Education.* Grand Rapids: Zondervan, 1972.

Miller, A. *Faith and Learning.* Westport, Conn.: Greenwood, 1960.

Moynihan, R. *The Necessary Learning: Liberal Arts and Science: A Defense and Reformation.* Washington, D.C.: University Press of America, 1989.

National Forum [Journal of the Phi Kappa Phi Honor Society]. Spring 1989.

Newman, John Henry. *The Idea of a University Defined and Illustrated: In Nine Discourses Delivered to the Catholics of Dublin.* Edited by M. J. Svaglic. New York: Holt, Rinehart, Winston, 1960.

Niebuhr, H. R. *Christ and Culture.* New York: Harper, 1951.

Oakley, Francis. *Community of Learning: The American College and the Liberal Arts Tradition.* New York: Oxford University Press, 1992.

Obitts, Stan. *Readings for Interterm.* Westmont College, 1972.

Parks, Sharon. *The Critical Years.* New York: Harper & Row, 1986.

Pattillo, M., and D. MacKenzie. *Church-Sponsored Higher Education in the U.S.* Report of the Danforth Commission. Washington, D.C.: American Council on Education, 1966.

Pelikan, Jaroslav. *Scholarship and Its Survival.* Princeton, N.J.: Carnegie Foundation for the Advancement of Teaching, 1983.

Perry, William G. *Forms of Intellectual and Ethical Development in the College Years.* New York: Holt, Rinehart, Winston, 1970.

Peterson, Michael. *Philosophy of Education.* Downers Grove, Ill.: InterVarsity Press, 1986.

Pieper, J. *Leisure: The Basis of Culture.* New York: New American Heritage Library, 1963.

Project on Liberal Learning, vol. 1, *The Challenge of Connecting Learning;* vol. 2, *Reports From the Fields.* Washington, D.C.: Association of American Colleges, 1991.

Ringenberg, William. *The Christian College: A History of Protestant Higher Education in America.* St. Paul: Christian College Consortium, 1984.

Ruscio, Kenneth. "The Distinctive Scholarship of the Selective Liberal Arts College," *Journal of Higher Education* 58, no. 2 (1987).

Sandin, Robert. *The Rehabilitation of Virtue: Foundation of Moral Education.* New York: Praeger, 1992.

Schenkat, Randolph J., et al. *It Stands to Reason: The Rationale and Implementation of a Development Based, Liberal Arts Oriented, Teacher Education Program.* Winona, Minn.: College of St. Teresa, 1985.

Shils, Edward. *The Academic Ethic.* Chicago: University of Chicago, 1984.

Silber, John. *Straight Shooting.* New York: Harper, 1989.

Smith, Huston. *The Purposes of Higher Education.* Westport, Conn.: Greenwood, 1971.

Smith, Page. *Killing the Spirit: Higher Education in America.* New York: Viking, 1990.

Sykes, Charles J. *ProfScam: Professors and the Demise of Higher Education.* New York: St. Martin's, 1988.

Tillich, Paul. *The Courage to Be.* New Haven, Conn.: Yale University Press, 1952.

Trueblood, David Elton. *The Idea of a College.* Three articles reprinted in *Faculty Dialogue,* Spring 1991, pp. 7–55. Cf. *The Idea of a College.* New York: Harper, 1959.

Whitehead, A. N. *The Aims of Education and other Essays.* New York: Macmillan, 1959.

Wilder, Amos N. *Liberal Learning and Religion.* Port Washington, N.Y.: Kennikat, 1951.

Wilshire, Bruce. *The Moral Collapse of the University.* Albany: SUNY Press, 1990.

Winter, David G., David C. McClelland, and Abigail J. Stewart. *A New Case for the Liberal Arts.* San Francisco: Jossey-Bass, 1981.

Wolterstorff, Nicholas. *Educating for Responsible Action.* Grand Rapids, Mich.: Eerdmanns, 1980.

———. *Reason within the Bounds of Religion.* Grand Rapids, Mich.: Eerdmanns, 1976.

Index

231

About the Author

Jim Mannoia grew up in Brazil, did laser physics as an undergraduate at MIT in the 1960s, switched to philosophy, and finished his Ph.D. in process metaphysics and philosophy of science at Washington University in St. Louis.

He taught physics at Grove City College in Pennsylvania and then philosophy at Westmont College in Santa Barbara, California, where he first began to do academic administration as associate academic dean. During a two-year leave of absence, he taught graduate and undergraduate philosophy at the University of Zimbabwe as a visiting professor and preached nearly every week as a tent-making missionary. He is an ordained elder in the Free Methodist Church. Within a few years of his return from Africa, he and his family moved to Houghton, New York, where he served as academic vice president and Dean of the College. In January 1999, he was appointed president at Greenville College, Illinois. His writing includes articles in process metaphysics, philosophy of science, and philosophy of education, including his first book, *What Is Science: An Introduction to the Structure and Methodology of Science*. His interests include his family (the name Mannoia is Sicilian), computers, cars, and travel.